CW00829210

1 MONTH OF
FREE
READING

at
www.ForgottenBooks.com

By purchasing this book you are eligible for one month membership to ForgottenBooks.com, giving you unlimited access to our entire collection of over 1,000,000 titles via our web site and mobile apps.

To claim your free month visit:
www.forgottenbooks.com/free905319

ISBN 978-0-265-89091-2
PIBN 10905319

From the collection of the

San Francisco, California
2008

BELL
TELEPHONE QUARTERLY

VOLUME XVI, 1937

INFORMATION DEPARTMENT
AMERICAN TELEPHONE AND TELEGRAPH COMPANY
195 Broadway, New York

PRINTED IN U. S. A.

BELL TELEPHONE QUARTERLY
VOLUME XVI, 1937

TABLE OF CONTENTS

BELL TELEPHONE QUARTERLY
VOLUME XVI, 1937
INDEX

LL TELEPHONE QUARTERLY

BELL TELEPHONE QUARTERLY

*A Medium of Suggestion
and a Record of Progress*

CONTENTS FOR JANUARY 1937

VOL. XVI   NO. 1

PUBLISHED QUARTERLY FOR THE BELL SYSTEM BY THE AMERICAN
TELEPHONE AND TELEGRAPH COMPANY. SUBSCRIPTION, $1.50 PER YEAR,
IN UNITED STATES; SINGLE COPIES, 50 CENTS

Address all communications to

INFORMATION DEPARTMENT
AMERICAN TELEPHONE AND TELEGRAPH COMPANY

195 Broadway, New York

Contributors to This Issue

WALTER S. GIFFORD

Harvard University, B.A., 1904. Entered the Bell System as clerk, Western Electric Co., Chicago, 1904; Assistant Secretary and Assistant Treasurer, 1905–08. American Telephone and Telegraph Co., New York, Statistician, 1908–11; Chief Statistician, 1911–16. Government service, as Supervising Director of the National Industrial Preparedness Campaign of the U. S. Naval Consulting Board, Director of the Council of National Defense, and Secretary of the U. S. Delegation of the Inter-Allied Munitions Council in Paris, 1916–18. American Telephone and Telegraph Company, Comptroller, 1918–19; Vice President, 1919–23; Executive Vice President, 1923–25; President, 1925–.

OLIVER E. BUCKLEY

Grinnell College, B.S., 1909, D.Sc. (Hon.), 1936; Cornell University, Ph.D., 1914. Instructor in Physics, Grinnell College, 1909–10. Engineering Department, Western Electric Company, 1914–17. Major, Signal Corps, in charge of Research Laboratory of Signal Corps in A. E. F., 1917–18. Engineering Department, Western Electric Company, which later became Bell Telephone Laboratories, 1918–; Assistant Director of Research, 1927–33; Director of Research, 1933–36; Executive Vice President, 1936–.

W. G. THOMPSON

Military College of South Carolina (The Citadel), B.S., 1914. American Telephone and Telegraph Company, Long Lines Department, Commercial Engineering section, 1914–15, 1916–20; Supervisor of Toll Rates, 1920–23; Commercial Engineer, 1923–28. Department of Operation and Engineering, 1928–29. Long Lines Department, Assistant to General Manager, 1929–30; title changed to Assistant to Vice President, 1930–.

T. C. SMITH

Purdue University, B.S. in M.E., 1910. New York Telephone Company, plant extension engineering, 1910–14. Engaged in electric light and power engineering, 1914–16. New York Telephone Company, general outside plant engineering and motor vehicle operation, 1916–21. American Telephone and Telegraph Company, Operation and Engineering Department, Plant Engineering Division, 1921–. Mr. Smith's work is concerned with automotive and construction apparatus engineering.

The American Communication Companies and National Preparedness*

IN accepting the invitation of the Secretary of War and the officers of the Army Industrial College to appear here and speak on the subject of The American Communication Companies and National Preparedness, it seems to me that a brief word as to my qualifications is in order.

With one short interruption during the period of the World War, when I served as Director of the Council of National Defense and of the Advisory Commission, practically all of my active life since graduating from college has been concerned with the problems of electrical communication and with the building up of an organization, the Bell System, designed to provide the people of the United States with the best, most comprehensive and most economical system of electrical communication which physical science and human organization make possible.

Specifically, my experience has covered not only the problems of the directing and operating units of the Bell System but likewise the problems of the Western Electric Company, which in our Bell System organization is responsible for the manufacture or supply of the physical things which our research and development organization, Bell Telephone Laboratories, develops and designs.

Even the interruption in this life work occasioned by the incidents of my World War duties was not really a break in the continuity of my connection with the problems of electrical communication, since many of the vital questions with which the Council had to deal were directly or indirectly concerned

---

* An address before the Army Industrial College, Washington, D. C., December 10, 1936.

3

with matters of electrical communication, either for the combat forces in Europe or at home or with the civilian activities which were their source.

While I am not myself a trained scientist or engineer, and so hardly competent to express a worth-while opinion on highly technical details, my more than thirty years of association with the problems and operations of the multitude of material instrumentalities on which the whole art and service of electrical communication is based has given me, I think, a proper appreciation of the major problems involved in the question we are here considering.

The Fundamental Problems Stated

As I see it, the fundamental problems concerned with electrical communication in connection with the national defense are not alone those which, when the emergency of war arises, will insure to the combat forces of the nation an adequate supply of communication material and an adequate personnel of men trained in its use and with an ability rapidly to instruct a larger number of other men to equal efficiency.

Of equal or even greater importance are two other problems which in my judgment must never be lost sight of if the primary objective of the military forces, victory, is to be achieved. One of these is that the material and personnel required initially for the combat forces (and which will, unaided, have to withstand the first shocks) must be arranged for in advance so as to be almost instantaneously available without producing an equally instantaneous disruption of the civilian service of communication.

The second problem which must not be lost sight of is that the demands of the combat forces on the civilian establishment, whether for material or personnel, must not so cripple the latter as to leave it incapable of providing for a suddenly enlarged and newly distributed demand for communication within the underlying service of supply.

4

We know from our experience during the World War, not only that the demands for electrical communication, both by telephone and telegraph, peak up enormously on the first impact of war, but, what is even more disconcerting, that the distribution of traffic undergoes violent change and that telephone and telegraph routes which under normal peace-time conditions are little used become overnight main arteries of traffic demand. Further, experience in the emergencies of both war and peace shows that the too rapid introduction of untrained personnel into the operating organization of an electrical communication system tends automatically to degrade the ability of the communication network to provide satisfactory service. Moreover, beyond a certain point further introduction of such personnel tends to accelerate the downward spiral.

Having stated the major problems as I see them, let me say now a word about my view as to our potential ability to cope with them.

MEETING THE PROBLEMS

As I see it, the United States above all other nations is most favored in this direction. While its normal telephone and telegraph facilities are operated by independent agencies rather than being concentrated within a single governmental administration, as is the case in most foreign countries, they can readily be made to function, if needed, as a single integrated whole. In addition, they have the advantage of certain stimuli of private initiative, which seems to be denied to political administrations whatever the form of government. Added to this is the fact that the Bell System, with its all-inclusive services of research and development, manufacture and operation, is not only by far the largest communication organization in the world, but is likewise, I think, generally recognized throughout the world as the most advanced in its development of electrical communication.

5

If in what follows I seem to dwell largely on the Bell System and on telephony, it is partly because of this predominant position of the Bell System in the whole art of electrical communication, and partly because the technical problems of telephony are in general more difficult than the technical problems of telegraphy and, when solved satisfactorily, carry in that solution generally the automatic solution of a host of telegraph problems.

With this preface related to the general aspects of our subjcet, let me now turn to a brief historical review and to some of what seem to me the more important details of the problem.

Lessons from the World War

What we might term the modern rôle in warfare of the electrical transmission of intelligence, particularly by telephone, is of very recent inception. It dates from 1917 and 1918, i.e., from the closing chapters of the World War. It therefore vied with chemical warfare and certain forms of mechanized warfare in the rapidity of its development. The military forces which went into the conflict in 1914 were equipped with simple forms of wire and radio telegraph and with wire telephones of a kind, but no radio telephones. Those that emerged from it, and especially the American Expeditionary Forces, had at their command a far-flung communication network involving not only thousands of miles of wire and cable together with fully developed telephone and telegraph exchanges and systems of the most modern sort, but also radio telephones with which flying aircraft could for the first time keep in touch with one another and with the ground, and with which naval ships could communicate by spoken word across hundreds of miles of water.

The rapid ascension of the telephone, both wire and radio, in military affairs was the direct consequence of certain epoch-making developments in the telephone art itself. Science contributed certain devices like the repeater, the vacuum tube

6

amplifier, the modulator and the electric wave filter, which were entirely new in principle, with the result that about 1914 or 1915 it became possible for the first time to say that the telephone was in a fair way to overcome all terrestrial distances. January, 1915, saw the opening of the first transcontinental telephone line linking New York and San Francisco, and in the summer and fall of the same year speech was successfully transmitted by radio from Arlington, Virginia, to Honolulu and across the Atlantic to Paris.

Work with the Army and the Navy

These two American accomplishments were quick to receive recognition from the United States Army and Navy. It was January, 1916, sixteen months prior to this country's entrance into the War, that we of the Bell System were asked to assist the Army and Navy communication people in determining how our new discoveries and developments could be adapted to their needs. It was in that month that j. j. Carty (later General Carty), then Chief Engineer of the American Telephone and Telegraph Company, read an important and confidential paper before the Army War College. This was at the request of General McComb, President of the College, and the paper was soon repeated before the Naval War College. Two months later, and again with the intention of demonstrating the military significance of some of the new developments for which the Telephone Company had been responsible, Mr. Carty arranged a demonstration in the course of which connections were established between the New Willard Hotel in Washington, where a distinguished audience was assembled, and the following points in sequence:

	Miles Distant from Washington
Seattle, Washington	3,700
Ottawa, Canada	780
El Paso, Texas	2,600
Jacksonville, Florida	820
San Francisco, California	3,400

The connection to El Paso brought in General Pershing, who was then stationed on the Mexican Border.

This demonstration was followed shortly by a request from Mr. Daniels, Secretary of the Navy, for a test of radio telephony between ships and between ship and shore. During the test, the Secretary from his office in Washington held frequent conversations with the Commander of the Battleship NEW HAMPSHIRE while it maneuvered off Hampton Roads. So pleased was the Navy with this demonstration that studies were at once authorized and urgently prosecuted for the purpose of adapting radio telephony to naval maneuvers generally. Similar developments were instituted for the purpose of perfecting radio telephone apparatus that would be applicable to army maneuvers and to aviation.

It was during the same year, 1916, that those familiar with the vital changes which the telephone art was undergoing began to realize the essentially new land line communication problems which the maintaining and direction of a huge American Army overseas would involve. To picture the situation then existing, I cannot do better than quote some post-war testimony of General Carty before the Committee on Military Affairs of the House of Representatives:

" There had been preparations made for war in the European terrain for forty years. When the war broke it was not possible for any of the European nations to provide a communication system adequate for the conduct of the war. It remained for the Signal Corps of the U. S. Army in nine months to construct a long distance telegraph and telephone system which the Governments of Europe had failed to do in forty years. We did that in nine months. There was a wire from Rome to Paris a great deal bigger than the wire we talk on from Washington to San Francisco, but they could not talk over it. . . .

" The Signal Corps built a system extending from Marseilles on the south to LeHavre on the north, and across the Channel to London, and equipped a line on to Liverpool; on the west their line went as far as Brest, and on the east as far as Germany. We were able to talk all over

8

the Continent. That gives you an idea of some of the work done by methods absolutely unknown to any of the nations engaged in the combat."

I do not need to remind this audience that the Signal Corps had behind it and at its disposal the facilities of the American telephone and telegraph industry. From its scientific laboratories came the new developments which surprised the armies of Europe. On the one hand, it produced the multifarious equipment—the telephone switchboards, cable and open-wire lines, loading coils and repeaters; on the other hand, it provided the trained personnel which the installation, maintenance and operation of such new equipment required. At the outbreak of the War, as I remember it, the Signal Corps staff of the Army numbered about 1,600; this the Bell System as their part of a coöperative undertaking matched three for one, supplying in the space of a few months some 4,500 engineers, installers and operators. The telegraph and independent telephone companies supplied a proportionally large number of trained men. As indicating the effectiveness of this assistance, I cannot do better than quote from a letter dated January 16, 1918, and written by General Edgar Russel, then Chief Signal Officer of the American Expeditionary Forces, to Mr. Carty:

" Let me again express my great appreciation of the splendid work you have done for us. Without your selection and organization of the officers and men you have contributed to this cause, I am sure our work would have been tremendously hampered. As it is, we are well ahead of the game, and the Signal Corps is receiving warm commendations from the Commander-in-Chief and the Line and Staff Departments."

We should note, however, that General Russel's letter sees only one of two very important aspects of the then existing situation. The supplying, in a minimum of time, of these 4,500 highly skilled individuals for military service had been arranged for with due regard to the point which I mentioned earlier as one of the fundamentals, namely, that of leaving essentially unhampered and uncrippled the ability of the nor-

9

mal service to cope with the problems of unprecedented demand and the training of new personnel.

It has been suggested that you would be interested in having me outline today my opinion as to whether the American communication industry is now in position to carry a war-time load. My answer is that we are better prepared in every way, should another emergency arise. Not only are we fortified by the experience gained during the World War, but since the Armistice the communication art has never for a moment ceased its progress. Engineering facilities and operating techniques of both telephony and telegraphy, by wire and radio, have advanced enormously in the past decade and a half. Many improved forms of equipment and many services which during the World War were unknown are now in current use. Some of these are distinctly attractive from the standpoint of military operations. Some, on the other hand, appear to present quite unappraised potentialities. I think it may be of interest if I comment briefly upon the more significant aspects of this post-war evolution.

OVERSEAS RADIO AND CABLE CHANNELS

During the World War, communication between this country and our military forces in Europe took place largely through a few submarine telegraph cables. Two or three of these cables actually were cut and the fear that others would go in the same manner was responsible for a very prolonged state of anxiety on the part of those responsible for maintaining transatlantic channels of communication. You may not know it, but the situation appeared so grave at one time that a special committee of distinguished engineers was organized by the State Department, with the coöperation of the War and Navy Departments, to develop and introduce immediately methods of operation which would very greatly increase the traffic carrying capacity of existing submarine cables.

This contrasts rather forcefully with the extent to which radio channels have today established the telephone and the telegraph as mediums of international communication. It is now possible from any telephone in the United States to reach practically every other country in the world; 66 nations or dominions is, I believe, the figure given by the latest count, or 93 per cent of all the telephones in the world. The significance of such a world-wide telephone network is incalculable in times of peace; in war, it may be equally vital in speeding urgent messages. At the present time, we witness every day the successful completion of scores of telephone conversations between this country and the various countries of Europe, South America and the Orient. Just by way of illustrating the progress in overseas telephone service since its inauguration in 1927, I might refer to a demonstration conversation held successfully in April, 1935, over a wire and radio circuit which completely encircled the earth. The speakers, of whom I was one, were in adjoining offices in New York City.

Moreover, overseas telegraphy by means of radio has, in the intervening nineteen years, made vast strides, there being direct channels now to practically all important countries. In regard to these, there has been a notable clarification of the situation since 1917. At that time, certain of the most important American radio stations were German-owned and had either to be closed down or to undergo a change of operating staff, with resulting delay and restriction of service. Since that time, control has been vested in American hands, thus simplifying war-time operating restrictions. Moreover, the equipment employed has improved in a variety of fundamental respects. The old mechanical alternators have given place to modern vacuum tube equipment for continuous wave signaling. Also, high speed automatic sending and receiving apparatus has entered the radio telegraph field as well as that of wire telegraphy.

11

Any consideration of the war-time use of radio channels, particularly those of high power for overseas communication, raises the question of secrecy and possible interruptions of service. The so-called privacy systems which we employ on our radio telephone circuits are very effective indeed so far as peace-time requirements are concerned. Like most telegraph ciphers, however, they are not unbreakable, a fact to which during a military campaign it would be necessary to give due weight. Moreover, all forms of radio are more or less vulnerable to intentional interference but I shall not presume to the extent of discussing this matter, with which doubtless you are already thoroughly familiar.

In passing, there is, however, one point connected with the fallibilities of radio transmission to which I would direct your attention. The vast progress in radio development, the obvious flexibility of its operation, and the glamor attendant upon its achievements, may have, I fear, tended to mask some of its as yet not overcome weaknesses, and to an extent have caused us to relegate the submarine telegraph cable to a too ancient category of outworn agencies. Added to the points of weakness of radio just mentioned must be a realization that the long swing periods of changing radio transmission which we attribute to sun spot disturbances are as yet little understood and we have no assurance as to exactly what will happen to all of our radio transmissions during the next period of maximum solar activity. If the results of this activity should exceed our present surmises and if perchance this maximum period should come at a time of emergency, we might find ourselves seriously crippled in our electrical communications if we place too much dependence on the one means which radio provides us.

From the standpoint, therefore, of both secrecy and continuity of service, the submarine cable is one of the mainstays of world communication, and hence it is very important to record here that although the cable is one of the oldest devices for electrical transmission of intelligence, the post-war epoch has witnessed a complete revolution in its design. The most modern type of cable now employed has approximately five times the message-carrying capacity of the pre-war non-loaded type. The first of these high speed telegraph cables was laid across the Atlantic in 1924 and others in various localities have since been placed in service. These cables are characterized by a continuous loading of the magnetic alloy, permalloy, and it is their reduced attenuation for signal currents which accounts for their high traffic capacity. Since the last of these high speed transatlantic cables was laid, shortly before the beginning of the depression, continued research and development work has indicated that cables with traffic capacity far in excess of that of the most modern now in operation can be produced. To the extent that cable communications are fundamental in time of war, the existence of these new circuits represents an important reinforcement of our international telegraph channels.

LAND LINE FACILITIES

The growth of our national telephone land line facilities since the World War has, if anything, been more prolific though perhaps less spectacular, than that of the overseas channels. To portray this domestic progress, I shall quote certain data which we keep for our own information and by means of which we attempt to see our telephone service as the user sees it. The average number of minutes required to establish a long distance connection dropped from 13.6 minutes in 1920 to 7.5 minutes in 1925 and again to 1.4 minutes in 1935. Correlatively, the percentage of long distance calls handled with the calling party remaining at the telephone rose from a negligible percentage in 1920 to 15 per cent in 1925 and again to 92 per cent in 1935. I shall not trouble you with even a cursory account of the increase and improvements in the American telephone plant and the changes in operating practices which

13

explain the progress revealed by these data. Underlying them there has been, however, a notable growth in American telephone facilities and this fact is in itself so fundamental to our discussion today that I will, in passing, call your attention to the following figures.

In United States	1920	1936
No. of telephones	13,329,400	18,450,000
No. of miles of wire in storm-proof toll cables	1,700,000	12,800,000
No. of miles of open toll wire	2,660,000	3,100,000

While similar figures for the other leading nations are not so vital from the standpoint of today's theme, they are of interest as signifying the world-wide recognition now accorded telephony. Thus Europe is today overlaid with a toll cable network containing some 5,500,000 miles of telephone wire, all having sprung into existence within the past ten years. The creation of this network marks what might almost be called a new era in telephone communication in Europe, and shows that the nations across the Atlantic have definitely ascended out of the primitive state described by General Carty before the House of Representatives, in which they had heavy copper circuits that were virtually useless for telephone purposes. Interconnecting most important European centers we now find this cable network—which in all respects is of the most modern type, and whose design, installation and operation are indicative of international coöperation on the part of the various telephone authorities.

Conference Telephone Service

Perhaps some of you will recall one of the items of the National Defense Day program in Washington on September 12, 1924. For that occasion, General Pershing was provided with a single telephone connection which included 23 other centers; he spoke from Washington with General Bullard in New York, General Hale in Chicago, General Duncan in Omaha and General Morton in San Francisco, and their words in turn were carried to Washington over transcontinental telephone lines and broadcast by 19 radio broadcasting stations in various parts of the country. I mention this occasion and the part which the telephone played in it because it was a forerunner of what we now call conference telephony. A few weeks ago, on the occasion of the celebration of the twenty-fifth anniversary of the Telephone Pioneers Association, as many as 265 banquet and assembly halls, scattered over the extent of the United States and Canada, were linked together on a conference circuit. In this case loud speaking receivers were provided at each hall and the arrangement was unquestionably the most extensive conference circuit ever established.

This form of call has within the past few years become a regular feature of American telephone service. From a telephone in this room, for instance, I could, through the regular traffic channels, place a call for several other parties simultaneously either within our local area or at remote points of the country, and within a reasonably short space of time be assured of a connection whereby I could be speaking to all of these points at the same time. They, in turn, could answer and their remarks would be heard by all of the other participants to the connection. I need not stress the importance of this type of service before a gathering of this sort. It can provide a rapid and yet personal contact between various headquarters—for instance, between Washington and the headquarters of various Corps Areas, or between various key points within an Area. The service is extremely flexible and is nation-wide in its extent. I might add that within recent months some of the European nations have undertaken to offer a corresponding service, and I understand that with them it now traverses national boundaries in certain instances.

Switched Telegraph Service

Turning next to the telegraph service, we encounter new developments which in their flexibility are similar to those long

15

characterizing the telephone service. Within recent years, there has grown up a considerable group of subscribers to a switched telegraph service, whereby any subscriber can at any time call any other subscriber and upon completion of the connection, transmit his message himself. This service involves printing telegraph machines so that as the message is transmitted it becomes available to both sender and receiver in the form of typewritten copy. Our latest figures show that the service now numbers over 10,000 subscribers who, for the most part, are business houses, factories, banks, etc. For military purposes, where secrecy is involved, automatic ciphering and deciphering printing telegraph machines could be used as readily as those regularly employed.

The average time of connection in the switched telegraph service is quite comparable with that in toll telephone service, being in the neighborhood of 1.3 minutes. The distance bridged by the average connection our traffic data show to be 420 miles. The average number of words per message is 200. I cite these figures merely to show that although this is a new service, we are nevertheless dealing with one which has attractive potentialities, and which in war-time might be of great assistance in coördinating national effort.

TELEPHOTOGRAPHY

Another development which some claim will be of value, especially for the transmission of maps to guide troop movements, is the electrical transmission of pictures. As you are all familiar with the quality of results obtainable with present-day equipment, I feel sure there is no need for me to enter upon a discussion of the subject.

OTHER TELEGRAPH DEVELOPMENTS

The instrumentality employed in the switched telegraph service, namely the printing telegraph machine, has in recent years been widely adopted by the commercial telegraph companies, both wire and radio, for handling private messages. It was not so long ago that the bulk of this telegraph traffic was transmitted and received by means of the key and Morse sounder. Today, probably 95 per cent of the traffic is handled by printers. Telegraphists who can read the Morse code are greatly reduced in numbers and their places have been taken by those familiar with a typewriter-like keyboard. This trend is one which has a certain significance from the standpoint of military communications. The weight and size of the printer do not lend it to field maneuvers. In an active campaign, it would be necessary to rely largely upon the trained ear of those who can read the telegraph codes.

But, fortunately, as one supply of trained telegraphists has dwindled, another source has sprung into existence. This new source comprises the small army of short-wave radio amateurs, estimated in this country to number perhaps 45,000, whose pastime is to communicate with one another through their low-powered transmitters. The results of a recent survey[1] indicate that in this body of radio amateurs there is probably an adequate supply of telegraphists for Army requirements, and I understand that through the Army amateur radio system a nucleus for meeting mobilization requirements is being defined.

Broadcasting

Turning next to broadcasting, we come to one of the most important of the post-war communication developments but one whose influence at a time of national emergency, although considerable, probably cannot be forecast with certainty. Upon the one hand, it permits the broadside circulation of propaganda, both friendly and enemy, although because of the geographical position of the United States the menace of subversive propaganda reaching us via broadcasting is probably of less moment than in the case of many other countries. How

[1] Report of the Hough-Bickelhaupt Board, 1934.

it can best be used to maintain national morale and assist in securing prompt and intelligent coöperation on the part of our vast population is a matter the details of which I will not attempt to picture. It seems to lend itself equally to the aims of the political party in control and to those of rebellious groups. In the latter category stands the recently attempted *coup d'etat* in Austria, wherein the revolutionists attempted to seize the broadcasting station simultaneously with their entrance into the Chancellery. In the former is the general strike which paralyzed England for a few days in 1926. I have heard it related that during that brief crisis when there were no newspapers, broadcasting did much to sustain the public morale and that one of the most reassuring messages which came over the radio was the sound of Big Ben striking the hour. This was in 1926, just after broadcasting had been born. Today, with its immensely greater coverage, its influence is doubtless proportionately larger. Reports from Russia tell of widespread use of radio broadcast for all sorts of purposes.

TELEVISION AND THE COAXIAL CABLE

While discussing the question of new equipment and services, such developments as television and the so-called coaxial cable deserve a word in passing. It is perhaps difficult at this stage of its development to assign to television any particular military value. The coaxial cable, on the other hand, because of its extremely simple physical structure, might find important uses behind the lines as a source of backbone communication channels, especially if quick methods of burying it underground prove practicable.

For military purposes wide band carrier systems which provide twelve or more independent telephone channels on each pair of ordinary telephone cable wires might prove of far more interest even than the wider band systems of the coaxial cable structure. In carrier on ordinary cable pairs, the four-wire system of operation is required; that is, the twelve west-bound transmissions are carried on one pair and the corresponding twelve east-bound transmissions on another pair shielded from the first. Thus two small shielded cable each containing, say, six pairs of wires, can provide for as many as seventy-two simultaneous two-way telephone conversations.

COMMUNICATION NEEDS IN CASE OF MOBILIZATION

Leaving this brief review of the more significant telephone and telegraph developments since the World War, we turn to the procurement problems which are destined to spring into existence should a grave national emergency arise. Due to the highly specialized character of the electrical communication art, both in regard to the diversity of equipment which it demands and the extended knowledge and training which its personnel must possess, these procurement problems are of special moment. At this time and place, and granting the existence of an emergency, it is not necessary to stress the elaborate requirements of the Army and Navy both for communication material and personnel. When these communication requirements expand suddenly, as they would were another war-time emergency to arise, they must be met promptly but not at the expense of the equally urgent requirements of the business and industrial world for the same effective communication service to which they have become accustomed in peace.

It is extremely fortunate that, in the handling of these difficult problems, the communication industries, which must be looked upon as the principal source of both trained personnel and specialized equipment, have been accorded sympathetic and intelligent coöperation by the Army and Navy, to the end that plans are now available whereby the necessary transposition of man-power and equipment could be made with what appears to be a minimum of dislocation in the established services.

Although many of you here are more familiar than I with these plans, it is my understanding that the estimated mobilization requirements of the U. S. Signal Corps for initial and subsequent mobilization will total around 6,000 men, including about 500 communication specialists required for the Corps Area Service Commands.

As to the procurement of 6,000 specialists, this must, as already mentioned, be accomplished smoothly, rapidly and without any derangement of the established services. It calls for the most efficient coöperation between the Corps Area Commands and communication companies in each Corps Area, to effect which it has been suggested that the Signal Corps establish a specialized recruiting group to be made up of Reserve Officers selected from the personnel of the four large communication companies. Should an emergency become imminent, these recruiting officers would be given the necessary instructions by the respective Corps Area Signal Officers, upon receipt of which the recruiting officers would immediately work out with their respective companies plans for selecting the personnel required.

Other essential plans have been laid with regard to the supply of communication material—wire, cable, switchboards, instruments, repeaters, radio apparatus, etc. Thus, the Western Electric Company, the manufacturing unit in the Bell System, knows quite clearly what the Signal Corps would call upon it for in case an emergency arose. Manufacturing schedules have been discussed together with delivery programs which satisfy both parties. These of course are coördinated with the probable civilian demands so as again to eliminate as far as possible any disturbing effects of a war upon the vital communication industry.

Similarly, for the Army cantonments which would spring into existence, contracts have been drawn up between the various communication companies and the Army and Navy which merely require signatures in order to set into motion a vast machinery of shipment and installation.

SPECIAL WAR-TIME CO-ORDINATION

While it was realized well in advance of the actual declaration of war in 1917 that mobilization of the nation's resources would require skillful coöperation, there unfortunately was not time enough to develop anything like the detailed schedule which we now have. It is not to be expected, however, that plans such as those to which I have just referred have been so skillfully prepared as to meet every emergency. Unforeseen situations are bound to arise, and to cope with these some purely war-time organization will be necessary, whose functions would be the expeditious coördination of civilian and military effort and the reconciliation of conflicting demands. It is conceivable, for example, that even with the far more extended telephone and telegraph plant which we have today, an emergency of such magnitude might arise as to call for a rationing of communication supplies and service. This need did definitely arise in 1917 and a coöperative committee on telegraphs and telephones under the chairmanship of Theodore N. Vail, at that time President of the American Telephone and Telegraph Company, established the necessary routines. In connection with this committee, it is significant that it came into existence prior to our entry into the World War and by the beginning of 1918, almost a year before the War closed, it had discharged its functions so satisfactorily that it became from then on inactive.

As to what emergency war-time organization ought to be established should another crisis arise, my view is that we should not attempt too detailed a forecast. Emergencies and threats of war are of so many different types, some minor and some major, that to plan far in advance the organizational machine required to cope with the situation seems of rather dubious value. We know from past experience that even in the case of a decidedly major emergency, such machinery can be created and caused to function in a surprisingly short time. My suggestion, therefore, would be to let our steps in this direction be dictated by the nature of the emergency, remembering that the primary function of the machinery is not to issue orders, but to bring together the national problems as they arise and the experts who are best qualified to attempt solutions. This was the chief rôle played by the Council of National Defense and its Advisory Commission together with their many coöperative organizations, such as the National Research Council.

As Director of the Council of National Defense and the Advisory Commission, I had an excellent opportunity of seeing how effectively such an arrangement can function. From the outset the purpose of the Council and the subordinate committees of the Council was to offer a channel through which the voluntary efforts of American industrial and professional life could be focused. The story of the way in which the members of these committees, practically all of them serving without compensation, rallied to aid in the common cause and the extent of the practical accomplishment of their voluntary service has probably not been equaled anywhere. The general spirit underlying these original committees was fundamentally that of business organizing itself in aid of the Government. The natural processes of administrative evolution gradually eliminated the old, large committee system in the case of the industrial committees and substituted for it a closely knit scheme of sections under the general head of the War Industries Board, in which each section head had general authority over all dealings with the industry with which he was particularly familiar. At the same time, the industries of the country rapidly organized to assist the Government in carrying on the War and created representative war-service committees of their own, thus simplifying and strengthening the method of coöperation of business with the Government.

22

The ways in which problems were brought before the Council and the method adopted in dealing with them varied greatly. At times they were discussed first by the Advisory Commission and brought before the Council with a recommendation. At other times they were brought to the attention of the Council through Government departments or other governmental organizations or through private citizens. The Council's general practice in handling questions which it did not itself act upon directly usually took one of three forms. Where the question apparently lay within the discretion of one of the executive departments or of an already existing Government agency, the Council referred the matter under discussion to this agency for executive action with or without a recommendation. In this way, questions of overlapping jurisdiction could frequently be settled. Where no agency for handling the matter existed and where some further investigation seemed advisable before a decision could be reached, the Council frequently referred the matter to the Advisory Commission for investigation or to one of the subordinate committees before action. Where the question was one of particular urgency and unusual authority was needed for its solution, the Council, after a thorough discussion, at times referred the matter directly to the President for final determination, usually with a recommendation.

From the first, there was not only a willingness but an affirmative desire to allocate to other agencies of the Government activities initiated by the Council and carried along by it to mature performance. The Council at all times resisted tendencies to cling to activities which could best be directed elsewhere. This policy was consistently maintained and was in harmony with one of the Council's prime functions, namely, to act as a sort of proving ground for problems dealing with public and governmental welfare specifically in respect of national defense. To cite a few examples as to how this policy worked out, the Committee on Transportation grew in due course into the Railroad Administration; out of the General Munitions Board came the War Industries Board; and out of the Committee on Coal Production grew the Fuel Administration. The Council was in no sense a fixed institution, but continued in a process of evolution rapid enough to keep abreast of the changing current of the times and yet conservative enough to prevent confusion through lack of proper coordination and control. It was therefore constantly ready to fill in the gaps and to assist regular departments of the Government in their efforts to expand and carry the new and huge burdens put up to them not only by the War but also by the aftermath of the War.

With this brief historical review of the functioning of the Council of National Defense, the picture which I have wanted to draw for you is complete. On the one hand, we have noted well-planned and well-understood, though quiescent, routines which are ready—for instant adoption in case of an emergency —to control the flow of communication services, of materials and of personnel both into the fighting services and into urgent civilian channels. Behind these routines, and without which they would be entirely ineffectual, stands the entire communication industry with its operating, its engineering and its research facilities. I have outlined very briefly the recent achievements of this industry in those respects in which they merit your consideration. Moreover, measured by such standards as you military experts have seen fit to exact, I understand that our capacity in all important respects appears adequate to a national emergency. Finally, to supplement the routines which, however carefully planned, can never cope with all the shifting variables of a prolonged campaign, we are provided from recent history with the example of a successfully functioning Council of National Defense to analyze, to recommend, and generally to coördinate the almost fabulous technical talent of the country. Our position, therefore, as to communications appears to be one of adequate preparedness.

WALTER S. GIFFORD

The Evolution of the Crystal Wave Filter*

ONE of the most impressive features of organized indus- trial research is the evolutionary character it assumes when carried on over a long period of time. New inventions and discoveries breed others. An invention made ten years or more ago to fill a particular need at the time finds applica- tion today in situations that could not possibly have been fore- seen when the original research was undertaken. Almost any important piece of telephone apparatus used in modern long- distance telephony would serve to illustrate this point. On examination, one would find in it contributions from researches conducted for purposes very remote from the needs which the apparatus now meets.

The crystal wave filter, employed at the terminals of new broad-band telephone transmission systems, is a convenient and fairly typical piece of apparatus to examine and discuss in this regard. It is not spectacular in appearance, and, in this respect, is characteristic of many of the more important and less publicized products of the laboratory. In external ap- pearance it is nothing more than a metal box measuring about 3 x 5 x 16 inches, and designed to mount on central-office frames in accordance with our regular telephone practice. Within the box are a few apparently very simple pieces of apparatus al- most as unimpressive as the box itself. No part of the assem- bly would attract particular attention from the casual observer, and yet it will reveal on careful study an interesting story of research.

A wave filter, of which the crystal filter under discussion is a special type, is a device that allows alternating current of cer- tain frequencies to pass readily through it, and opposes a high

* Presented at a meeting of the Institute of Physics in New York, N. Y., October 30, 1936.

25

impedance to currents at all other frequencies. Wave filters find many uses in modern telephony. In this instance, the filter is part of a broad-band telephone transmission system: that is, a system which transmits a large number of conversations simultaneously over a single telephone line. The line may be a pair of open wires on poles, a pair of small wires inside a lead-covered cable, or it may be a coaxial line consisting of a copper pipe which carries a centrally disposed insulated wire. This latter type of line is of special interest at the moment, since a first practical trial of it is now being made. Figure 2 shows the construction of the coaxial cable recently installed between New York City and Philadelphia. This cable contains two coaxial lines, one to carry speech in each direction, and each capable of carrying several hundred independent speech channels.

The transmission of several conversations simultaneously over a single circuit, which in recent years has become quite commonplace, is itself a remarkable achievement of communication research. It is accomplished by transforming currents of the voice range, the region from about 250 to 3,000 cycles, into currents of higher frequencies. A different frequency band is allotted to each of the conversations transmitted, just as different frequency bands are allotted to different programs in radio broadcast transmission. Not only does the same circuit serve to transmit a large number of conversations at different frequencies, but the same amplifier or repeater can serve for all speech channels, with great resultant economy.

With this type of transmission, known as "carrier transmission," the message carrying capacity of a circuit is determined by the width of the frequency band that the line and its associated apparatus are capable of transmitting effectively. If the available band width of the coaxial line is 1,000,000 cycles, for example, and if a frequency band 4,000 cycles wide is allotted to each speech channel, 250 independent telephone conversations can be conducted over two of these coaxial pipes.

26

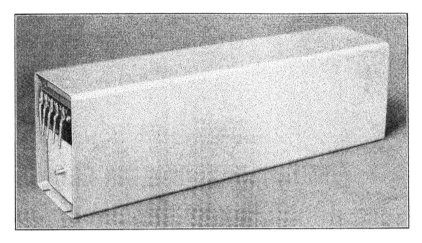

FIG. 1. IN THE CRYSTAL WAVE FILTER FOR BROAD-BAND TELEPHONY, AN AUSTERELY SIMPLE EXTERIOR COVERS A MOST INTERESTING COMBINATION OF RESEARCH PRODUCTS ORIGINATING IN DIVERSE FIELDS.

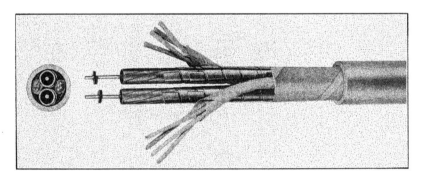

FIG. 2   A SAMPLE OF THE COAXIAL CABLE USED ON THE EXPERIMENTAL CIRCUIT BETWEEN NEW YORK AND PHILADELPHIA.

Crystal wave filters are used at each end of such a circuit— one for each speech channel transmitted in each direction. At the entering end, the filter serves to limit the transformed speech frequencies to those which fall within the assigned band, thus assuring that none gets into other bands to interfere with the speech in other channels. At the outgoing end, the filter serves to select a band of frequencies appropriate to it, and to guide the speech within that band to apparatus that returns it to its original form by relocating the frequency components in their normal positions.

To cover the entire range of frequencies that such a coaxial line can transmit would appear to require 250 filters at each terminal, each designed for a particular band of frequencies. In the interest of economy, however, only 12 different designs of terminal filters are used. These provide twelve 4,000-cycle channels, extending from 60,000 to 108,000 cycles, and each of these 48,000 cycle bands is then treated as a unit, and by a second step of modulation is relocated in its appropriate position on the frequency scale.

Filters play a very important part in the economy of broad-band telephone systems. This is partly because so many of them must be used—four for each two-way conversation— which puts a premium on low cost and physical compactness. But what is fully as important is frequency compactness, which determines the width of band that must be allotted to a speech channel. Because of the sharp cut-off of the crystal wave filter, it is practicable and economical to space the speech channels only 4,000 cycles apart.

If we removed the cover from one of these crystal filters, we should find a very simple assembly, consisting of four quartz plates, four metal boxes containing inductance coils wound on toroidal cores of compressed powdered permalloy, two other metal boxes containing mica condensers, and eight tiny variable air condensers for the fine adjustments. Any of the essential parts of this filter would serve to illustrate the evolutionary

27

character of development. Let us examine in this regard first the network itself, second the crystal, third the combination of the network with the crystal, and finally the coil. In each case we shall see evidence of contributions from many diverse directions.

To find the beginnings of the evolutionary train of thought which produced the network, we must go back more than thirty years to the time when Dr. G. A. Campbell, then of the American Telephone and Telegraph Company, was studying the possibilities of improving long-distance telephone transmission by loading, i.e., by inserting inductance coils in series with the line at regular intervals. Campbell did not stop with determining what inductance the coils should have and how they should be spaced, but went further and computed the characteristics of such a line for frequencies both within and beyond the range of those used in telephony. He discovered that the coil-loaded line, which transmitted telephone currents more efficiently because of inductance added by the coils, transmitted high frequency currents less efficiently because the inductance, instead of being distributed uniformly, was concentrated at the points where coils were inserted. The transition from improved transmission at low frequencies to impaired transmission at high frequencies was very striking. The loaded line was said to have a definite cut-off frequency, which was a function of inductance of the coils and their spacing along the line.

The loaded line is now looked upon as a low-pass filter, the loading coils providing series inductance and the line wires shunt capacitance. Campbell was inspired by his discovery to study the general case of a reiterative ladder type network in which the reactances of rungs and side arms of the ladder were generalized. Two specific forms of the ladder type network are shown schematically in Figure 3. One is a low-pass and the other a band-pass filter. Within the frequency limits of the pass band, the filter transmits currents without attenuation, but outside of the limits, currents are rapidly attenuated.

28

Important variations of this network were later derived by K. S. Johnson, G. C. Reier, O. J. Zobel, and others, which made it possible to make combinations of filters to meet almost any practical requirements of band width and of terminating impedance, as well as to avoid reflections of waves at filter terminals.

Campbell later made another great advance in network theory when he derived the lattice type structure, shown in Figure 4. This criss-cross network is a much more flexible tool than

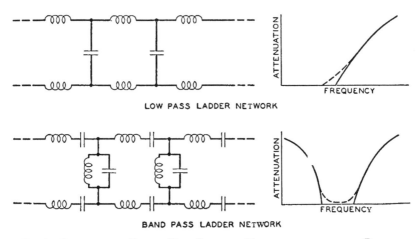

LOW PASS LADDER NETWORK

BAND PASS LADDER NETWORK

FIG. 3. SCHEMATIC OF LADDER TYPE LOW-PASS FILTER, ABOVE, AND OF A BAND-PASS FILTER, BELOW. THE RESPECTIVE ATTENUATION CHARACTERISTICS ARE SHOWN AT THE RIGHT.

its predecessor of the ladder type. Sharper cut-offs at the edges of the band are obtained with it, and a greater range of characteristics becomes possible in practical filter design. One might expect that further complication of the network would lead to still further possibilities in these directions, but Campbell proved that the lattice structure was as effective as any symmetrical structure that could be derived from combinations of simple inductance and capacitance, thus greatly simplifying the task of later students.

It is unfortunate that it does not seem possible to explain

the action of a filter simply in mechanical terms. A tuned circuit of inductance and capacitance is accurately analogous to a weight supported by a spring. One can devise a mechanical filter likewise from weights and springs in place of inductances and capacitances. One can even observe that it acts as a wave filter; but the explanation of its action is far too complicated to treat other than with mathematical equations, which we need not go into here.

When Campbell's wave filter was first developed, no extensive practical need was apparent for it, but it was nevertheless quickly recognized as a tool of great potential value, and

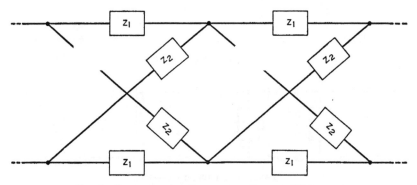

FIG. 4. SCHEMATIC OF GENERALIZED LATTICE NETWORK.

the need for it was not long in coming. The earliest commercial use of a wave filter in a telephone transmission system was made in the first transcontinental line in 1915 to prevent singing in telephone repeaters at frequencies above the voice range. A more extensive demand was created with the introduction of carrier telephone systems in 1916. From these beginnings the use of filters has expanded with great rapidity. Today we find the study of filters and related networks among the most important and productive activities of the Laboratories. Some twenty or more mathematically trained men now devote their entire time to network design, and a staff of five mathematicians is continuously engaged in research in this field.

Some indication of the importance of filters and related networks could be given by mentioning the large amount of money invested in them, but in another sense their actual value far exceeds any estimate in dollars and cents, for without filters many of the savings made in recent developments of long-distance telephony could not have been realized and advances now impending would have been quite impossible. Indeed, the invention of the electric wave filter should be ranked as one of the most important in the history of telephony.

Until quite recently, nearly all of the filters developed for telephone transmission systems have been made from combinations of simple inductances and capacitances in ladder or lattice circuit structures, or in arrangements derived from those simple types. With all such filters, the sharpness of cut-off at the edges of the pass band is dependent on the resistance associated with the filter elements. Condensers can readily be built with low resistance, but practical inductances invariably embody at least the resistance of the the copper wire of which they are wound, and if they employ magnetic cores, resistance is also contributed by hysteresis and eddy currents. It is true that the resistance could be made small by making the coils large, but this quickly runs into practical difficulties at telephone frequencies.

A possible escape from this limitation is to use in place of an inductance coil a mechanical element coupled to the electric circuit in such a way that its mass or inertia appears in the electrical circuit as inductance. Mechanical vibrating systems may be made with extremely small damping so that little mechanical resistance need accompany the inductance so secured. The stiffness of the spring supporting the mechanical mass will, of course, appear as capacity in the electrical circuit, and this must be taken into account.

The quartz crystal filter might be called a semi-mechanical filter. It is an electrical filter, but it uses mechanical mass to provide some of its inductance elements. The mass in this case is that of the crystal itself. This mass is transformed into inductance, and the stiffness of the crystal is transformed into capacitance, through the "piezo-electric" effect. Quartz is a crystal which generates an electromotive force when subjected to a mechanical stress; conversely, it changes shape when subject to electrical stress. Quartz has another property which is very important. It is a very stable material and can be obtained in large crystals of a high degree of purity. Indeed, we find by X-ray examination that the orderliness of the arrangement of its atoms is extreme.

Let us review some of the steps which led to the introduction of quartz into the filter circuit. The piezo-electric effect has been known since 1880, when it was discovered by the Brothers Curie, but it was not until about 1917 that the effect began to receive serious consideration for practical uses. Indeed, there was no possibility of making much practical use of the effect until the vacuum tube amplifier became available. During the period of the World War, A. M. Nicholson, of the Bell Laboratories, made numerous experiments on devices employing rochelle-salt crystals, which display remarkably high piezo activity. With them he made microphones and loud speakers, and demonstrated a great variety of possible practical applications. About the same time Professor Langevin of France was making practical trials of quartz crystal oscillators driven by vacuum tubes to generate high-frequency sound under water for use in the detection of submarines. Langevin's use of the crystal in this manner inspired others to experiment with it. Professor Cady in this country recognized the value of the quartz crystal vacuum tube oscillator as a source of radio frequencies of high precision. Following Cady's lead, experimenters in the Bell Laboratories developed crystals accurately compensated for temperature changes, and in this way produced frequency controls of very great precision. Today we find nearly all radio broadcasting stations equipped with quartz crystal controls, and we also find them in small radio transmitters such as those used in airplanes or in police patrol cars.

In its use as an oscillator, the quartz crystal with its attached electrodes behaves much as a simple electric circuit comprising an inductance and two capacitances connected as in Figure 5. However, it is not possible practically to duplicate the performance of the crystal with actual coils and condensers. To build the equivalent circuit would demand coils having less than a hundredth of the resistance-to-reactance ratio of those which are available.

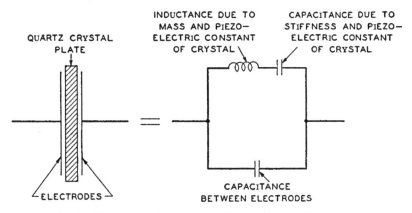

FIG. 5. EQUIVALENT CIRCUIT OF A QUARTZ-CRYSTAL OSCILLATOR.

L. Espenschied, at that time of the American Telephone and Telegraph Company, first suggested that a ladder-type filter of sharp cut-off could be made by employing piezo crystals to supply equivalent inductance without the added resistance that is unavoidable when inductance is obtained by the use of coils. The band width that could be obtained with crystals in the ladder network, however, was too narrow to give it a very wide field of application. With this type of filter employing quartz crystals, the ratio of the upper to lower cut-off frequencies had to be less than 1.008, which means that for a 60-kc. carrier the pass band could be only about 480 cycles.

W. P. Mason, of the Bell Laboratories, studied the application of crystals to Campbell's lattice-type network in 1929, and found that by adding an inductance in series with each crystal element in the lattice, the ratio of the upper to lower cut-off frequencies could be increased to 1.135.[1] This made the crystal filter a practical device meeting the requirements of a band-pass filter for broad band carrier telephony. Crystal

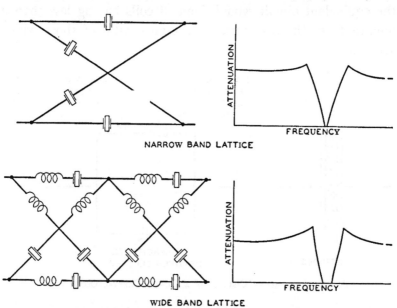

NARROW BAND LATTICE

WIDE BAND LATTICE

FIG. 6. USING CRYSTALS ALONE, ABOVE, ONLY A VERY NARROW PASS BAND CAN BE OBTAINED, BUT THE ADDITION OF INDUCTANCE, IN SERIES WITH THE CRYSTAL, MAKES IT POSSIBLE TO WIDEN OUT THE BAND OVER FIFTEEN FOLD.

filters with and without the added inductances are shown with their characteristics in Figure 6.

Further studies by Mason indicated that the inductances in the side and lattice arms could be wound on the same core and placed in the side arms as indicated in Figure 7, which is a schematic of the actual filter used in the coaxial cable system.

[1] Space does not permit a full explanation of this and other steps in the design of the network. The reader is referred to Mason's original paper in the *Bell System Technical Journal*, July, 1934.

A bridging resistance was also inserted between the sections to help in sharpening the cut-off. In addition to these modifi-cations, the circuit finally evolved contains added capacitances in multiple with the crystal. These capacitances serve to con-

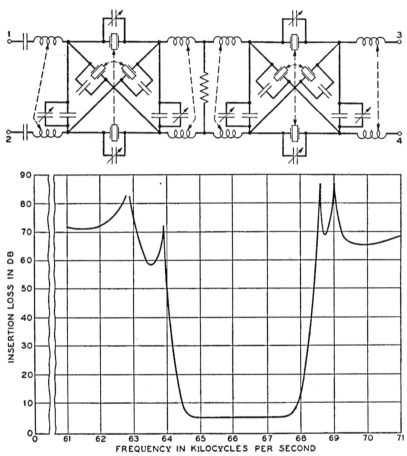

FIG. 7. SCHEMATIC DIAGRAM OF A QUARTZ-CRYSTAL BAND-PASS FILTER, ABOVE, AND THE FILTER CHARACTERISTICS, BELOW.

trol the width of the pass band and to permit fine adjustment.

In the lattice-type network as developed by Mason and em-bodied in the filter under discussion, the quartz crystals are cut in the shape of thin rectangles from 2.4 to 4.2 cm. long, and with a width of about 50 per cent, and a thickness of 2 or 3 per cent, of the length. The two broad surfaces of the plate are coated with aluminum deposited from the vapor in a vacuum chamber. This process, now quite familiar to physicists, is the same as that employed in making astronomical mirrors. Electrical contact is made to the metal surfaces through the supporting points.

Such a crystal has several modes in which it may vibrate when excited with alternating voltage of appropriate frequency. There are five simple modes of vibration: two parallel to the edges of the plate, one perpendicular to the surface of the plate, one in flexure, and one in shear. The crystal may also vibrate in combinations and overtones of these modes, any of which may be excited with proper combination of exciting frequency and size and form of crystal. For this filter "longitudinal vibrations" are used, the length of the crystal determining the natural frequency of vibration. Crystals of four different frequencies are used for each filter, but the twelve different designs of filters employed for the groups of twelve 4,000-cycle channels in each of the 48,000-cycle bands are almost identical except for the dimensions of their crystals.

Although it is the length of the crystal plate which principally determines the natural frequency for longitudinal vibrations, the other dimensions are not merely a matter of convenience. Both width and thickness affect the natural frequency through internal elastic coupling among the several modes of vibration. They also, of course, affect the impedance of the crystal. Further, it is not enough to have a crystal which vibrates at the desired frequency. It is necessary too that it should not vibrate at unwanted frequencies. For if there should be a mode of vibration in the attenuating range near the cut-off frequency of the filter, the filter would pass frequencies which it is desired to exclude.

The first filters of this type were made with crystals cut with their thickness parallel to the X or electric axis of the crystal, their width being along the Z or optic axis, and the length along the Y or mechanical axis. It was found that crystals cut in this manner had a strong coupling to a shear mode of vibration, which would introduce an additional resonance at a frequency 40 per cent higher than the desired frequency. This had the effect of introducing an added pass band at this point, which was undesirable. By studying the elastic constants and modes of vibration of quartz, Mason proved that by cutting the crystal so that its major axis made a small angle (about 18.5°) with the mechanical axis, as shown in Figure 8, there would be no coupling between the longitudinal and shear modes of vibration, and accordingly the crystals for the filter were cut in this manner.

In the circuit diagram of the filter, shown in Figure 7, there are eight crystal elements, whereas in the actual physical structure there are only four. This has been made possible by making one crystal serve for two. The aluminum plating is applied in two parts with a narrow unplated strip separating them. Electrically, therefore, there are two crystals, but mechanically there is only one.

The coils in this filter are also of special interest as a product of research. Their function is to provide inductance where more is required in the filter network than is provided by the equivalent inductance of the crystal itself. Since the filter is to be used at high frequencies, in this case up to 108,000 cycles, the coils must have very low alternating-current losses. Air-core coils can be made which will meet the electrical requirements, but the space occupied, as well as the large magnetic fields, is objectionable, and so cores of magnetic material are employed, but it must be a material with extremely low hysteresis and eddy current loss. The requirement is met by a core of compressed powder of molybdenum permalloy. This material is itself one of remarkably high intrinsic permeability and low hysteresis, and by insulating the separate grains of the powder from which the core is pressed, eddy currents are kept very small.

These coils have another property which is quite important

37

in this application. They maintain the same inductance over a very wide range of temperatures. This is unusual in coils with ferromagnetic cores, since permeability in general increases rather rapidly with rise of temperature. Molybdenum-permalloy is no exception in this regard, but its increase of permeability with temperature has in this case been compensated by incorporating with it a small proportion of an alloy whose permeability decreases rapidly with temperature. The

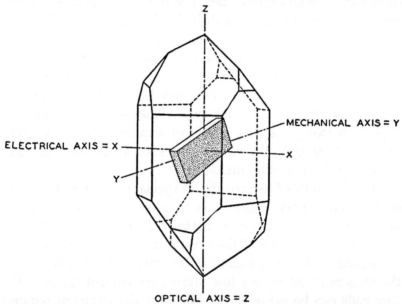

MECHANICAL AXIS = Y

ELECTRICAL AXIS = X

OPTICAL AXIS = Z

FIG. 8. THE QUARTZ PLATES ARE CUT WITH THEIR FACE PERPENDICULAR TO THE ELECTRICAL AXIS OF THE CRYSTAL, AND WITH ENDS AND SIDES MAKING A SMALL ANGLE WITH THE MECHANICAL AND OPTICAL AXES.

resulting combination displays negligible change of permeability over the range of temperatures to which it is subjected in use.

The evolution of this core presents still another interesting illustration of physical research extending over a long period of time. In this case we must go back thirty years to the first application of inductive loading to telephone lines. The problem then, as now, was to obtain inductance with as little added resistance as possible. The best that could be done in the first loading coils was to use fine iron wire for the core. This wire had to be drawn to .004-inch diameter to hold the eddy-current loss to the required low value, and this feature made the coils very expensive.

The iron-wire core was soon succeeded by a core of compressed powdered electrolytic iron, the separate grains of which were insulated by a thin coating of shellac. This iron-powder core was used in loading coils from 1916 to 1927, when it was succeeded by the smaller permalloy-powder core, which in turn is now being succeeded by the still smaller and cheaper molybdenum-permalloy-powder core.

Permalloy is a nickel-iron alloy of very high permeability and low hysteresis, which was first developed for loading submarine telegraph cables. It is a tough, malleable metal, and considerable development work was required to produce a satisfactory method of reducing it to powdered form. After the molybdenum permalloy has been powdered, the individual particles must be insulated. The insulation must be thin, so as not to introduce too large a magnetic gap between adjacent grains; it must withstand the effect of compressing the grains into a solid mass of nearly the density of solid permalloy; it must be refractory, so as not to be broken down in subsequent heat treatment; and it must retain its insulating quality through compression and heat treatment.

With the crystal wave filter, as with all other products of research, the task of producing the practical apparatus in form for manufacture and use was not completed with the solution of the problems to which I have referred. No less important are the many steps of engineering development that had to be taken to insure that the apparatus could be made economically and would always work. Among such steps were the development of methods of cutting and plating crystals, the development of a successful mounting for the crystal, provision for precise adjustment, shielding from electrical interference, and protection from moisture. In these features of the development we would find similar evidence of evolution.

Although it is impossible in a few pages to bring out the effort that has been expended in the past thirty years in developing this unimposing but important exhibit, enough has been given, I trust, to explain what was meant by the statement that industrial research is an evolutionary process. A consequential feature of industrial research is that it is a long time in the doing and calls for patience not only from the investigator but from his financial supporters.

Another striking feature which is characteristic of nearly all research is that applications are found in quite unexpected fields. In this case, researches on the loaded telephone line, the transatlantic cable, the use of crystal to detect submarine, the study of the diffusion of impurities through metals, the plating of metals by evaporation, all found application in a way which could not possibly have been anticipated while the fundamental work was being done.

But the most important feature of all is one which the preceding discussion has done little to bring out. It has to do with the character of the men who brought this filter into being, and the spirit of investigation which guided them. Men of many types, working in different fields of research, have contributed their bit to this development, but these men all have certain characteristics in common: good minds as a foundation, many years of learning in the fundamentals of their science and the methods of research, and a coöperative attitude; for without coöperation of individuals these synthetic products of research could never be produced. Above all else, however, they had " the spirit to adventure, the wit to question, and the wisdom to accept and use "[2] which seems to me the best summary of the requirements for a research worker.

OLIVER E. BUCKLEY

[2] H. D. Arnold, in the BELL TELEPHONE QUARTERLY, April, 1932, page 96.

Making Neighbors of Nations

An Anniversary

MAN against the Atlantic—what high adventure that struggle has brought since the venturesome voyage by the Santa Maria and its determined commander! Nearly 350 years after Columbus another significant transatlantic crossing was made by the " Great Western," which was the first of the transatlantic liners. Its trip from Bristol, England, to New York took only two weeks. A few years later, in 1858, the first transatlantic cable was laid, and communication across the Atlantic was no longer dependent on water transport.

In the years prior to the turn of the century, men of science were learning things about electric impulses, which showed a surprising readiness to jump off metal conductors and travel through the air; and in 1901, one of the young men investigating these phenomena, Guglielmo Marconi, startled the world by flashing " International S " through the air across the broad Atlantic. During the next quarter of a century research and development brought about still further advances in transportation and in communications. A striking parallel occurred in that, during this period, science turned to the air as a new medium for operations in the fields of both communication and transportation.

While the airplane was becoming a scientific and commercial achievement, telephone engineers were working zealously at turning wireless impulses into speech—teaching them to carry syllables, just as Alexander Graham Bell had taught the impulses from a wet cell battery to carry syllables along a wire. In 1927, there occurred two other significant victories over the Atlantic—one by transportation, when Lindbergh, in May, flew a single-engined airplane non-stop from New York to Paris; and the other by communications when on January 7, 1927, just ten years ago this month, the work of the scientists and engineers in the field of radiotelephony culminated in the inauguration of telephone service across the Atlantic between New York and London. Now, on this tenth anniversary of the bridging of the Atlantic by telephone, it may be of interest to glance backward over the record.

Much has been written upon the fundamentals and technique of radiotelephony as demonstrated and applied in overseas service. The advances in the science are indeed remarkable. They are part, however, of the story of engineering achievement which it is not the intention to tell here. This article is merely intended as a brief history and outline of the scope of Bell System overseas telephone service and the steps by which the infant service of ten years ago is attaining full stature.

As far back as 1914, Bell System engineers were looking forward to the possibility of projecting the human voice across oceans. The high vacuum tube had been developed sufficiently to offer the key to the attainment of radiotelephony. The famous Arlington tests with Paris, Panama, and Hawaii were made in 1915. Despite interruption by the war, prospects of actually applying radiotelephony for service across the Atlantic began to take form by 1923. To put to practical use this new science meant pioneering in an untried field and risking a considerable expenditure in apparatus on both sides of the ocean.

The first efforts were concentrated on spanning the Atlantic between the nearest practicable points. Along the Great Circle route the closest land was the British Isles, although in those days there was considerable doubt that a radiotelephone circuit would work successfully over such a distance. The British General Post Office had available a toll wire network extending from London throughout Great Britain and also, in coöperation with other European telephone administrations, had developed

42

an extensive toll layout to many European countries. The favorable distance factor and the existence of the wire networks at both ends, coupled with the further advantages of a common language and the potential traffic volume to be expected between the two great financial centers of New York and London, led to the establishment of the first link (a long wave channel) across the Atlantic as a New York-London circuit.

EARLY EXTENSIONS OF TRANSATLANTIC SERVICE

Shortly following the opening of this circuit, the service was extended beyond the terminals of the radio circuit by means of the wire toll lines at each end, so that by the end of 1927 all of the United States and Cuba, together with a part of Canada, was interconnected with Great Britain.

How best to extend service to the countries on the European continent was the next problem. It appeared that, at least during the early development years of the radiotelephone service, the best and most reliable way to serve such countries was by utilizing the extensive wire telephone network radiating from London to the principal European countries, in combination with the radio link which had been established.

By this means service was extended in 1928 to many of the countries in western Europe, such as Belgium, the Netherlands, Germany, Sweden, France, Denmark, Norway, Switzerland, Spain, Austria, Hungary, and Czechoslovakia. Although for some years to come the volume of traffic to the continent appeared likely to be small, it seemed that direct circuits to the larger countries in Europe eventually would be required. The tentative plans for the future, as then formulated, took this probability into account.

A second important step in the overseas plan was to strengthen the initial radio link to provide a more reliable pathway across the Atlantic. Bell System engineers had been studying and testing short waves. The results indicated that

43

with highly directional antennas a satisfactory overseas circuit could be obtained with much less power than was required for the long wave circuit. Furthermore, the short wave characteristics would conveniently supplement the long wave characteristics, since the two types of circuit were found to be affected differently by varying radio transmission conditions.

In order to insure reliable telephone service for any considerable volume of transatlantic traffic, it was deemed desirable to build up the New York-London route as the "backbone" route. Therefore, three short wave channels were designed to supplement the long wave circuit, the first short wave channel being placed in service in June, 1928. With the later installation of the remaining two short wave channels in 1929, there was available a four circuit group, diversified as to type of radio channel and with sufficient capacity and a fair degree of reliability to care for the future transatlantic demand as it arose.

Toward the end of 1929, most of North America, including part of Mexico, was connected for service with Europe. Several additional European countries, such as Italy, had also been added to the transatlantic telephone network.

Overseas Fundamental Plan

In July of 1929, applying the experience gained with the early transatlantic radio circuits to Europe, a fundamental plan for overseas service was formulated, with the aim of placing the United States in communication with the rest of the world as rapidly as technical developments and the prospects for traffic warranted. The fulfillment of this plan for a world telephone network radiating from the United States westward and southward as well as eastward was the next important step in the pioneering stage of overseas service.

It may be of interest at this point to note that of the thirty countries outside of Europe considered at that time for the extension of service, twenty-three are now served and two more will soon be added.

HEADING SOUTH

The first move toward the world plan was soon made. Looking southward, arrangements were completed with the Compania Internacional de Radio, a subsidiary of the International Telephone and Telegraph Corporation, located in Argentina, to establish a short wave radiotelephone circuit between New York and Buenos Aires. This circuit was opened in April, 1930, and provided service between North America and Argentina, Chile and Uruguay—the latter two countries being reached by wire lines from Buenos Aires.

In 1931, a direct connection was also established with Rio de Janeiro, Brazil, utilizing the same stations at this end as were used for Buenos Aires, the new connection providing service to the telephone network of Brazil.

Later, in 1932, Lima, Peru was added as a direct connection, and by 1935 Paraguay was also connected, being reached by wire lines from Buenos Aires.

TRANSPACIFIC AND THE FAR EAST

Meanwhile, the radiotelephone continued its steady march across the world in other directions. Having bridged the Atlantic and connected North and South America, the telephone dared to challenge the mighty Pacific. The fundamental plan pointed the way for a transpacific station and so, in December, 1931, from radiotelephone centers established near San Francisco, a short wave channel was provided between that city and Honolulu, Hawaiian Islands. This circuit, used in combination with the wire lines and the inter-island short wave radiotelephone system of the Mutual Telephone Company of Hawaii, binds closer to the mainland that distant bit of American territory.

The transpacific station was utilized in March, 1933, for a further jump west. A direct connection was established between San Francisco and Manila, through arrangements with the Philippine Long Distance Telephone Company, providing service to that easternmost outpost, the Philippine Islands.

Some years back, in 1931, Java and Sumatra in the Netherlands Indies, those famed islands of travel and adventure, had been added for service by a combination of facilities reaching half way round the world *eastward* from the United States. The makeup of the route was unusual: transatlantic radio channel New York to London; wire lines London to Amsterdam; and radio again between Amsterdam and Bandoeng, on the island of Java. Bandoeng had short wave connections with Sumatra to complete the last link in the chain. This was a long route with several switches and types of facilities, so, in order to shorten and simplify the route, in 1934 direct connection was established with Bandoeng from San Francisco *westward*.

Late in 1934, direct connection was made between San Francisco and Tokyo, thus providing service to Japan, some five thousand miles distant and nearly a day earlier in time. Incidentally, the wide time difference on the transpacific channel causes many special problems of operation and scheduling and, of course, is somewhat of a handicap as regards the short period during which the business days on the two sides of the Pacific overlap. Nevertheless, it is surprising how easily both the user and the operating force adapt themselves to the jumping calendar.

Finally, to nearly complete the roster of far eastern countries, it should be mentioned that tests are under way, looking toward service with China.

Around the World by Telephone

It may be well to digress a moment to tell of a rather significant event arising out of the change from *eastward* to *west-*

ward in the route to Java. When this change in route was an accomplished fact, the overseas telephone network had spanned the world. To mark this achievement an "Around the World" circuit was set up on April 25, 1935, with the co-operation of the Netherlands Indies Telephone Administration, the British Post Office, and others. Starting and terminating at New York, this circuit was composed of a New York-London radiotelephone channel, wire lines between London and Amsterdam, a radio link again between Amsterdam and Bandoeng, another radio channel from Bandoeng to San Francisco, and, finally, wire lines from San Francisco to New York. Sitting in one room at 32 Sixth Avenue, the Long Lines building in New York, Walter S. Gifford, President of the American Telephone and Telegraph Company, conversed around the world with T. G. Miller, Vice-President in charge of the Long Lines Department, who was seated in the next room.

CARIBBEAN AND ATLANTIC COAST

While the march westward was on, still further expansion was taking place along the Atlantic coast.

Late in 1932 a new radiotelephone center to serve Central America and the Caribbean area was established near Miami, Florida. A short wave channel was provided which was first used for connection to Nassau, in the Bahama Islands. This Caribbean circuit, operated on a "party line" basis, was designed so as to serve a number of countries direct. Venezuela and Colombia were also connected for service shortly thereafter, by arrangements with telephone companies which operate in these territories and which are allied with the Associated Telephone and Telegraph Company. In collaboration with the Tropical Radio Telegraph Company, operating in Central America, the countries of Panama (including the Canal Zone), Costa Rica, Guatemala, and Nicaragua were added for service in 1933 and Honduras in 1935. The Dominican Republic was also connected for service with the Miami station in 1935.

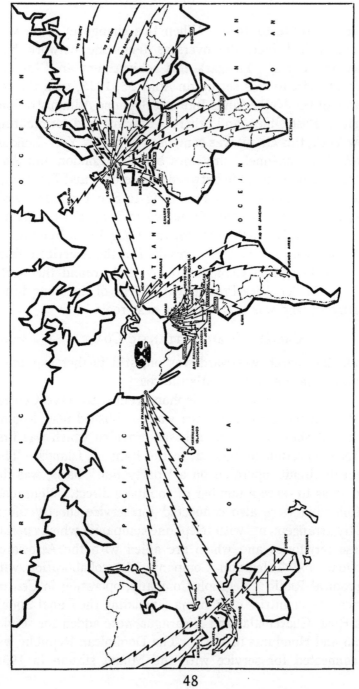

OVERSEAS TELEPHONE CONNECTIONS OF THE AMERICAN TELEPHONE AND TELEGRAPH COMPANY AND ASSOCIATED COMPANIES.

Puerto Rico, Jamaica, and Salvador followed in 1936. Thus, service to most of the countries and islands of the Caribbean area is well established.

Farther north on the Atlantic coast, in 1931, a short wave channel was established between New York and Hamilton, Bermuda, linking this well-known island into the overseas telephone network.

Now, turning back to the first overseas route, the transatlantic, a few of the more unusual extensions of the scope of service along that route are worthy of attention.

LATER EXTENSIONS ON THE TRANSATLANTIC ROUTE

Service to Australia was opened in 1930, using the New York-London and the London-Sidney channels, the first case of two radio links in tandem. South Africa, Egypt, and Siam were added, using similar tandem radio channels, in 1932, and also India in 1933. Palestine was reached through Egypt in 1933 and Syria in 1934 by means of wire lines beyond the radio terminal at Cairo. Algeria, French Morocco, Tunisia, and French Indo-China were added for service in 1934, all being reached through England and France, which latter country has radio circuits to these distant territories. Iceland was reached in 1935 by means of tandem radio links via London, and Kenya in Africa was added, by the same means, in 1936.

On December 1, 1936, a direct short wave radiotelephone channel was established between Paris and New York to carry the traffic between France and the United States. This single direct circuit is supplemented by the use of the New York-London "backbone" circuit group for periods when the direct New York-Paris circuit is not in service. As conditions warrant, it is planned that other countries in continental Europe will be reached by direct connections from the United States.

Today there is available, to the public of the United States, telephone service to nearly seventy countries and territories

49

scattered throughout the globe, and to the neighboring nations of Canada, Cuba, and Mexico. To the latter territories, of course, service has been available for many years by wire lines.

At this point a glance at the route layout may be of interest. Of the nearly seventy countries and territories reached, there are now twenty-two with which the United States has direct connections. The other forty-odd territories are reached via the countries with which the direct connections are made. The circuits radiating from the United States are centered at three focal points:—New York, which is the terminal point for the transatlantic and the most distant southern routes, has direct connections with England, France, Argentina, Brazil, Peru, and with Bermuda; Miami, which is the terminal for the Caribbean area, has connections with the Bahamas, Dominican Republic, Jamaica, Puerto Rico, various points in Central America, Colombia, and Venezuela; San Francisco, which is the terminal for the transpacific area, has connections with Hawaii, Japan, Java, the Philippines, and will connect soon with China. It should be noted that much of the service at present is on a party-line basis, that is, several countries are served by a single transmitting channel from this end which is switched between the distant terminals as traffic requires. Undoubtedly, as traffic develops, individual circuits or circuit groups will be required for the larger countries. Although there are, naturally, some departures, it is surprising how closely the present network follows the fundamental plans outlined early in the development of overseas service.

SERVICE ARRANGEMENTS AND RATES

Overseas service is closely akin to the telephone service given within the Bell System, but as it is rendered jointly with foreign administrations or companies outside the Bell System and is provided by radio rather than by wire, there are some essential differences in the type of services offered and in the arrangements under which it is given. In many instances the service is rendered under circumstances where both the time of day and the language are different at each end of the route. Further, there is the necessity of developing methods which will appeal to the public of various countries which may have telephone service, habits and methods differing widely from those in the Bell System. In this connection it may be well to point out that the Bell System does not own nor have any financial interest in any of the distant ends of the overseas radiotelephone services.

The arrangements for overseas service with the various companies and administrations in the overseas territories may be of interest. For each territory with which there is a direct connection there is executed a so-called "service agreement" which, in general, is not unlike a Bell System "connecting company agreement." These agreements, in brief:—provide that each company or administration shall establish and maintain the requisite facilities for the service at its end; cover the basis for the rates and the exchange of currencies; and specify methods for the collection and division of revenues. Also contained therein are commitments as to the use of standardized practices and uniformity of accounts. The arrangements with the twenty-two overseas administrations directly connecting with the Bell System by radiotelephone are practically the same, except for some minor differences. The service between the United States and each territory with direct connections is operated jointly by the Bell System on one side and the company or administration on the distant side, and the division of the revenue from the radiotelephone haul is divided equally between the two sides, each side bearing its own expenses. In fact, except for ship-shore service, where the revenue is divided one-third to the ship station and two-thirds to the shore station (because of the greater power and more extensive operating furnished by the shore station), the overseas services are truly joint partnerships on a "fifty-fifty" basis. Although

51

these fundamental arrangements, as can be readily seen, are quite simple, the necessary details of handling the service by joint agreement as to the commercial practices, traffic procedures, plant operating methods and engineering standards are, of course, manifold in number and often complex in character.

The following table shows the direct overseas routes from the United States, and the name of the administration which is the contracting party at the other end of the direct connection. It is opportune here to say that the sincere and hearty cooperation of the overseas administrations interchanging traffic with the Bell System has been one of the most important factors in the establishment, extension, and improvement of the overseas telephone service.

Route	Connecting Administration
New York—London, England	General Post Office—British Gov't
New York—Paris, France	Dept. of Posts, Telegraphs & Telephones—French Gov't
New York—Buenos Aires, Arg.	Compania Internacional de Radio
New York—Rio de Janeiro, Brazil	Companhia Radio Internacional
New York—Lima, Peru	Compania Peruana de Telefonos
New York—Hamilton, Bermuda	Halifax & Bermudas Cable Co.
San Francisco—Honolulu, Hawaii	Mutual Telephone Company
San Francisco—Manila, Philip. Is.	Philippine Long Distance Tel. Co.
San Francisco—Bandoeng, Netherland Indies	Dept. of Posts, Telegraphs & Telephones—Netherlands Indies Gov't
San Francisco—Tokyo, Japan	Dept. of Telecom.—Japanese Gov't
Miami—Nassau, Bahama Is.	Government of the Bahama Islands
Miami—Bogota, Colombia *	Compania Telefonica Central
Miami—Caracas, Venezuela	Compania Anonima Nacional Telefonos de Venezuela
Miami—San Jose, Costa Rica	Tropical Radio Telegraph Company
Miami—Panama City, Panama	Tropical Radio Telegraph Company
Miami—Guatemala City, Guat.	Tropical Radio Telegraph Company
Miami—Managua, Nicaragua	Tropical Radio Telegraph Company
Miami—Tegucigalpa, Honduras †	Tropical Radio Telegraph Company
Miami—Ciudad Trujillo, Dom.	Compania Dominicana de Telefonos
Miami—San Salvador, El Sal.	Government of El Salvador
Miami—San Juan, Puerto Rico	Porto Rico Telephone Company
Miami—Kingston, Jamaica	Jamaica Telephone Company

* There are two other direct connections with Colombia from Miami, one with Barranquilla and the other with El Centro.

† There is another connection to La Lima, Honduras.

The rates for overseas service on the New York-London route between Great Britain and the east coast of the United States were first established as $75.00 for the initial three minutes and $25.00 for each additional minute. The United States, and later the remainder of North America, were divided into large rate zones and zone charges were added to the base rate mentioned, for calls beyond the first zone. This zone system, modified somewhat as to zones and zone charges, is still in effect for overseas service. On the European side a similar zone plan is in effect for countries reached by wire lines beyond the radio terminal. On other routes to countries in South America and the Far East, rate zones have also been set up in certain of the foreign territories where long wire hauls beyond the radio terminals are involved.

Early in 1928, the transatlantic rates were reduced to $45.00 for the initial period and $15.00 for each additional minute, and again in May, 1930, were further reduced, this time to $30.00 and $10.00. In the meantime, similar rates had been introduced on the new routes which were opening up, ranging in level from $30.00 on routes such as the South American and transpacific to a $12.00 rate for the Miami-Nassau channel, which is one of the shortest radiotelephone links radiating from the United States. Night rates were introduced on the transatlantic route, which is the only route operated at present during the entire twenty-four hours, in June, 1935, at a level 30 per cent lower than the day rate.

Between July and November, 1936, the rates on most of the overseas routes from the United States were reduced from 30 per cent to 50 per cent, while at the same time Sunday rates approximately 30 per cent lower than the weekday rates were introduced on practically all routes. Today the rates on direct routes usually range from $21.00 for weekday service and $15.00 for Sunday service on most of the longer routes down to $7.50 for weekdays and $5.25 on Sundays on the shorter radiotelephone routes.

53

PASSING OF PIONEERING STAGE

The pioneering stage of the overseas development is now passed. The establishment of most of the important fundamental primary routes is well along and service is extended to almost all of the larger countries. In fact, the number of telephones which may be reached from any Bell or Bell connected telephone comprises 93 per cent of the world's telephones.

Strengthening and improving this present radiotelephone network and the service it renders is the next step in the up-building of overseas telephone service. In fact, plans are now under way to improve the transatlantic short wave circuits within the next two years and in the near future to provide direct service to additional European countries.

Elsewhere in the world, while the overseas telephone network from the United States has been growing, radiotelephone services have been established radiating from other countries, so that today many of the larger countries have rather extensive systems. Of these larger nations, Great Britain, France, Germany, Italy, Holland, and Spain of the European nations; Japan, in the Far East; and Argentina and Brazil in South America, in particular have actively developed overseas radiotelephone routes, so that along the usually travelled world lanes everywhere one now finds the overseas telephone paralleling the age-old trade routes.

USE OF THE SERVICE

Since that first year of overseas service, when the traffic averaged only a few messages a day (about 2,000 messages were handled in 1927), the volume has increased from both the addition of new territories and from growth in calls with countries already connected until today, at recent levels, the total overseas traffic on a yearly basis would approximate

50,000 messages. Of these, the transatlantic traffic generally ranges from 60 to 65 per cent.

Although no recent analysis has been made, it is estimated that about half the day-to-day traffic volume is comprised of business calls and the rest is made up of calls relating to social or personal matters. This usage is by all types of business and people. Probably the greatest use of the service is for the transaction of financial matters. World happenings of widespread interest, such as the events at the time of the abdication of King Edward VIII, and the devaluation of the monies of various countries, often bring sudden sharp peaks in the traffic load. But day in and day out the increasing volume consists of calls made, in the main, because there is a work-a-day job to be done in finance, in sales, in engineering, in manufacturing, and because there is the need to keep families or friends in touch with each other. What, a short ten years ago, was a great adventure in crossing the seas by telephone has now become a familiar experience to many in the everyday conduct of their affairs. And yet there remains the thrill which always seems to be associated with ocean voyages by voice or in person, and why wouldn't it be a rather thrilling experience, however often it happened, to hear a "hello mother!" or a real Yankee "Howdy Jim!" from Cape Town or Manila! Yet for all the wonder of it, the service is already in use regularly as one of the modern conveniences of 20th Century life.

In one phase of human life the overseas telephone has filled a need that could have been filled by no other means—except perhaps television. To members of a family separated by thousands of miles there is nothing that quite equals the elation of hearing each other's voices. Especially at holiday time is the need for this contact strong, and so each year has witnessed a tremendous increase in the volume of Christmas and New Year's greetings across the seas by telephone.

In 1935, the transatlantic traffic on Christmas day totalled 246 messages, and on all overseas routes 358 messages. In the holiday season just passed, the overseas traffic on Christmas was 674 messages, an increase of 88 per cent over the year before; and on New Year's Day of this year, 365 overseas messages were handled, over three times as many as on that same day last year. From the results it will be seen that it was a truly Merry Christmas and Happy New Year for the Overseas Telephone Service, coming just at the appropriate time to add to its pride in celebrating its tenth birthday on January 7, 1937.

W. G. THOMPSON

Equipping the Telephone Fleet

IN an article published in the QUARTERLY of January, 1936, under the title "Engineering the Telephone Fleet," body equipment for Bell System motor vehicles was discussed. This large and gradually growing fleet, now numbering some 17,500 vehicles, is constantly changing, due to the replacement of worn out and obsolete cars, trucks, and associated equipment and to the addition of units to care for growth. New vehicles are always supplied with the latest equipment, to provide maximum assistance to the men engaged in the various kinds of work necessary to the construction and maintenance of the Bell System's outside plant. Through this process, the design standards of the motor vehicle equipment are constantly being improved.

Various kinds of equipment which are associated with the vehicles are described in this article in some detail. These include: trailers for carrying materials and tools which cannot be conveniently or economically carried on the trucks; trailers for serving as storehouses for the men when the units do not need to be moved frequently enough to warrant the continual use of a car or truck; devices to improve the economy and utility of the vehicles in telephone work; various types of power operated equipment especially adapted to assist the gangs in the many kinds of work they have to do; and other accessory devices which are hand operated.

Generally speaking, this equipment has been designed or adapted to field requirements by Bell System engineers. It is observed in service, so that improvements can be made, better fitting it to existing requirements; and as new conditions arise, the designs are modified to meet them.

57

TRAILERS FOR CARRYING POLES AND OTHER MATERIALS

Transporting new telephone poles from the yards out to the line and hauling old poles away from the locations where they are removed becomes a big operation in the aggregate when it is considered that in the neighborhood of a million poles a year are set by the telephone companies. Generally speaking, the poles are transported on medium or heavy duty two wheel trailers (Figure 1) upon which the load of poles is practically balanced.

These trailers are equipped with an extensible tongue, which is connected to a towing hook built into the rear of the truck when medium length and short poles are carried. For transporting very long poles, the first pole loaded on the trailer bolsters is placed in the middle of the load and permitted to project ahead of the rest of the load, so that when the tongue and poles are properly lashed together this center pole, with a suitable draw bar fastened to its front end, serves as the tongue.

It has been found to be most satisfactory to bind the pole loads with wire rope by means of small hand operated winches especially designed for this purpose. Of course, the removable sliding stanchions, two on each side, also help to hold the load in place.

These trailers in the medium and heavy duty sizes weigh 2,900 and 3,800 pounds respectively, and carry loads of from three to eight tons. In keeping with the somewhat higher road speeds now prevalent with pneumatic tired trucks, these trailers are being built with dual pneumatic tires instead of the solid tires which have been used generally in the past. Also, electric brakes, which are operated by a rheostat in the cab convenient to the truck driver, have been found advantageous. In some instances, vacuum booster operated hydraulic brakes have been used. They, too, are operated from the cab by remote control.

There has been for some time a tendency in telephone work

FIG. 1. BALANCED LOAD OF POLES CARRIED ON " HP " OR " MP " TRAILER.

FIG. 2. JUNK ON " SLP " TRAILER.

FIG. 3. LIGHT POLE LOAD ON " SLP " TRAILER.

FIG. 4. SPLICER'S
EQUIPMENT IN "S"
TRAILER.

FIG 5 (BELOW).
"PCP" TRAILER
WITH SADDLES FOR
CARRYING REELS OF
CABLE.

FIG. 6. WITH SADDLES DETACHED, "PCP" TRAILER IS EQUIPPED WITH BOLSTERS
FOR POLE HAULING.

Fig. 7. (above).
Winch Loading
Trailer, Type
"WL," in Posi-
tion to Start to
Load a Reel.

Fig. 8 (left).
Reel Being
Drawn Up on
"WL" Trailer
by Winch Line.

Fig. 9. Reel
of Cable in Trav-
eling Position,
"WL" Trailer.

TRACTION LOAD-
ING " TL " TRAIL-
ER. FIG. 10 (TOP):
JACK-KNIFED
READY TO PICK
UP REEL. FIG. 11
(CENTER): LIFT-
ING REEL, WITH
TRACKS LOCKED.
FIG. 12 (BOTTOM):
IN TRAVELING PO-
SITION.

toward the use of lighter trucks. The carrying of heavy materials, such as reels of cable or suspension strand, loads of crossarms, etc., by suitable trailers relieves the trucks of these loads. Practically no weight is added to the truck by the balanced trailer loads, as in the case of the poles mentioned above. As an additional advantage, the single axle trailers require a minimum of storage space.

A light type of trailer (Figure 2) is used for carrying coils of wire, crossarms, tree trimmings, etc. This trailer weighs about 850 pounds and has a carrying capacity up to about two tons. It, like other telephone trailers, is of the two wheel type, in order to provide maximum ease in maneuvering, is light in weight in relation to carrying capacity, and is low in first and maintenance costs.

This trailer serves a dual purpose. With the removable sides and ends of the box body taken off (Figure 3), it becomes a light duty pole trailer. The tongue being short and of the fixed type, it is necessary always to use the center pole as a tongue.

Splicers' Trailers

Another type of trailer (Figure 4) is used in a different class of work by telephone gangs. Many cable splicing jobs require a considerable length of time. In such service this small trailer, with its box body having suitable compartments and racks, provides a convenient place for splicer and helper to keep their tools, sleeving, solder, paraffin, etc. At night the body is locked, a lantern is secured in a screen holder on top, and the unit can be left on the job.

For very short distances between splices the men may move the trailer along the street by hand. For moves of greater distance it is either trailed behind a vehicle or, for long hauls at usual road speeds, it may be carried in a truck. This trailer weighs approximately 420 pounds and ordinarily carries a load of about 450 pounds. There are many hundreds of these splicers' trailers in service in the Bell System.

HEAVY DUTY TRAILERS FOR REELS OF CABLE, ETC.

It is evident that special provision must be made for transporting reels of cable, which ordinarily may weigh up to 6,000 pounds each. One type of trailer for this work (Figure 5) carries the reel on a spindle with the design so arranged that the balance will always be slightly heavy toward the front or tongue end.

This cable reel trailer is loaded by placing the spindle through the center of the reel, raising the trailer tongue by hand until the back lips of the saddles hook under the spindle ends, and then pulling the tongue down with the truck winch rope. As the tongue is lowered, the spindle rolls forward on the saddles into the front brackets, where it is pinned.

Reels up to seven feet in diameter and 37 inches wide can be handled by this trailer, which weighs about 2,700 pounds. With this equipment the cable can be pulled from the reel while it is supported on the trailer spindle, thus obviating the necessity of unloading it and swinging the reel on a spindle supported by means of jacks.

By removing the detachable saddles and adding the pole bolsters, which also can be quickly attached or detached, this unit can be easily changed into a pole trailer (Figure 6). Since it has a non-extensible tongue, one of the poles in the load is used as a tongue.

For delivering the very heavy reels of armored cable on cross country jobs away from the highway, special trailers have been developed which are of heavier, stronger construction than the highway trailers and which have special provision for supporting the loads over soft ground. The so-called "Winch Loading Trailer" for this purpose (Figure 7) is loaded by means of a hinged yoke which is lowered back from the trailer by the winch rope until it rests against stops so that the steel rope slings can be hooked under the ends of the cable reel spindle. Then the winch rope pulls the yoke forward, swinging the reel free of the ground (Figure 8). By continuing to pull the yoke forward (Figure 9), the spindle slides up the guide until it can be locked at the top by means of hinged hooks.

It will be noted that two pairs of dual rubber tires are used on each bogie or wheel carriage supporting this trailer. The tires are so spaced that, where required by very soft ground, a steel track of hinged pads can be thrown over both dual wheels, with centering lugs between the dual tires. These are detachable and are not shown in the pictures.

Some tractors used in delivering reels of cable off the road do not have winches. For such a condition, the traction loading trailer (Figure 10) can be used. This type is sometimes referred to as a " Jack-Knife Trailer."

In loading this trailer, one of the caterpillar tracks is pinned so the wheels will not move, and the tractor is backed up, throwing the trailer frame and spindle hooks back and down so that the reel spindle can be caught. The tractor then moves ahead slowly (Figure 11), thus raising the reel until the jack-knifed trailer frame is pulled forward into the traveling position (Figure 12) and locked. The tongue is extended when a reel happens to rest in a hole, thus permitting the lowering of the spindle hooks quite low to pick it up.

The winch loading and traction loading trailers, as shown, weigh about 4,500 and 4,400 pounds respectively. They carry reels of cable weighing up to 10,000 pounds each, and measuring 46 inches wide by seven feet in diameter. These trailers have also been used to advantage in delivering heavy loading pots by hanging them from the cable reel spindle.

Truck Power-Take-Offs and Power Winches

The most frequently used device of power equipment on the truck is the power winch, and the simplest winch installation is the single drum type (Figure 13). The illustration shows the winch mounted on the chassis just before the truck body is installed. The cast steel winch drum upon which the steel winch rope is wound may be connected to the shaft by a jaw clutch, so that when desired the drum can be permitted to turn freely on its shaft, as in paying out the winch line. When the clutch lever at one end of the drum is pushed in one direction it engages the clutch and in the other direction it releases the clutch. Then at a farther position this lever action puts a brake upon the drum so that it can be prevented from spinning too fast if rope is being pulled off.

By different gear reductions and engine speeds, almost any desired rope speed can be secured, from 20 to 270 feet per minute. The winch will exert a line pull of 10,000 pounds, or even more for a short time. The heavy rope pulls introduce very great pressures between the driving worm and wheel (Figure 14), located in the case at the end of the drum. In fact, the pressure between these gear teeth may exceed seven tons at times because the teeth are closer to the shaft than the rope leaving the drum. In order satisfactorily to withstand these conditions, the gears and worms are very accurately cut from high grade especially selected bronze and steel respectively, and they run in a special extreme pressure lubricant.

At the end of the worm shaft away from the sprocket, there is a safety device in the form of an automatic brake (Figure 14) which works when the drum rotates in the reverse direction only and which will not permit the dropping out of control of a suspended load on the winch line due to overhauling of the gears. This is a very important feature in erecting poles and handling cable reels.

As viewed from beneath the chassis (Figure 15), the drive for this particular winch comes from a power take-off attached to the side of the truck transmission. A propeller shaft leads from the power take-off to an auxiliary transmission under the winch frame. From a sprocket on the shaft leading out of the auxiliary transmission a silent chain transmits the power

FIG 13. SINGLE DRUM POWER WINCH "SL12–RRC–82," WITH DRUM CLUTCH AND BRAKE.

FIG. 14. OPERATING MECHANISM INSIDE THE POWER WINCH.

FIG. 15 (BELOW). VIEW OF WINCH, POWER TAKE-OFF, AND AUXILIARY TRANSMISSION, FROM BENEATH.

FIG. 16. DOUBLE DRUM POWER WINCH "LFRC–82–LFR"

FIG. 17 (BELOW). "HC" EARTH
BORING MACHINE READY TO START A
HOLE

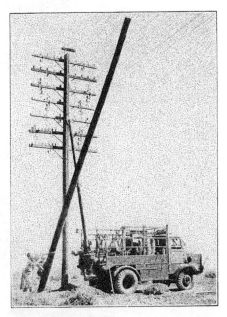

FIG 18 (ABOVE). ERECTING 40-FOOT POLE
WITH TELESCOPING DERRICK ON "HC"
EARTH BORING MACHINE. (NOTE HIGH
TRACTION TIRES ON FOUR WHEEL DRIVE
TYPE OF TRUCK.)

FIG. 19. DERRICK TELESCOPED AND BORING MACHINE LOWERED TO TRAVELING POSITION.

FIG. 21. DROP WIRE REEL ON "LI" BODY.

FIG. 22. LADDER PLAT-
FORM IN SERVICE.

FIG. 23 (BELOW). LAD-
DER PLATFORM IN CARRY-
ING POSITION ON 1½ TON
" LC–104 " TRUCK

up to the winch. A lever in the cab selects the desired gear combination in this auxiliary transmission.

For some conditions of operation, as for instance in handling a pole derrick with both a boom line and a fall line, a double drum winch (Figure 16) is required. Each drum is driven independently. A complete double drum winch, together with its power take-off, drive chains, mounting brackets and levers, adds about 970 pounds to the weight of a truck. For the single drum winch which is illustrated, this figure is about 650 pounds.

EQUIPMENT FOR SETTING POLES

Where a considerable amount of pole work is to be done, the use of the latest type heavy duty earth boring machine is advantageous (Figure 17). A truck of the four wheel drive type using high traction tires on all wheels can reach almost any location where it may be desired to dig the hole and set a pole. Ordinarily the actual digging of a six foot hole 20 inches in diameter requires two or three minutes.

The new telescoping tubular derrick (Figure 18), which is an integral part of the machine, can be extended or telescoped by power controlled by the earth boring machine operator. Also, the usual power operated leveling worms of the machine are used to tilt or straighten the derrick either sidewise or front and rear. These features are very convenient when erecting poles into wire lines or among tree limbs.

When it is desired to travel a short distance between pole holes, ordinarily the derrick is telescoped and carried in the erected position. However, when moves of any considerable distance are contemplated, the derrick is telescoped by power and then one of the power operated leveling worms lowers the machine into the truck body (Figure 19).

The earth boring machine mechanism as it is attached to the truck (Figure 17) consists of a tubular case with suitable brackets for the attaching bolts. At the rear end of the tube is an intermediate case connected to it by a swivel joint. At-

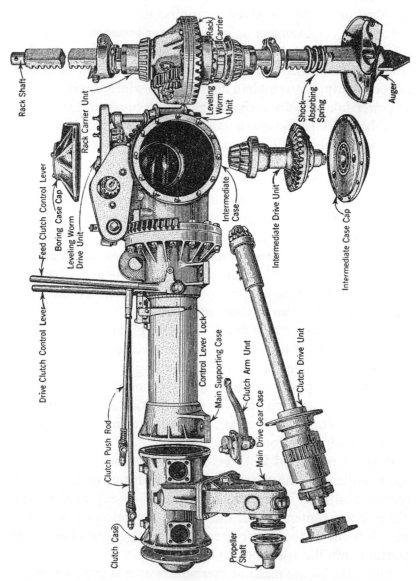

FIG. 20. "EXPLODED" VIEW OF "HC" EARTH BORING MACHINE; DERRICK NOT SHOWN.

tached to one side of the intermediate case by another swivel joint is the boring head case. The operation of these two swivel joints by power accomplishes the leveling of the boring head case so that the hole can be dug vertically regardless of any slope upon which the truck may be standing.

The mechanism of the boring unit, which is shown in an exploded view in Figure 20, is carried inside the three above mentioned cases upon anti-friction bearings throughout. All control for boring, and for raising and lowering the auger, is through the two operating levers, each of which connects with a clutch and a brake. Power from the clutches to the auger rack shaft is transmitted by two lines of shafts consisting of solid shafts working inside quill or hollow shafts, pairs of bevel gears being used at each point where there is a change in direction. The inner or solid shafts are responsible for rotating the auger and the quill shafts for raising and lowering it.

The complete truck, chassis, cab, body and earth boring machine weigh about 14,500 pounds. The weight of the boring machine mechanism alone is about 3,000 pounds.

REELS FOR DROP WIRE

Thousands of half ton cars, somewhat lighter vehicles than those discussed thus far, serve men who use insulated drop wire for making connections from poles to buildings. These cars are equipped for carrying a drop wire reel (Figure 21), which can be used on the car or on the ground for paying out or winding coils of wire. These reels are convenient to handle, as they weigh only about 30 pounds, and they have an automatic brake to prevent the spool from over-running and snarling the wire.

AERIAL WORK

Recently much interest has been shown in, and a considerable amount of experimental field work done with, a device called the ladder platform (Figure 22). This consists of an especially designed, very strongly built extension ladder having a platform near its top where one or two men can work. The ladder is always carried and supported in the truck. When in use, its bottom is pinned to the floor in a swivel joint, so that before the man ascends he can readily swing the ladder around to any position on the sides or back of the truck, where it is supported by a strong steel ring permanently mounted on the truck body. The ladder is also arranged so that it can be extended or shortened by one man.

This device is used for maintenance work, such as inspection and repair of aerial cable, tree trimming, etc. When the job is such that the truck is moved with the workman on the platform, a telephone connection is ordinarily maintained between him and the driver to insure coördination.

To take down the ladder for moving long distances, it is first telescoped down to its shortest length and swung around to rest on a straight bar on the front side of and below the ring. Then the pivot pin is pulled from the floor and the ladder balanced on the cross bar, after which it is lowered to a horizontal position (Figure 23).

It is planned to use the ladder platform with light maintenance trucks of 1½ tons capacity, such as that illustrated in Figure 23. The permanent ring adds about 200 pounds to the weight of the standard body and the ladder with its platform weighs about 214 pounds.

In all the designs of automotive equipment for telephone outside plant use mentioned above and the many others in this same general class, particular attention has been paid to safety of operation as well as convenience for the men and economy in performing the work. It is needless to say that the use of these and the many other similar items of equipment greatly expedites the work, which is of distinct value in the day to day gang performance but is doubly important during times of emergency.

When automotive equipment is transferred from one section

of the country to another, as is often necessary in clearing up storm damage, etc., it is very advantageous to have uniformity of equipment, so that the specially organized forces can function immediately in accordance with the methods followed in their usual work. Also, of course, the large degree to which the equipment is now uniform leads to the purchase of a relatively large volume of each item, so that purchasing advantages are realized, as well as improved manufacturing arrangements, more satisfactory inspection of the different types of units before they leave the factories, and more prompt availability of the various kinds of new equipment as the requirements for them arise at any points among the field forces throughout the country.

T. C. SMITH

A Northwest Winter—and the Telephone

Editor's Note:

The following report was compiled at the headquarters of the North-western Bell Telephone Company under the heading, " A Brief Resumé of the Effect on Telephone Service of the Abnormal Weather Conditions prevailing during the Winter of 1935–1936." The document was written for internal circulation only, but since it constitutes an interesting revelation of telephone operating conditions, and of the operating point of view, during a Northwest winter, it is printed here with the thought that all Bell System readers will take pride in the record.

" THE coldest winter weather in its history" was the announcement of the Federal Weather Bureau regarding the extended period of subnormal and subzero weather prevailing in our territory from December 24, 1935, to the latter part of February, 1936. This record-breaking situation, with temperatures below zero for consecutive periods of from 25 to 30 days and with lows of 34 degrees below zero in Iowa, 35 in Nebraska, 52 in South Dakota, 55 in Minnesota, and 56 in North Dakota, was accompanied by frequent snows and high winds, these causing drifts in places of 25 feet or more which, in spite of all the efforts of the railroad and highway crews, slowed up and at times completely paralyzed all forms of transportation, leaving many communities and families isolated. The snowfall during the period varied from 2 feet to 5 feet throughout the territory. On many days the combined conditions of cold and blinding blizzard rendered it quite dangerous to attempt cross-country travel by any means of locomotion.

Naturally such a situation affected the business and social activities of the entire population and resulted in the most severe and prolonged test of our facilities and service that has ever been experienced. Peak days on which the community use of telephones was more than double the normal volume

68

were the rule rather than the exception, while toll business during the worst period of the winter ranged from 25 to more than 150 per cent above normal.

Effect on Telephone Facilities and Service

Our outside plant is well designed for these conditions and in an excellent state of upkeep, as is evidenced by the fact that practically the only type of plant failure was wire breaks due to extremely low temperatures. This type of trouble is always experienced with low temperature but is usually not serious. In spite of the fact that this cold-weather wire-break trouble has been studied for many years and has been minimized by certain refinements in design, no economical means of complete elimination appears to be available. The strain placed on wire during an extremely cold period might be illustrated by the fact that a 130 foot span having 14 inches of sag at 100 degrees above zero will contract until the sag is about 3 inches at 40 degrees below zero. Defects in the wire from wear or other causes are likely to result in breaks when the additional strain is applied.

Out of a total of 4,500 toll circuits in the plant, less than 10 per cent were out of service, due to this cause, for comparatively short periods during the days of the most severe temperature and wind conditions. These troubles, fortunately, were not concentrated, and only a few of the smallest communities at isolated points served by only one or two circuits were without telephone service for more than one day.

While troubles in connection with rural station service, both owned stations and service station companies, were not abnormal, the effect of failures of these lines frequently cut off families from any form of communication.

In many communities, the central office equipment, particularly the manual equipment, in spite of additional operators,

69

etc., was unable to handle the traffic as promptly as usual because of the abnormal number of calls.

In the dial cities, there was evidence of prolonged overloads which were noticeable to the customer by failure to obtain the dial tone and by encountering busy trunk groups. In Des Moines, additional trunks and rearrangements brought some relief. In Minneapolis, spare switchboard positions were cut into service where available, and interoffice trunk groups were enlarged both in Minneapolis and Omaha.

Traffic to tourist bureaus and street car, bus, taxi, railroad, and coal companies was probably the heaviest of any one type of business. In Minneapolis, the Yellow Cab Company was flooded with calls for a period of several days. In some cases, because of busy lines to schools, the operators helped by furnishing information as to which schools were closed.

In only one or two instances were peg counts of local use of telephone equipment taken on the day of the heaviest traffic. However, the record of the high recorded day at representative exchanges, as tabulated on the following page, furnishes some information as to increased traffic, of which Sioux City, Iowa, taken on February 7, is probably the most representative of the peak loads recorded.

Except for a somewhat slower answering time, due to overloads, we have no evidence of where telephone service failed to serve the purpose for which it was designed.

It is difficult to estimate how many millions of dollars of additional investment would be required to maintain the normal speed of the telephone service in emergencies of this kind. Beyond anything that we could do with regard to adding facilities in our own plant, there would still be the necessity of customers providing themselves with much additional service. For example, the railroads and coal companies, the newspapers, highway departments, etc., would need to have a large increase in their telephone facilities and personnel to maintain a normal service during such periods as they have just experienced.

Exchange	Local Traffic			Toll Traffic		
	Normal	High Recorded Day	Per Cent Increase	Normal	High Recorded Day	Per Cent Increase
Des Moines, Iowa	316,427	439,779	39	2,750	4,782	74
Cedar Rapids, Iowa	111,279	147,317	32	1,500	2,490	66
Sioux City, Iowa	140,099	316,513	126	1,150	1,791	56
Mason City, Iowa	37,238	55,420	49	850	1,324	56
Waterloo, Iowa	66,278	79,815	20	1,000	1,800	80
Davenport, Iowa	105,000	142,003	35	850	1,469	73
Omaha, Nebraska	430,000	735,000	71	2,700	3,874	43
Grand Island, Nebraska	26,000	51,225	97	385	575	50
Norfolk, Nebraska	14,850	28,000	90	440	670	52
North Platte, Nebraska	15,524	27,730	79	200	289	45
Sioux Falls, S. Dakota	70,000	133,000	90	825	1,285	56
Minneapolis, Minnesota	911,580	1,045,416	15	3,650	4,640	27
St. Paul, Minnesota	512,000	595,000	16	1,550	2,167	40
Duluth, Minnesota	144,000	204,306	42	725	852	18
Fargo, North Dakota	84,071	100,306	19	629	878	39
Grand Forks, North Dakota	41,188	50,845	23	326	478	46

EMPLOYEE PERFORMANCE

Meeting this emergency taxed the initiative and morale of the organization severely. The alertness and ingenuity of the District and other supervisory people were continuously demonstrated in their promptness in sensing the rapid increase in demands and in planning and assembling forces as well as in meeting many specific difficulties. The spirit shown by the operators, installers, repairmen, and other groups was excellent. Many unusual problems were encountered and met with ingenuity. Ex-employees whom we occasionally hire responded to the needs of the service with the same spirit as those regularly employed. The regular employees, without exception, willingly gave up personal plans and scheduled days off to help meet the conditions by working long hours at top speed as the occasion might demand.

In many cases transportation was provided by the members

of other departments. Taxicabs and cars rented from "Drive-It-Yourself" companies were used extensively. When other means of transportation failed, the employees frequently walked in order to be at work on time. Many operators arranged to stay with friends nearer the offices, or their supervisors provided sleeping facilities in or near the exchange. One outstanding example of devotion to duty was the case of an operator in Sioux City who, on the morning of February 8, reported for duty after walking two miles against a 38-mile wind in a temperature of 18 degrees below zero.

The efforts of our Plant forces were directed toward giving preference to toll line troubles on circuits leading to towns that were isolated. This was done under the most severe conditions. The general use of motor vehicles and equipment had to be abandoned and our forces resorted to other means of transportation, such as snowmobiles, skis, snowshoes, railroad trains, railroad speeders, horses, and, in two cases, an airplane. Two types of snowmobiles were used, one type propelled by a chain track similar to an army tank and the other provided with skis in front and rear with motive power supplied by an engine equipped with an airplane propeller. In North Dakota, officials of the Great Northern and Northern Pacific Railway Companies extended every practicable aid to us in clearing trouble. They permitted the use of their section men and speeders in every case where we asked for such help.

In many of the smaller exchanges, especially magneto, where the local forces realized that some of the rural subscribers were more isolated than others, daily tests of these circuits were made. Where it was determined that trouble existed or that a portion of the customers on any one line were out of service, the last customer reached was asked to check the remainder of the stations and make temporary repairs of broken wire, with the understanding, of course, that proper remuneration would be paid for the time they spent on the work.

However, in spite of the use of all other possible means of transportation, much of the trouble necessitated walking for considerable distances. In one instance a repairman walked 19 mile in one day to clear toll line trouble with temperatures 15 below zero and a strong wind. In another case two men were forced to spend most of Christmas day in a small town consisting of a grain elevator and a few other buildings. In several cases workmen walked from 10 to 12 miles a day through deep snow and traveled more than 60 miles on foot during a calendar week.

While the ingenuity of employees in getting to and from work and in clearing trouble on rural service and circuits leading to towns that were isolated were probably more thrilling, the performance of the forces in carrying on the routine work of the exchange, the handling of the central office equipment under tremendously overloaded conditions, and the installing of the greatest net gain in stations during any similar period since 1920 provided an accomplishment equal in performance and worthy of the highest praise and commendation.

In all of the above activities and hardship, every effort was made to protect the health and safety of the employees, it being of particular interest that no serious cases of accident or illness developed during the period.

Uses Made of Telephone Service

With rail and highway transportation hampered and mail service badly crippled, telephone subscribers were forced to rely upon the telephone considerably more than under normal conditions. In many cases, telephone service became the only substitute for all these other public services. It was the one service which enabled families, business, government, and communities to maintain contact. The state highway commissions and county officials used it extensively in connection with their efforts to open highways. The railroads used it in connection with the clearing of snowbound rights-of-way. Train crews engaged in clearing rights-of-way reported frequently from the nearest available telephone. Train dispatchers checked the progress of these crews by calling farmers along the railroad. In a number of exchanges, it was extensively used for calling the homes of children attending consolidated schools, informing the parents not to start their children out, etc. On the days when the school busses were running, many calls were made to see if they arrived safely.

Farmers who were able to get into town called their neighbors to see if there were any supplies they could bring to them in order to save them a trip during the bad weather. Merchants in towns would call the farmers and make deliveries of coal and other commodities by traveling along main highways, with farmers meeting them at specified points to obtain supplies. Travelers in blocked trains and automobiles sought shelter in nearby homes. Telephone calls informed their families of their safety.

At Corydon, Iowa, on Saturday, February 8, the day of the worst blizzard, a water main broke and the entire town was deprived of water for three days. The telephone was used to inform the people of this situation and when water would again be available.

In communities where there was a shortage of bread, milk, or other commodities, dealers used the telephone to locate sources of supply. The C. C. C. Camp located near Camp Brook, South Dakota, placed an emergency call for food. Fort Meade and the Highway Maintenance Department at Sturgis organized caravan of snowplows, trucks, and men as a rescue party to carry food to this camp. Similar means were used to reach other inland towns located in the northwestern part of the state.

Stores experienced a great increase in orders by telephone. Many stores put on extra help to answer telephones and make deliveries.

A number of cases were reported where farmers who had discontinued their service for a considerable period, but where the telephones were still in place in their residences, reconnected their own telephones and called the local manager explaining what had been done and of their intent to come in and arrange for the reëstablishment of their service as soon as possible.

Snowbound homes and communities reported cases of critical illness by telephone so that snowplows and highway crews could open the roads and bring aid. Physicians found it difficult, and in many cases impossible, to reach their patients and gave instructions by telephone for the care of the sick. Some cases which are typical of the general conditions may be briefly mentioned as follows:

An ambulance carrying a patient from Persia, Iowa, to Council Bluffs at night was stalled south of Underwood. The driver went to the nearest farm house, called the operator at McClelland, who summoned farmers to shovel a path for the ambulance, which then went on to its destination.

The son of a farmer living nine miles west of Pocahontas, Iowa, became ill with an acute case of appendicitis. The telephone in that home was a service station out of Verina but was out of order. The farmer walked to a neighbor who had Pocahontas service and from there called a doctor, who was unable to reach the farm but gave instructions as to treatment over the telephone. The next day the boy's condition was much worse. Neighbors who had kept in touch with the family called for a snowplow, which was able to proceed within a quarter of a mile of the farm house. The boy was carried to where the road was open and in a neighbor's car, with the snowplow breaking the trail, they reached Gilmore City and from there Fort Dodge, where an emergency operation was performed. The distance traveled was only 50 miles but eleven hours were required for the journey.

A doctor at Valley Junction, Iowa, had three rural patients

who could not be reached by the road and had to be treated by telephone. The doctor states that the telephone was the only means of contact between these people and the outside world.

At Virginia, Minnesota, the night operator received a call for a doctor and, sensing something unusual, she called for several until one was found. When the doctor arrived he found four people overcome by escaping gas from a frozen gas main; a pulmotor was obtained, and the victims saved.

The operator at Grand Marais, Minnesota, succeeded in summoning help for a stricken family 70 miles north of that town. A trapper living on the Canadian side with his family walked 10 miles to the nearest telephone and asked the operator to send help to his home. He reported that one child was dead and the rest of the family seriously ill. The operator communicated with Canadian officials and obtained help from that source.

The manager at Howells, Nebraska, was advised by a doctor that the telephone of a farmer residing seven miles in the country was out-of-order and that one of the children was seriously ill with scarlet fever. The manager walked 14 miles to repair the telephone, the roads being covered with snow-drifts from four to eight feet in depth.

During the storm of February 3, the towns of Springfield and Gann Valley, South Dakota, were isolated as far as long distance service was concerned. The trouble was reached and repaired by using a saddle horse for transportation. At Gann Valley there was an epidemic of measles and no doctor was available. The telephone service enabled the people of these communities to communicate with doctors in neighboring towns.

Eight cases are on record where babies were brought into the world by following instructions given by doctors over the telephone. A resident just outside of the city limits of Omaha called their family physician on Saturday night, February 8, regarding a confinement case. The doctor's car became stranded in snow several blocks from the home and he could not make his way there even on foot. He backed out and drove into town, from where he telephoned the home. The father, having assisted the doctor at the births of three previous children, was given specific instructions by telephone, which he carried out successfully alone. The doctor was unable to get to the home until Monday but he kept in touch by telephone and when he did arrive he pronounced everything satisfactory with regard to the birth of the baby girl.

On account of the deep snow making it impossible to get through, a doctor at Atkinson, Nebraska, gave instructions over the telephone for the handling of three confinement cases.

Other similar situations were reported from Faribault, Minnesota; Wayne, Nebraska; LeMars, Iowa; and Canton, South Dakota.

Public Reactions, Both Critical and Commendatory

Of all the expressed reactions from the public, it is difficult to pick out any of a definitely unfavorable nature; there were hundreds of a most favorable character. At a few exchanges, principally in the larger towns where the operators were handling a peak load of calls, some criticisms were received to the effect that service was slow.

In Des Moines, after experiencing for several days the enormous overloads of local calls with resultant lack of promptness in completion of calls, it was decided to interview personally several hundred of our customers. We chose those who had contacted the Repair Department concerning delays, busies, no dial tone, etc., and of the nearly 500 interviewed substantially all were interested in our problem and appreciated our contacting them and there was not a single case of serious dissatisfaction with the service. Similar programmed interviews with large groups of subscribers in other exchanges where delayed service developed met with the same results.

77

Public reactions were in general favorable. Newspapers gave considerable space to the weather and to its effect on telephone service. Several papers ran suitable feature articles on the latter. Advertisements were inserted in papers where appropriate. All of these apparently gave telephone users a tolerant understanding of the situation and as a result the service was better than they expected.

A doctor, who has always been hypercritical of the service, called the Chief Operator to express appreciation of the fine service under trying circumstances.

Other comments received at various exchanges may be quoted as follows:

"I have received more value from my service during the past few weeks than I pay for it for an entire year."

"Our telephone was the only contact with the outside world for over a week. I cannot see how anyone can get along without one."

"Telephone instructions received from the doctor who could not reach my farm were responsible for saving the life of my daughter."

"If it had not been for the help of your agent, I would have lost my wife and three children."

"We don't know what we would have done if it had not been possible to secure help by telephone."

"First aid instructions received by telephone saved my hands from amputation after they were badly frozen."

Many compliments and thanks have been received for the services rendered and much consideration has been shown the operators.

One banker who sensed the situation during the December 24 storm gave orders that all use of the telephone in the bank must stop during the storm except in cases of extreme necessity.

On the evening of February 7, during the height of the most severe blizzard in Grand Island, Nebraska, a number of men from the Episcopal Church called at our Grand Island office and were shown through the building. All of these men were high in their praise of the service, and especially were they complimentary relative to the manner in which the girls handled the terrific volume of calls while these men were observing them at work.

At Litchfield, Minnesota, when one of our operators offered to pay a taxi driver for taking her home, he refused payment, saying "the telephone operators have done so many good things for us during this stormy weather that I would not think of accepting payment from you for a ride, or from any of the operators."

Another interesting example of willingness on the part of the forces to volunteer help to others in an emergency was obtained from Mr. Bayard H. Paine, one of the State Supreme Court Judges of Nebraska, who called at our office immediately following a severe blizzard. He informed us that while on his way to Grand Island, Nebraska, during the storm his car ran off the road into a ditch and a passer-by agreed to send him a wrecking car from the nearest town. When this car arrived he found that it was a light wrecking car. He stated that after considerable effort, covering a period of two hours, during which time the wrecking car became stalled in the ditch also, a large telephone truck came along. Mr. Paine called attention to the fact that in spite of these telephone men being out on an emergency trouble, the big truck stopped alongside his car, some of the men jumped out, looked over the situation, pulled out a cable from inside the truck, and without any ceremony hooked the cable on the front end of the wrecking car and pulled both cars out of the ditch up on to the road. Two of the men jumped out of the truck, unhooked the cable, placed it in the truck, waved their hands, and the truck went on about its work. Mr. Paine marveled at the fine coöperative spirit which prompted these men, busy with their own emergency repair work, to stop and assist an unfortunate person such as he, and the spirit in which they did so. He expressed regret that it was not possible for him even to thank them, as they merely waved their hands and left without thought of compensation or reward for their service.

Our manager at Buffalo, Minnesota, repaired a service station line containing seven stations when he learned that the lineman was ill and unable to take care of it. The subscribers expressed their gratitude for giving them this service when it was so badly needed.

The manager at Cambridge, Minnesota, repaired a broken service station line when he found that the lineman was snowed in. Many other instances of assistance to service station companies were evident throughout the period.

Conclusion

The alertness and ingenuity of employees and the splendid spirit shown by them in maintaining throughout this trying situation a high quality of continuous service is impressive. This is particularly true when, in reviewing the various reports, it is realized that this performance was not local to any one community or area but was typical of all communities and all areas within the Company's territory, including the territories of subsidiary companies.

While naturally pleased with such an accomplishment, the Company's organization has recognized the importance of surveying and recording in detail any equipment and operating failures, interruptions or delays, with the view of minimizing the effect of similar conditions through refinements, adjustments or expansion where sound administrative analysis indicates that it is appropriate.

Notes on Recent Occurrences

PRESENTATION OF JOHN J. CARTY MEDAL AND
AWARD FOR THE ADVANCEMENT OF SCIENCE

IN connection with the presentation on November 17, 1936, by the National Academy of Sciences of the John J. Carty Medal and Award to Dr. Edmund Beecher Wilson, Professor Emeritus of Zoölogy, Columbia University, the following presentation address was made by Dr. Frank B. Jewett, Vice President of the American Telephone and Telegraph Company:

MR. PRESIDENT: In connection with presenting Dr. Edmund Beecher Wilson to you for receipt of the John J. Carty Medal and Award for the Advancement of Science, voted to him last spring by the Academy, it is appropriate that a word both as to the history of the medal and award and Dr. Wilson's qualifications for it should be made. I am happy that it falls to my lot as Chairman of the Carty Medal Committee to make these few remarks.

The late General John J. Carty, in whose honor this medal and award were established, was for many years a distinguished member of the National Academy of Sciences. His major activity throughout his active life was concerned with the development of electrical communication. At the time of his death on December 27, 1932, it can be said without fear of contradiction that he was recognized to be the most distinguished communication engineer in the world. This distinction had long been his and when, on June 30, 1930, he retired for age from active service as Vice President of the American Telephone and Telegraph Company, his associates in the Bell System sought for some appropriate way in which to signalize their esteem for him and for his contributions to science and engineering. Recognizing as they did the wide and scholarly sweep of his intellectual and scientific interests and his deep and abiding faith in the value of the National Academy of Sciences as a powerful instrumentality for the advancement of science in the United States, they decided that nothing could be more appropriate nor more pleasing to General Carty than the establishment of a perpetual medal and award in the Academy to be named for him.

The result of this decision was that the Directors of the American Telephone and Telegraph Company, acting for themselves, the stockholders of the Company, and the employees, all of whom recognized their great debt to General Carty, gave to the Academy the sum of $25,000 to be held in trust, with the income available periodically for the bestowal of a gold medal and a monetary award. In addition to this, General Carty's immediate associates in the management of the American Telephone and Telegraph Company, as a token of their particular admiration and esteem, arranged for the design of the medal and the making of the dies needed for striking it.

In order that with the passage of time the medal and award should achieve a real distinction, and because of the catholicity of General Carty's interest in the whole domain of science, the donors in their Deed of Gift specified only two major requirements. The first and lesser of these requirements was that the medal and award should not be bestowed oftener than once in two years. As a part of this condition it was specified that with every award the net accumulated income since the time of the last award should be given to the recipient along with the medal and certificate.

The second and major condition specified by the donors was that the award should be to an individual for noteworthy and distinguished accomplishment in any field of science coming within the scope of the charter of the National Academy of Sciences, and should be either for specific accomplishment or for general service in the advancement of fundamental and applied science; and further, that there should be no limitation placed on the individual sought to be honored by virtue of race, nationality or creed. The method of selecting the candidates to be voted on by the Academy and the method of taking such vote was left entirely to the discretion of the Academy.

Under the conditions of this Deed of Gift, the Academy is assured at all times of complete and untrammeled freedom to bestow this particular honor periodically on anyone anywhere and for any achievement in the field of its present or future interest, whenever in its judgment such bestowal is appropriate.

Thus far since its establishment the medal has been bestowed but once, and that through unanimous vote of the Academy on General Carty himself. Fortunately, this evidence of esteem was made before General Carty's death and was a source of the deepest gratification to him. Unfortunately, presentation of the medal had to be made posthumously.

On this occasion the action of the Academy last spring was on the unanimous recommendation of the Carty Medal Committee. This recommendation was made after long and painstaking consideration. In presenting Dr. Wilson to you I feel I can do no better than to quote from the report of the Committee as follows:

> " In recent years, Professor Wilson has stood preëminent in the field of zoölogy, and the influence he has had on two generations of biologists is of a very high order. His individual researches on experimental embryology are classical, and his papers on cytology have been fundamental. His great book, ' The Cell in Development and Inheritance,' has perhaps influenced subsequent biological thought more than any other book produced in this country.

> " In arriving at its present decision to recommend Professor Wilson, the Committee has been guided by the terms of the Deed of Gift, which as they relate to the recipient's qualifications read as follows:

>> ' The award may be either for specific accomplishment in some field of science, or for general service in the advancement of fundamental and applied science.'

> " In view of his outstanding contributions, the Committee has no hesitancy in suggesting that Professor Wilson's selection is appro-

priate both as to specific accomplishment and general service, and we, its members, believe that every consideration points to him as one eminently qualified to receive the Carty medal."

It is now therefore my very great pleasure to present Professor Wilson for the Carty Medal and Certificate, and its accompanying Award, which in this case I understand to have a value of $3000.

GOLD MEDAL IS AWARDED BELL TELEPHONE LABORATORIES

THE award of a gold medal for 1937 by the American Institute of the City of New York to the Bell Telephone Laboratories has recently been announced. The gold medal, given annually by the American Institute in recognition of outstanding accomplishment in research, was awarded to the Bell Telephone Laboratories "for researches in electrical science which, applied to communication, have promoted understanding, security and commerce among peoples by transmitting human thought instantly throughout the world." The medal will be presented at a meeting of the Institute to be held on February 4, and will be accepted by Dr. Frank B. Jewett, President of the Laboratories. The American Institute of the City of New York was incorporated in 1828 for the purpose of "encouraging and promoting domestic industry in this State and in the United States."

RADIOTELEPHONE SERVICE IS OPENED TO LINER ON THE PACIFIC RUN

SHIP–TO–SHORE telephone service, which has been available for several years with a score of liners on the Atlantic, was extended to the Pacific Ocean recently when service was opened between this country and the steamship Chichibu Maru of the Nippon Yusen Kaisha (Japanese Mail Steamship Company).

The service to the Chichibu Maru is available throughout the ship's voyage, which touches Honolulu, Yokohama, Kobe, Shanghai and Hong Kong, and to all Bell and Bell-connecting telephones in the United States, Canada, Cuba and Mexico. The ship is 17,500 tons, one of the three largest ships in N. Y. K.'s fleet.

Contact with the Chichibu Maru utilizes the radio facilities at Dixon and Point Reyes, Cal., Bell System short wave transmitting and receiving stations respectively. These stations are already used for telephone service with Hawaii and the Orient, and for the past five years have been used in giving telephone service with the Empress of Britain, Canadian Pacific liner, during part of her annual round-the-world cruise.

FIRST DIRECT RADIOTELEPHONE CHANNEL TO CONTINENT OPENED ON DECEMBER 1

THE Bell System made its first direct contact with continental Europe on December 1, 1936, when a short wave radio telephone circuit was opened between stations of the American Telephone and Telegraph Company in New Jersey and stations of the French Ministry of Posts, Telegraphs and Telephones near Paris.

Before the opening of the new radio link, service between Bell and Bell-connecting telephones and those in France was handled through London. Service was originally established with Paris on March 28, 1928.

The transmitting stations for the direct circuit are at Lawrenceville, N. J., and Pontoise, France, while the receiving centers are at Netcong, N. J., and Noiseau, France. The circuit between New York and Paris totals about 3,600 miles in length. The cost of a three-minute conversation between the two cities is $21 on week-days and $15 at night and on Sundays.

It is interesting to recall that it was in Paris that the first spoken words to be transmitted by radio across the Atlantic were heard. In 1915, through the courtesy of the French Government, Bell System engineers were permitted to set up receiving apparatus in the Eiffel Tower, in an attempt to pick up speech sent out by other telephone engineers from Arlington, Va. These experiments, ending successfully with the transmission of intelligible speech, marked an important milestone in the development of the radio telephone system which now enable the Bell System subscriber to reach about ninety-three per cent of the world's telephones.

LARGEST WIRE HOOK–UP EVER ESTABLISHED UNITES MANY PIONEER GROUPS

PRESIDENT Walter S. Gifford of the American Telephone and Telegraph Company was the principal speaker at the international celebration of the Twenty-fifth Anniversary of the Telephone Pioneers of America, held on November 19. Over the largest wire hook-up ever established, Mr. Gifford addressed about 40,000 telephone people, gathered in 268 meetings in 234 cities in this country and Canada. The telephone hook-up extended from St. John, New Brunswick, to San Diego, Calif., and from Miami, Fla., to Edmonton, Alberta. More than 25,000 miles of telephone wires linked together the various groups, all of whom listened to the same speeches and heard the same entertainment.

Mr. Gifford was introduced to his vast audience by Chester I. Barnard, head of the international body of Pioneers and President of the New Jersey Bell Telephone Company, who was attending a meeting of the G. H. McCully Chapter of the Pioneers in Newark. From a meeting at the Hotel Commodore in New York of the Edward J. Hall Chapter of the Pioneers, of which he is a member, Mr. Gifford addressed his fellow Pioneers gathered in groups throughout the North American Continent. The international hook-up was introduced by President Barnard. Others who spoke were J. E. Macpherson, Senior Vice President of the Pioneers and Vice President of the Bell Telephone Company of Canada, who spoke from St. John, New Brunswick; and James L. Kilpatrick, President of the New York Telephone Company and President-elect of the Pioneers, who spoke from a meeting of the Empire Chapter at the Hotel Astor in New York.

ELL TELEPHONE QUARTERLY

MEETING THE CHALLENGE OF SLEET
AND FLOOD

THE TELEPHONE BUSINESS OFFICE

LANGUAGE AND THE TELEPHONE ART

SCIENCE RESEARCH IN ELECTRICAL
COMMUNICATION

BELL TELEPHONE

QUARTERLY

*A Medium of Suggestion
and a Record of Progress*

CONTENTS FOR APRIL 1937

VOL. XVI   NO. 2

PUBLISHED QUARTERLY FOR THE BELL SYSTEM BY THE AMERICAN
TELEPHONE AND TELEGRAPH COMPANY. SUBSCRIPTION, $1.50 PER YEAR,
IN UNITED STATES; SINGLE COPIES, 50 CENTS

Address all communications to

INFORMATION DEPARTMENT
AMERICAN TELEPHONE AND TELEGRAPH COMPANY
195 Broadway, New York

Contributors to This Issue

JUDSON S. BRADLEY

Yale University, B.A., 1918. Private, U. S. Army Ambulance Service with the Italian Army, 1917–19. Assistant editor, managing editor, *The Yale Alumni Weekly,* 1920–24. Southern New England Telephone Company, copy manager, advertising manager, 1925–28. American Telephone and Telegraph Company, Department of Operation and Engineering, Sales Section, 1928–30; Information Department, 1930–.

ROBERT P. JUDY

Pomona College, B.A., 1920. Associated Oil Company of Wyoming, Purchasing Agent, 1920–22. Southern California Telephone Company, Commercial Department, 1922–27. American Telephone and Telegraph Company, Department of Operation and Engineering, Commercial Division, 1927–; Commercial Results and Practices Engineer, 1934–.

FRANK B. JEWETT

Throop Polytechnic Institute (now California Institute of Technology), B.A., 1898; University of Chicago, Ph.D., 1902. Several honorary degrees. Instructor in Physics and Electrical Engineering, Massachusetts Institute of Technology, 1902–04. American Telephone and Telegraph Company, Transmission and Protection Engineer, 1904–1912; Western Electric Company, Assistant Chief Engineer, Chief Engineer, Vice President, 1912–25; Vice President, American Telephone and Telegraph Company, in charge of Development and Research Department, and President, Bell Telephone Laboratories, 1925–.

STERLING PATTERSON

Yale University, Ph.B., 1915. Reporter, *New York Tribune,* 1915–17. First Lieutenant, U. S. Air Service, 1917–19. Western Electric Company, Public Relations Department, and Editor, *Western Electric News,* 1919–30; Editorial Director, 1930–33. American Telephone and Telegraph Company, Information Department, 1933–.

Meeting the Challenge of Sleet and Flood

NATURE smote the Ohio River valley with heavy hand late in January, bearing hardship, suffering, destruction and death on flood waters which in the lower part of the river reached levels never before known. Cities, towns, hamlets, cross-roads settlements alike experienced the devastating force of a mighty stream gone berserk.

The floods in the Spring of 1936 covered a wider geographical area, exacting their toll from Maine to Maryland and the Virginias as well as along the Ohio. It was the communities along the upper reaches of that river and its tributaries which suffered then; this year, by contrast, it was principally from below Wheeling, W. Va., to the confluence with the Mississippi that the sullen, murky flood reared its crest to new heights, spread further to each side its greedy inundation.

Fortunately, ours is not only a vast country but a unified one. The same newspapers which carried early accounts of the misery and loss in the stricken territory carried also reports of the immediate, orderly, far-flung mobilization of every means to bring it aid: not only National Guard units and, in some instances, Federal troops, but the Coast Guard, the Public Health Service, Army Engineers, CCC and WPA workers and, as a matter of course, the Red Cross. Mobilized also, and equally as a matter of course, were the resources—the man-power, the supply service, the productive capacity and the operating, engineering and administrative capabilities—of the Bell System.

Well do the men and women of the Bell System know that catastrophe places upon them a double responsibility; for the same forces which inflict damage and destruction on all other property are no more sparing of telephone plant, while bringing at the same time all the more urgent need for communication. So with this flood: telephone calls within, into, and out of the affected areas by individuals, by industry, by the press, by the arms of rescue and rehabilitation multiplied many-fold, making abnormal demands upon plant which, because of damage, was in certain cases and for longer or shorter periods inadequate to provide even normal service.

So they swung into action on a front that included not only the flood area but such distant points as New York City and Jacksonville, Chicago and New Orleans: operators, plant men, engineers, commercial department people, executives, in the operating companies; Long Lines repair and maintenance men, repeater attendants, operators, traffic and circuit engineers; manufacturing, distributing, transportation, installation forces in the Western Electric Company; power supply and other specialists from the Bell Laboratories; and, in the A. T. and T. Co. headquarters organization, those who could best advise on problems anticipated or to be met.

MOBILIZATION FOR THE ONE GREAT TASK

A systematic mobilization of man power—*and* woman power —was directed at these three aspects of the one great task: To take in advance every possible precaution to protect the equipment and the service against the flood. If and when these precautions are unavailing, to maintain the service as long as power and a switchboard and a line are left to use and one person left to use them. And, if the waters are finally victorious wholly or in part, the plant is crippled or goes dead and service is greatly curtailed or suspends, to restore the plant and resume the service at the earliest moment humanly possible.

On the Ohio, in the early days of February, there might have been seen at one time stirring, determined, wearying efforts to achieve all three of those objects.

In the cities and towns first affected, where now the flood was receding, the work of restoration was in full swing: equipment was being dried out, or replaced from emergency shipments; the huge task of inspecting, repairing, renewing outside plant was surging ahead with augmented forces, which were in turn receiving the full support of the service of supply; the entire effort, through long hours of work along predetermined lines, was to restore the service to normal with the least possible delay.

Further down the river, the second stage of the battle was in progress: to hold out or to pump out the water—to protect the equipment by any and every means—to keep as many lines up as might be or to establish emergency circuits when all others had failed—to man the switchboards as long as calls could go through. In many a central office so circumstanced, operators, plant men, and others either slept and ate within the building or resorted to boats for transportation; stores of food and sometimes of water were laid up; emergency generators furnished the power or stood ready to be hooked up; and safe exit for all by boat or other means was instantly available if the fight must become, after all, flight.

WAITING—AND KEEPING THE SERVICE GOING

Still lower in the Ohio River Valley, as at Cairo, Ill., for example, where the waters lingered for days a scant six inches below the top of the city's 60-foot sea wall while the second floor of the central office is at a level equivalent to the 54-foot stage of the river, the first phase of the fight against the flood was taking place: preparation. Here everything had been done that could be done. Records and equipment were moved, emergency power was provided against need, men and women knew their individual duties should there come the sound of the flood alarm, transportation to safety was at hand. There remained only to furnish telephone service to Red Cross, National Guard, army engineers and the other forces of rescue and relief in the evacuated city—and to wait. Just wait. Wait until, at long last, the river's level began to fall, slowly, almost imperceptibly, and word went forth that the immediate danger was past.

And below Cairo? Below Cairo is the Mississippi. What of *it?* Why, from Cairo to New Orleans pretty much the same story: foresight, preparation, watchful waiting. From the Ohio to the Gulf, means and men are at hand to protect equipment, to maintain circuits, against a crest full 10 feet higher than there is slightest likelihood that even this greatest of all floods will reach.

That, then, is in broad perspective the view which early February discloses. The aftermath will be written in days and weeks and months of anxiety, of unremitting labor, of problems met, faced, overcome. The sequel will be told, without fanfare, in normal telephone service.

NATURE'S FIRST ONSLAUGHT WAS WITH SLEET

The flood was Nature's second onslaught in quick succession, however, not the first—at any rate so far as concerns the telephone system and its business of carrying messages. As a series of curtain raisers to the Ohio River's savage outbreak, multiple sleet storms struck heavily over an area coinciding in part with that which was later to suffer from the rising waters but extending for many hundreds of miles beyond it.

Sleet! It rarely makes newspaper headlines, except for local summaries of transportation and communication facilities interrupted. It causes relatively little damage to property in general, it seldom disrupts social and commercial life, it drives before it no horde of hapless refugees, as does a major flood. But of the continuing flow of intercommunication—the pulsing of the relationship between one group, one place, and another —over open wire lines, sleet is, by and large, the most relentless enemy.

From the early days of January up even to the start of the flood emergency, sleet storms—in some territories three or more, in others two, and in some only one—laid wires in icy tangles and poles in splintered rows across a big part of the country. The area affected forms a wide swath extending from southwestern Texas in a northeasterly direction across parts of Oklahoma, Kansas, Arkansas, and Missouri; into a corner of Iowa; across west central Illinois and the lower part of Indiana; and along the western sections of Tennessee and Kentucky.

The Storms Did Enormous Damage

The damage to telephone plant by this succession of sleet storms was tremendous. In the territory of the Southwestern Bell Telephone Company alone, as the result of the first sleet storm, 25,000 poles were down or broken over an area of 175,000 square miles, 2,500 toll circuits were out of service, 60 towns were isolated at one time or another, and 710,000 spans of wire (18,000 wire miles) would have to be replaced before repairs were complete. Subsequent sleet storms, although less wide-spread, did additional damage. Some 2,000 plant men, including crews rushed into the area from adjoining Bell System companies, were called on to undertake restoration of the damage. The same storm, striking the western section of Illinois Bell territory, took down nearly 3,000 poles, isolating a number of important toll centers as well as causing many exchange wire breaks. If the damage from this and subsequent sleet storms was less heavy in the territories of the other Associated Companies affected, it was principally because they were there less wide-spread. And there were many instances of tired plant gangs, working long hours to restore the service to full usefulness after one sleet storm, which were called on to do again much of what they had recently accomplished, or to rush to another section of the territory to restore service on an emergency basis, as one storm followed another.

Throughout this whole vast sleet-ridden area, rapid surveys of damage were followed by the assignment of plant forces summoned from far and near to meet the critical necessity of restoring service. Closely coördinated with this rallying of man power were the emergency shipments from Western Electric factories and distributing houses straight to the points of greatest need: poles and cross arms by the thousands, line and pole hardware by tons, innumerable thousands of feet of wire, other equipment as needed and on demand, speeding by truck and train to those places in the stricken area where they were most sorely needed. Standardized items all, ready to take their place and do their part anywhere in the Bell System, and ready also to the hand of any Bell-trained man, no matter from what section of the country nor from which Operating Company he had been dispatched to help in the restoration of the service. Men and supplies! The ones schooled and the others manufactured to work together, as is the Bell System way, together they can confront, can overcome even so far-flung a test of skill and resources as last January's sleet.

WEARY MEN WHO FACED THE FLOOD

That, obviously, is but a moment's glance at the vast picture of the sleet storms and what they did. The whole story cannot possibly be told now, any more than can a comprehensive account of the flood which followed. So much is given here because it forms in part a background to the story of the flood. For it was in many cases those same plant men, weary from days and even weeks of heavy work in restoration of sleet damage—the same foremen, supervisors, executives—the same companies and territories, in other words, which were confronted with a flood of size and force never before known.

For the full length of the Ohio River, the flood story can be narrated in terms of damage done: of lines under water or washed out, of central offices partly flooded or almost wholly inundated or even carried away; of service continued under the utmost difficulty and often danger, and of service suspended for a while when there remained no longer any means to give it; of work carried on through utterly trying circumstances,

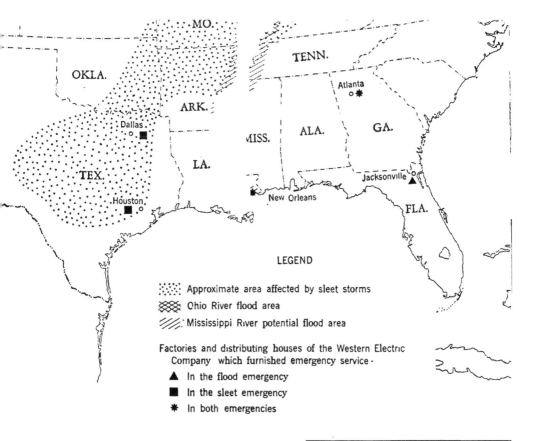

LEGEND

::::: Approximate area affected by sleet storms

⧄⧄ Ohio River flood area

⫽⫽ Mississippi River potential flood area

Factories and distributing houses of the Western Electric Company which furnished emergency service ·

▲ In the flood emergency

■ In the sleet emergency

✳ In both emergencies

*T*HE photographs on the following pages have been selected from several hundred in an attempt to visualize for the reader something of the conditions which prevailed over a large part of the middle West during last January and February, from the onslaught of the sleet through the several stages of the battle against flood waters. As illustrations for the article " Meeting the Challenge of Sleet and Flood," they were not chosen as typical of the situation in the territory of any one telephone company but as representative of the conditions faced, in greater or less degree, by eight Bell System operating companies. They tell, as adequately as is possible in limited space, the story of the loyalty to the service that is traditional with Bell System workers, save for one important omission: operators' work under stress does not lend itself to pictorial treatment, and their faithfulness and courage cannot be captured by the lens.

Desolation in much of Northern Missouri was sleet's aftermath.

It was cold in Indiana as, entering the sleet zone, this line gang stopped to put chains on their truck.

Four cross-arms of this terminal pole just outside Quincy, Ill., succumbed to the gleaming sleet which has no beauty in a plant man's eyes.

Atop a pole near Moberly, Mo.

Heavy was Nature's burden the wires bore. These are in Camp Point, Ill.

Emergency shipments leaving Western Electric's Hawthorne Works by night for sleet-stricken areas. Left: drop wire for Louisville, Ky. Right: line wire for Quincy, Ill.

Why the wires went down in Indiana

Long Lines Plant crews raising circuits north of Cairo, Ill., by bolting ex.
the tops of the poles or relocating crossarms in preparation for possible *f*

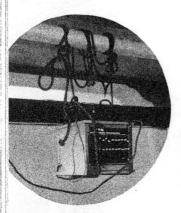

A pickle barrel kept this Pittsburgh P.B.X. out of high water—and trouble.

Business as usual through this P.B.X., with trunks cut through on night connections to second floor extensions.

With wate
on the Po
Va. centre

cuits near New Albany, Ind., were kept out of trouble at this point.

Up she comes!

Swinging the main frame up to the ceiling made it possible to maintain service at Marietta, O.

Unloading emergency power equipment from Harriman, Tenn., at Beuchell for transportation to Louisville by truck.

This shed was built to house emergency motor generators rushed to Ci LaGrange, Ind., and Milwaukee, Wis.

Boats and improvised life belts were included among the preparations in Cairo, Ill., against the eventuality that the water might overtop the sea wall.

Not the warfare, t of the . central o Louisville had bec

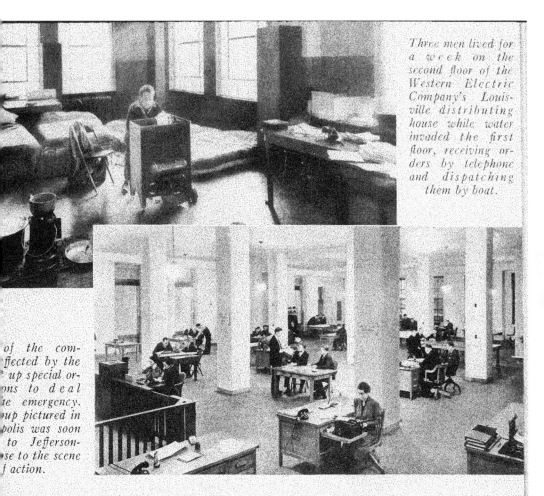

Three men lived for a week on the second floor of the Western Electric Company's Louisville distributing house while water invaded the first floor, receiving orders by telephone and dispatching them by boat.

of the com-
fected by the
up special or-
ns to deal
te emergency.
up pictured in
olis was soon
to Jefferson-
se to the scene
action.

When flood relief assumed major proportions, the disaster staff of the Red Cross took over the Assembly Hall at National Headquarters in Washington. Telephones were quickly provided by stringing cables from wall to wall overhead and dropping wires to the desks. In this picture the installers are still at work.

The Red Cross supplied the boat these Long Lines men are using along the Memphis-Little Rock toll lead.

Nautical hitch-hiking.

Stout fella!

The good ship " Bell Telephone Long Lines" is beached for temporary repairs.

Stringing drop wire in Marietta, O.

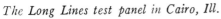

The Long Lines test panel in Cairo, Ill.

gs and
k e p i
ater-
wn in
e man-
utside
a n s -
n d .,
h o n e
l i n g .
at the

Operators reporting for duty in Marietta, O.

This operator clambered up the fire-escape and through the window into the central office in Jeffersonville, Ind. Next day, leaving, she stepped out of the window directly into a boat.

Supplies entering the second-floor central office in Mound City, Ill. Although the town was practically evacuated, service was maintained to aid in relief and levee patrol work.

Boatmen rowing operators away from the Jeffersonville central office in a downpour, after orders had been received that the office be evacuated.

Half of Cincinnati's 88-position outward toll switchboard. For hours upon hours, during the emergency, every position was filled.

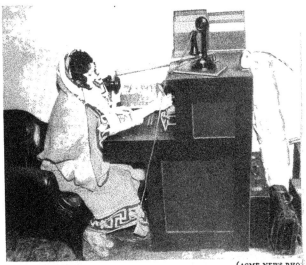

(ACME NEWS PHO

This P.B.X. operator in a hotel in Portsmouth, O., carried on in the same spirit as her sister operators throughout the flood area.

Temporary dormitories were generally provided for operators whose homes were flooded out or for whom high water made transportation difficult or dangerous. This picture was taken in Evansville, Ind.

r tele-
ut the
cluded
phoid.

Truck convoy waiting at the railroad for the arrival of emergency supplies for Louisville.

Tank trucks delivering in Cincinnati for use in and for cooling emer charging sets.

With no electric power Louisville, a truck wi hoists food and water the ninth floor.

Pickaback to restore a subscriber's service.

"Low bridge" through the telephone building's front door in Marietta, O.

Impromptu cafeteria set up in Evansville, Ind., to provide hot food during the flood emergency.

Borne by raging current, this tree-trunk threatened to demolish the house in the background, at Cypress, Ind. Telephone men working nearby snapped a steel cable around it, shown at left of picture, and anchored it securely to a sturdy tree.

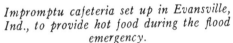

to here" went the water on the New Albany, Ind., test desk.

y telephone men were among the sed amateur radio operators who ed relief and rescue messages. ng them was this St. Louis West- Electric installer, owner of his own teur station and a member of the Naval Communication Reserve.

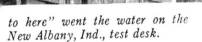

Lines must be cleared of debris left by receding waters.

Following the water's devastation comes the scourge of muck. This scene, which might be anywhere in the flood's wake, happens to be in Louisville.

Battered victim.

Water goes but trouble remains on the Gallipolis-Portsmouth line.

Water rose above the key shelf in the second-floor operating room in Jeffersonville, Ind.

Plant Department quarters in New Albany, Ind. The high-water level leaves its record on the wall.

Western Electric's installation forces tear out what's left of a switchboard in order to start anew.

Night scene at the Western Electric Company's St. Louis distributing house as cross-arms are being pinned, braced and loaded into a waiting freight car.

This reel of cable, being loaded at the Hawthorne Works for the Indiana emergency zone, is one of a 5-car shipment of 169,300 linear feet of cable contained on 84 reels.

A general view of the wire shipping section in Western Electric's Point Breeze plant. The fully wrapped coils of wire in the background are being placed aboard a fast freight bound for a distributing house in the flood zone.

when emergency generators maintained power where otherwise there was none and when water had to be brought in tanks because the regular supply had failed. So also can it be read in tales of ingenuity and quick thinking: of the central office kept in service with water deep on the frame-room floor because the main frame and test desk could be hauled up to the ceiling; of the town kept in touch with the outside world through magneto switchboards rushed to a nearby Long Lines repeater station when the local connecting company's central office went out of service for an indefinite period; of the vitally important link to a distant broadcasting station kept open by applying carrier current to the metallic lines at the upper and lower outside corners of a 4-cross-arm pole line, even though for 15 miles that line was under water. Most certainly the story can be told in terms of heroism, of devotion to duty far beyond the strict requirements of the job: of men risking their lives to install or repair or protect an important circuit; of other men working laboriously and without thought of self at whatever the emergency required; of men and women sticking to their posts while the same water which lapped higher each moment in the central office also engulfed their homes and their possessions; of women staying for days on days in telephone buildings without elevator power or even adequate water facilities so that they might handle the calls of Red Cross, government and other relief bodies, and all messages contributing to the alleviation of the situation.

In such terms as these can the story of the flood, and of the telephone men and women in the flood area, be told. But not here, not now. The canvas is too big, the scene too close at hand.

Out of the picture already stand, however, certain bold features. They represent the various arms of the Bell System as a whole mobilized to the assistance of the flooded territory.

Not only did plant crews from neighboring Associated Companies respond to the need; Long Lines maintenance forces were rushed into the area, some of them from great distances, some equipped with boats and some others obtaining boats locally. Ahead of the flood they worked feverishly to protect the circuits into and through the river valley from the onward march of the waters. Where the waters rose, they were there to maintain the lines and to restore at the earliest feasible moment those which went out. To these men, and to their fellows on the localized battle grounds, is due the principal credit that few important points in the Ohio Valley were without telephone contact with the outside world for longer than brief intervals.

THE WIRES WERE VITAL LINKS

Upon these long-haul circuits, during the early days of the flood, depended in great part the orderly organization of the nation's resources for rescue and relief work, and, indeed, accurate news regarding each community's needs. Outward long distance calls mounted rapidly. On Sunday, January 24, for example, the number of outward long distance calls from Cincinnati was 330 per cent above normal, from Louisville 184 per cent, and from Memphis 60 per cent above normal. The number of calls varied widely during the whole flood period, but a week later, on January 31, outward long distance calls from Cincinnati were still 84 per cent above normal, from Louisville 135 per cent, and from Memphis 70 per cent. Similar increases occurred in other cities, the effect of the flood crisis being reflected in marked traffic increases in such cities as Pittsburgh, Cleveland, Chicago and St. Louis.

To meet this sudden uprush of traffic, and to bring relief to operators who had been working at the switchboards under great pressure and trying conditions for many hours at a time, operators who volunteered for the service were sent from New York, Philadelphia, Cleveland, Detroit, Chicago, St. Louis, Kansas City, and Dallas to places where their help was most needed, particularly Cincinnati, Louisville, and Memphis. Former operators in the flood area, realizing the emergency, also offered their services, and were accepted.

The Western Electric Company, source of emergency and replacement supplies and equipment for the Bell System, was already making large shipments into the sleet-stricken territory when first warning came of the flood catastrophe in the Ohio Valley. Throughout its widely distributed facilities east of the Rockies it set in motion its machinery for meeting major emergencies.

The Supply Service Plays Its Important Part

Its principal factories and its distributing houses were placed on a 24-hour basis, ready to handle emergency shipments at any hour. Distribution and traffic specialists worked in day and night shifts, expediting shipments by train, plane, ship, and truck. The company's mobile crews of switchboard installers were placed at the disposal of the Associated Companies and some thousand men were held ready to join forces with other telephone men at an instant's notice.

With this plan of operation placed in effect virtually over night, emergency shipments commenced to speed toward the flood scene. Orders placed by the Distributing Houses and shipped by the factories or suppliers, almost without exception in a few hours after receipt, rapidly mounted to impressive totals. In just a little more than two weeks, these totals included thirty-five sections of No. 12 switchboards, 28,750 hand telephone sets, 23,700 subscriber sets, 38,610,000 conductor feet of rubber covered wire, 216,200,000 conductor feet of cable, 325,000 pounds of pole-line hardware. When the total extent of the damage is finally known and requirements ascertained, these totals will doubtless be greatly exceeded.

Contributing their share to the maintenance of service in the flood territory were power specialists from the Bell Telephone Laboratories and the American Telephone and Telegraph Company headquarters organization who went from New York to assist the operating companies in engineering and establishing emergency sources of current. In a number of instances, in both the large cities and in smaller communities, it was these emergency generators which saved the day and kept the service in operation when the normal supply of electric power had failed completely.

So in terms of the coördination and coöperation of the Bell System can this story of the Ohio River flood be told: of men and women coming to the aid of other men and women who were there in the thick of it; of the supply system and the men and women in back of that; of the scientists and the specialists and their resources of information and experience. Almost wholly in terms of men and women can and must the story of the telephone's victory over these unleashed waters be told. But these same men and women it is who form this country's nationwide telephone system. So the story can be told, too, in some part, in terms of the value of that organization, its heritage, its unity, its will to serve.

JUDSON S. BRADLEY

The Telephone Business Office

THE telephone business office is provided to meet the needs of customers in arranging for new service, changes in service or the disconnection of service; securing information about bills or charges; or taking up any of the many questions that may arise between them and the Telephone Company. In other words, the business office is the customer's normal point of contact for direct dealings, in person, by telephone or by correspondence, concerning all phases of his business transactions with the Company.

Depending upon the community served and the varying requirements of small and large cities, business offices range from the small offices with one or two employees who handle all phases of customer transactions, up to the very large offices of 100 to 200 employees. In these larger offices one or more groups may specialize in handling all telephone and correspondence transactions together with the bulk of the record work associated with customers' service; another group may be engaged in handling solely the "public office" transactions (i.e., where customers visit the office in person); while separate groups also may take care of the preparation of service orders, the disposition of money received from customers in payment of bills, coin box collection work, etc. In the intermediate sized offices some of these functions frequently are combined to advantage under one group; for example, the office may be arranged so that the representatives handling telephone and correspondence transactions also may take care of the customers calling at the office in person.

There are more than 5,000 business offices of these varying sizes in the Bell System, with over 15,000 people engaged in work in these offices. Aside from the payment of bills, customers initiate by personal visit to the office, by telephone call, or by correspondence nearly forty-two million transactions with the business offices each year. Impressions they secure in this way as to the efficiency and courtesy of the Company unquestionably contribute a great deal to their opinion of the Telephone Company.

IMPROVEMENT IN BUSINESS OFFICE SERVICE A CONTINUOUS ACTIVITY

It is, therefore, highly important that there be an adequate number of conveniently located offices with suitable facilities and equipment and capable personnel well trained in a wide range of telephone matters.

Consideration of business office service and its improvement has involved, and will continue to involve, many related factors, such as the location of offices, building designs, interior layouts and arrangements, office equipment and appliances, selection and training of personnel for their duties, and adjustment of the force to handle the fluctuating volumes of customer transactions. Consequently, this work is under continuous study throughout the System. The headquarters staff of the American Telephone and Telegraph Company has worked with the Associated Companies in designing improvements, as well as assisting in their introduction and application. Rapid strides have been made during recent years in improving the layout and equipment of business offices, providing more of them and in improving all phases of their operation.

To the customer who prefers to transact his business with the Company by telephone or correspondence, these improvements are apparent to him only by the more prompt, accurate and efficient handling of his business and by the pleasing manner of the business office representative.

For the customer who wishes to call personally at the business office, however, the greater ease, convenience and physical comfort with which he may transact his business in this manner has been particularly apparent and pleasing. The progress during recent years in improving this phase of business office service, as described more fully in the remainder of this article, is illustrative of the improvement which has been made in business office operations as a whole.

Meeting the "Public Office" Requirements of Customers

Of the nearly forty-two million transactions which customers initiate with the business office each year, about twelve million, or 30 per cent, are by personal visit to the public offices. In addition, a fairly sizeable portion of the customers prefer to pay their monthly bills by coming to the nearest available public office. While one public office in each of the smaller cities usually is sufficient to meet the customers' convenience in these respects, in the larger cities or metropolitan areas, several such offices may be required. Adequate coverage from the customers' standpoint involves consideration of such factors as geographical conditions, community of interest, and the availability of reliable transportation facilities. In addition, growth of the community, changes in transportation facilities, etc., frequently lead to changes in location or the establishment of additional public offices. As an illustration of the attention given this matter of conveniently located public offices during the last ten years, in the 72 cities in which over half the customers of the Bell System are located, the number of such offices has been increased 77 per cent, to meet the changing requirements of customers due to growth and other related factors.

Improvements in "Public Office" Arrangements and Facilities

A few years ago, most of the public offices in the larger cities were of the conventional "counter" type, as shown by Figure 1, although in some offices turrets or screens were built into the counters to segregate the positions at which representatives were located, as shown by Figure 2. Customers stood at the counter while transacting their business with the representatives or while waiting for attention during busy periods. Early in 1926, however, the New York Telephone Company introduced an experimental public office in Brooklyn where the counter was eliminated entirely, with the exception of that part devoted to receiving payments, and each public office representative equipped with a desk at which a customer could be comfortably seated while transacting his business. The advantages of this type of office over the " counter " type became quickly apparent and a number of offices in the New York Company and other Associated Companies were similarly equipped. Experience indicated that, in order to assure quiet working conditions, it was desirable to construct partitions in the larger offices so as to segregate the public office from the remainder of the business office, where the two were at the same location.

Pictures of two so-called " counterless " public offices are shown in Figures 3 and 4. These particular offices are designed to handle only those transactions with customers who visit the office in person, telephone and correspondence transactions being handled by an entirely separate force. Also shown in Figures 5 and 6, however, are pictures of the counterless arrangement subsequently introduced in the so-called combined office; that is, where the same representatives handle all transactions with customers whether they are by personal visit, telephone or correspondence. It will be noted that these offices are not materially different in appearance from the purely public offices, since they also are designed to permit customers being seated at a representative's desk during the interview.

Where necessary, the manager, or a representative acting as a floor director, arranges for customers to be waited upon

102

FIG. 1. A TYPICAL "COUNTER" TYPE PUBLIC OFFICE.

FIG. 2. A "COUNTER" TYPE PUBLIC OFFICE, SHOWING THE TURRET CONSTRUCTION AND POSITIONS AT WHICH REPRESENTATIVES ARE LOCATED

FIG. 3. A PUBLIC OFFICE, WHERE CUSTOMERS TRANSACTING THEIR TELEPHONE BUSINESS IN PERSON MAY BE SEATED IN COMFORTABLE CHAIRS DURING THE INTERVIEW. ONLY PERSONAL VISIT TRANS-ACTIONS ARE HANDLED IN THIS OFFICE.

FIG 4. A PUBLIC OFFICE, SIMILAR TO THAT SHOWN IN FIGURE 3 BUT DIFFERING SLIGHTLY WITH RESPECT TO ARCHITECTURAL DETAILS.

Fig. 5. A Business Office of the Combined Type. Personal Visit, Telephone and Correspondence Transactions are Handled by the Same Representatives, the Necessary Office Records Being Filed in Specially Designed Desk Drawers. This Arrangement Is Confined Mostly to Offices in the Smaller Cities.

Fig. 6. A Business Office, Similar to That Shown in Figure 5 but Differing Slightly with Respect to Architectural Details.

7. Payment Counter with Grille Work Enclosing Tellers' Positions   This Counter
. Remodeled, as Shown in Figure 8, at the Time of Converting the Office to the Counterless Arrangement.

. 8   Open Type Payment Counter Used in Counterless Offices. This is the Remodeled
                                            ounterless Arrange-

EQUIPMENT DISPLAY LO-
THE PUBLIC OFFICE AD-
O THE WAITING SPACE.

FIG. 10 INTERIOR OF A "CUS-
TOMBR'S ROOM," WHICH HAS A
DIRECT ENTRANCE FROM THE
PUBLIC OFFICE.

FIG. 11. PUBLIC TELEPHONE A
DIRECTORY FACILITIES IN A PU
LIC OFFICE, LOCATED ADJACE
TO THE WAITING SPACE.

FIG 12. DISPLAY WINDOWS, SHOWING USE FOR INFORMATIONAL AND PROMOTIONAL PURPOSES.

FIGS. 13 AND 14.   SMALL COUNTERLESS BUSINESS OFFICES, SHOWING DESKS EQUIPPED FOR RECEIVING PAYMENTS.

FIGS. 15 AND 16   SMALL COUNTERLESS BUSINESS OFFICES, SHOWING DESKS EQUIPPED FOR RECEIVING PAYMENTS.

and escorts them to the proper desk. Comfortable chairs, settees or davenports usually are provided for the use of customers who may be required to wait for a few minutes when all the desks occasionally are being utilized, and for the convenience of those persons who are merely accompanying a customer. In many cases, of course, simple inquiries by customers may be answered courteously and quickly by the manager or floor director when greeting the customer, thereby speeding up the handling of customers' business in such cases.

One of the principal advantages of the counterless arrangement, of course, is that it permits customers to be seated during the interview. This is particularly appreciated by elderly persons or those having physical infirmities. There are, however, many other important advantages. Discussions between the customer and the representative are not readily overheard by other customers, since ample space is left between desks, thereby encouraging private conversations which customers so frequently desire when discussing their individual telephone business. The physical strain on representatives who might otherwise be required to stand throughout the greater portion of the day is reduced and their prestige is enhanced in the customers' minds by being seated at desks instead of standing behind a counter. The entire atmosphere of the office is quietly businesslike, and the comfortable arrangements tend to encourage courtesy and patience on the part of both customer and representative, which frequently facilitate the work of securing the facts concerning a difficult or complicated situation and arriving at a mutually satisfactory agreement as to the action to be taken. In addition, the establishment of a new business office with the counterless arrangement requires less capital investment, since it eliminates a major item of expense, the construction of a suitable counter.

With the counterless arrangement other improvements in the design, arrangement and furnishings of the public office also were introduced. For example, the old type metal cages and grille work enclosing the payment counter were obviously out of place in the setting which resulted from removing the rest of the counter and providing attractive desks, chairs and other facilities. As a means of further assisting in furnishing a pleasing and personal service, as well as improving the general appearance of the offices, an open type payment counter was developed which does not require metal cages or grille work. The pictures in Figures 7 and 8, which are of the same counter before and after conversion of the office to the counterless arrangement, show the radical differences in appearance of these two types of payment counters. The open type counter is designed to permit tellers while seated to receive and pass money over the counter with ease and to converse freely with the customer without the obstacle of a grille or screen in between. At the same time, the counter on the teller's side is designed to provide adequate protection of money, and on the customers' side such features as a shelf on which customers may place small packages when making payments and openings in the face of the counter for disposing of envelopes and other waste paper frequently are provided. The payment counter in a public office is always located near the entrance, or between the entrances if there is more than one, so that it may be easily seen and reached by customers.

A great deal of study has been given to the design and arrangement of these new type offices as a whole, to the end that the improvements may be in keeping with the stability, dignity and character of the business. It was found practicable to provide attractive and convenient offices appropriate to the locality they serve, without involving or even giving the impression of extravagance, and in many cases this was accomplished at less cost than would have been incurred with the counter arrangement. Based on the experience of the Companies, considerable information with respect to the selection and planning of business offices was accumulated, which is now in use throughout the System. Among the features being given consideration in the planning of new public offices in addition to those mentioned previously, are (1) the provision of appropriate equipment displays, consisting of the simpler types of services which may be demonstrated readily to customers, located near the entrance or adjacent to the waiting section, as illustrated in Figure 9; (2) "Customers' rooms" with a direct entrance from the public office, where customers desiring to place a large number of local or long distance calls may do so with privacy and comfort, as shown in Figure 10; (3) adequate public telephone and directory facilities located where they may be seen readily and used without disturbing other customers, a typical arrangement of which is shown in Figure 11; and (4) display windows for use of informational and promotional displays, such as shown in Figure 12.

Extent of Introduction of Counterless Offices

The counterless arrangement for public offices was extended gradually to offices of varying sizes and was found to be adaptable readily to large or small office conditions. While new offices may be established at less expense with the counterless arrangement, as compared with the counter plan, and small counter offices readily converted to this arrangement, in many of the larger counter offices the "out-of-pocket" conversion expense is such that, in general, conversions of these offices have been confined to cases where major changes, additions, or moves were needed for other reasons. Nevertheless, during the last ten years a considerable proportion of the larger offices have been converted to the counterless arrangement, as shown by the chart in Figure 17, and conversion of most of the remaining offices in this group is planned coincident with other contemplated changes. There are relatively few in the large group of offices serving communities with less than 1,000 telephones, which are not now on the counterless basis. In these smaller offices, where all of the business office work may be handled by one or two representatives, the payment counter also has been eliminated in many instances by remodeling one desk to facilitate receiving payments, a transaction requiring so little time that customers usually do not prefer to sit down. Figures 13, 14, 15 and 16 illustrate the arrangement now

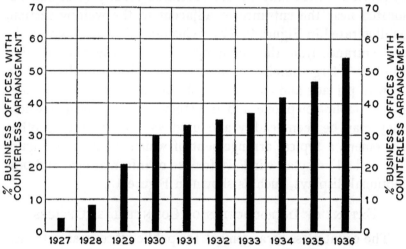

FIG. 17. BELL SYSTEM COUNTERLESS OFFICES IN CITIES HAVING 1000 OR MORE TELEPHONES.

widely in use in small counterless offices requiring only a few representatives.

While it is desirable to locate a public office in that section of the area served which is most convenient to the largest number of customers, in most cities it has not been found necessary to have quarters in the busiest portion of the principal business district. Frequently Company-owned buildings, either administration or central office buildings, may be located sufficiently close to a focal point in the community to permit including a public office, or a complete business office, on the ground floor. A number of additional public offices of the counterless type have been located in such buildings in the larger cities during the last few years.

R. P. JUDY

Language and the Telephone Art

NEXT to man himself—the how and why of his living, moving and being—probably the most interesting thing in the world is the speech of man.

Sounds becoming words; words expressing thoughts; thoughts stimulating actions; actions translated into history. Words,— the media through which man makes known his aspirations and his fears; through which are recorded the experience of the past so that the race, generation by generation, may improve; speech—one of the characteristics which makes man the highest animal. Can anything be more significant than words?

Where do they come from? What causes them to be born? How do they creep into the living tongue? What gropings for knowledge, what accomplishments, what hardships, obscured by mists of the past, lie behind words in daily use?

Forsythia is not merely an arbitrary term, designating a yellow, spring-flowering shrub, so well known to all of us that many think it native to our continent. It is, at the same time, a memorial to William Forsyth, British horticulturist, who discovered the species in the wilds of China. *Macadam* is a monument to the inventor of a road surfacing process, as well as a common name for the process, itself. *Volt* is a measure of electrical intensity, but it is, likewise, a tribute to Volta, the physicist.

Back of words like *volt* and *ohm* and *ampere* stand shades of scientists, great ghosts that whisper (if we but pause to listen) of man's eternal struggle with the unknown and of the success which sometimes crowns the effort of gifted individuals. There is in such words acknowledgment of a debt to the past and encouragement for the future.

Consider, for a moment, a name (it is both noun and verb) so common to American speech that it is doubtful that a day passes without some reference to it by half, or more, of the population of the United States. That word is *telephone*. It derives from two Greek words: one, meaning "afar"; the other, "voice" or "sound."

In the American Telephone Historical Library at 195 Broadway there is on file a letter which Alexander Graham Bell wrote to an unnamed correspondent on April 9, 1888. It begins as follows:

Dear Sir:

> Your note of the 7th inst. just received. It will give me much pleasure to be of assistance in discovering " the father and the birthday of the word ' Telephone.' . . ."

The inventor refers, then, to a number of sources, contributing to a justification of the word. He mentions "the Telephonium or music telegraph of M. Sudre" and describes it as "a trumpet or bugle that could be heard three miles whereby 'musical speech' could be produced, depending on the combination of the seven notes—Re, Mi, Fa, etc." He quotes Dr. Romershausen, the author of "The Telephone, an Acoustic Means of Communication" as proposing in 1838 "a means of speech communication . . . through the use of far-reaching transmission of sound in narrow tubes." He takes notice of the glorified speaking tubes proposed by a clergyman named Gautier and an Englishman named Dick. And of Reis' instrument, which Bell contended, incidentally, would transmit pitch only and not other qualities and was, therefore, incapable of transmitting genuine speech, he wrote:

> I need hardly refer to the use of the word "Telephone" by Reis and others about 1860 to designate an apparatus for transmitting musical pitch—and specially the pitch of the human voice.

Nor did he omit Elisha Gray's use of the word. He wrote:

> . . . about that time (1877) an apparatus composed of tuning forks and resonators was exhibited in this country by Mr. Elisha

Gray of Chicago as a " telephone." We were both lecturing on the " telephone " at the same time. He lectured upon the " telephone " alone—while mine were lectures on " The Electric Speaking Telephone."

Bell cited a passage from a letter he had written to Gray, dated March 2, 1877, which was used as evidence in certain Bell patent cases, as follows:

I have not generally alluded to your name in connection with the invention of the electric " telephone " for we seem to attach different significancies to the word. I apply the term only to an apparatus for transmitting the voice (which makes it strictly in accordance with the derivation of the word) whereas you seem to use the term as expressive of any apparatus for the transmission of *musical* tones by the electrical current.

With a discussion of transmission of sounds over wooden rods, threads, the "lovers' telegraph " and other means, Bell's letter closed.

One sentence, appearing early in the communication, was this: " I christened my apparatus ' The Electric Speaking Telephone ' but the world has abbreviated it to ' Telephone ' alone."

In the light of events, the statement has weight. For the word *telephone,* in modern usage, compresses within its three syllables the whole history of the development of voice communication from Dr. Bell's basic patent to the coaxial cable.

Not long ago, listening to a radio program featuring the competitive offerings of amateur performers, I heard the announcement that the winning amateur could not be determined until judges had read the *decibels* measuring the volume of the audience's applause. That very day I had written, in an article not for publication in a telephone periodical but for consumption by the general public—" To a man, the busy hum of a tea-party is so much sound and fury, measurable in decibels." I was, as it were, an eye-witness to the introduction to living language of a term created by telephony.

All of us are aware that from foreign countries, from the

lower strata of society, from the arts, picturesque terms emerge, bubble for a while in the cauldron of slang, and eventually take their places—many of them—as respected members of our linguistic community. Thus, British army men brought back from India the word *pukka,* meaning " thoroughgoing " or " complete." A *pukka* officer is, for example, an officer and a gentleman, virtually above criticism. From Africa the troops brought us *trek,* a march. The underworld has given us *gunman* and *racketeer.* The painter contributes *highlight* in the sense of accent, while the new wave of swing music is producing an avalanche of strange phrases, at present meaningless gibberish to the average man, but perhaps destined in time to enliven his vocabulary.

The Laboratories' Contribution to the Language

The laboratory, too, does its share in giving variety to everyday speech. *PBX,* due, no doubt, to the public contact with Private Branch Exchange operators, is gaining a foothold. *Sidetone,* though defined by engineers as " reproduction by the telephone receiver of a telephone set of sounds actuating the telephone transmitter of the same telephone set " is, in the sense of a continuous, irrelevant sound, coming into common talk. *Microphone,* or, oftener, " the mike " (to engineers, a synonym for " telephone transmitter ") is, by way of radio and talking motion pictures, a part of everyman's verbal equipment. And now *decibel* is, more and more, being employed by the man in the street as meaning a unit measure of sound volume.

To engineers, *decibel* does not mean quite that. It is an international word, a synonym for the obsolete term " transmission unit," and is abbreviated, officially, " db." It is one-tenth (deci) of a " bel." The last syllable derives from Bell, the inventor of the telephone, just as another unit, of the same nature as decibel but differing from it in magnitude and quite

110

unknown as yet in ordinary speech—the " neper "—stems from Napier, the inventor of natural logarithms.

All right, the average man says, a decibel is a tenth of a bel. So what is a bel?   And the engineer replies: " A bel is the unit of measure of the ratio of two amounts of power, the number of bels corresponding to any given ratio of two amounts of power being the logarithm, to the base 10, of this ratio."   And he might add, " The practical unit is the decibel."

An Engineer Defines the Decibel

But, if the engineer happened to have a soft spot in his heart for the layman, he might say, as John Mills does, in his "A Fugue in Cycles and Bels," " The ' decibel' scale of the communication engineer is now generally accepted. By its use comparisons may be conveniently expressed; acoustic power, or its electrical equivalent while in process of transmission, may be referred to some standard and quantitatively described as so many units above or below the standard.

" The unit is the ' bel,' named after the inventor of the telephone—but its submultiple, the euphonious ' decibel,' abbreviated ' db,' is much more commonly used. It does not stand for any definite amount of power but rather for a specific percentage increment.

" Imagine that one listens alternately to two musical notes identical in pitch and for the moment of equal intensity.   Then one of the sounds is slightly increased and the comparison repeated; and so on, until to the ear the notes appear to differ in loudness. The minimum perceptible difference in intensity is thus determined for the conditions of the experiment, that is, for a definite pitch of note and a definite initial sensation.

" Repeat the experiment, keeping the stronger of the two tones steady and increasing the intensity of the other until it is just perceptibly louder. Another level of sensation is thus attained. Successive sensations, it will be found, arise from amounts of acoustic power which form an increasing series like

111

the value of a bank account in compound interest. The average increase in acoustic power which the ear can detect is about twenty-five per cent. On that basis each level corresponds to a power 1.25 times that of the next lower level. Each level in the series represents a step of one decibel. (A bank account which increases at that rate of twenty-five per cent would double on the third interest date and be ten times its original value on the tenth.) Each level in this series of acoustic power represents a step of one decibel; ten steps and one has a power level ten times that from which he started, a whole bel higher.

"Applying this scale, for describing acoustic power, to speech engineers have found that very loud speech is about twenty decibels higher than speech is on the average, and very faint speech about twenty decibels below average. Ordinarily then speech covers a power range of forty decibels. Since for every ten decibels power increases ten times, this range represents an increase of ten thousand times. When one argues his acoustic power is probably, therefore, about ten thousand times greater than it need be."

TELEPHONY IS A BORROWER OF WORDS

The situation of the telephone engineer with respect to his terminology differs somewhat from that of the biologist or the medical man. The latter, following academic tradition, derives words, when need for a new one arises, from Greek or Latin or, perhaps, from the physician most closely associated with the study of a specific irregularity. Thus, a type of paralysis is called *Parkinson's Disease;* or, the capacity of living tissue to recover from injury is described in medicine as *vis medicatrix naturae.*

It is true, of course, that some telephone words, such as *microphone,* stem from ancient tongues. By and large, however, the communication vocabulary—due in the main to the development of the industry by practical rather than cloistered men—has been built up by borrowing from other arts and crafts. The telephone *plug* took its name from a similar device used in telegraphy. The hole in the switchboard into which a plug fits is called a *jack* (it was first known as a jack-knife switch) because its movable parts resemble an old-fashioned Barlow. When voice currents were stepped up as they passed through an intermediate telephone office, the amplifying devices were termed *repeaters,* after a set of repeating relays in telegraphy, though no one can, to be sure, hear a telephone repeater repeating conversation.

INITIALS SOMETIMES FORM NAMES

Ultimately, telephony reached a point at which prior arts failed to supply terms. Some of the descriptive phrases thus evolved were cumbersome. In the early days of transoceanic telephony, for example, a good many cabled references had to be made to the *voice operated device anti-singing.* Obviously, this had to be contracted. It was called by its initials—*vodas,* and it is so known to-day. If you hear a telephone engineer mention vodas, he will be referring to a little black box in a transoceanic circuit, which clears an electrical pathway ahead of a speaker's voice and at the same time blocks a return path to his ear. Were this not done, serious interference between various parts of the two-way transmission system would result.

One of the problems of transoceanic radio telephony—the necessity of sending out as much radio power as possible to override static—has brought the word *vogad* into our vocabulary. This *voice operated gain adjusting device* operates on the speech coming into the control office to iron out the differences between loud voices and weak ones. When a loud talker begins, the vogad quickly adjusts the circuits so as to reduce the volume, if necessary, to a point where the radio transmitter is fully loaded and no more. If the next talker should be a weak one, the vogad will increase the volume until the full-load point is reached.

In any speaker's voice, be it loud or weak, there is a range

113

of 1,000 to 1 between the loudest and the faintest sounds. If the fainter sounds could be amplified, they would override the static better, and if the louder sounds were not amplified, the radio transmitter would not be overloaded. A device which does this is called the *compandor,* because it *com*presses the range at the transmitter to be only 30 to 1, and ex*pands* it at the receiver to be the full 1,000 to 1 again. When static is heavy, this device often makes usable a radio channel which otherwise would be too noisy.

A more euphonious group of telephone words are those formed by joining syllables which suggest properties of the material itself. The famous *permalloy* is an *alloy* of iron and nickel whose *perm*eability to magnetism is very high. Its younger sister *perminvar* is an alloy whose *perm*eability is nearly *inva*riable with changes of magnetism. A *varistor* is a device, for example a copper oxide rectifier, whose res*ist*ance *var*ies with the applied voltage.

Just as *decibel* is creeping into the talk of the man on the street, so we may expect to meet at some time in the future *vodas* and *permalloy* and *varistor.*

Engineers are not especially happy over this transmutation. Sticklers for accuracy (as they should be, of course), they object to the distorted meaning, which almost invariably is applied by the average user of a word lifted from technicians. The process cannot be avoided, however. It should, indeed, be recognized not alone as a means by which common speech is enriched, but as unconscious tribute paid to technical skill which makes possible the steady forward march of the telephone art.

STERLING PATTERSON

114

Science Research in Electrical Communication

Excerpts from an Address Before The Bond Club of New York, February 19, 1937, by Dr. Frank B. Jewett, Vice-President, American Telephone & Telegraph Company; President, Bell Telephone Laboratories, Inc.

DURING the past thirty years, and most actively within the period of twenty years, we have been living in an age in which there has been an increasingly vast stream of new knowledge coming into the world. Primarily, it comes, of course, from the fundamental research laboratories of our great institutions of learning. Much, if not all, of that new stream of knowledge is potentially applicable to practical things, and the fact that it is a large stream and an ever increasing stream is becoming more and more obvious and more and more utilized by so-called "practical people."

The recognition accorded the industrial research organizations associated with businesses which are grounded on science has been growing, both in numbers, in size, and in efficiency. From my thirty years in an industrial organization with practically the whole of that time on the research phase, and incidentally, in contact with much research in fields quite outside of communication, it seems to me that in many kinds of activity, industrial research is probably the most important thing that a business can concern itself with if it has regard for its future well-being and its future safety.

If one looks back over industrial history one finds the gravestones which indicate the dangers of not possessing a forward-looking knowledge and utilization of the things which are potentially available in the field of science.

If you want examples of how dangerous it is to assume fixation for a present situation either for a nation, a vast industry or even a part of an industry, you can pick out almost any number for your illustrations. I will give you three that come to mind. The first affects the integrity of a nation's economy: the situation in Chile, where you had a whole national economy, based in the last analysis on the sanctity of one raw material, sodium nitrate. The world's supply of fixed nitrogen was largely dependent upon the Chilean supply, and the whole economy of the nation was based on the income from the exploitation of that natural resource. But out of science has come, in the last two decades, means for producing fixed nitrogen, artificially, which destroyed or largely destroyed the basis of that economy.

Take another case where an industry grew out of science— take our electric street railroads, our interurban roads, which twenty-five or thirty years ago were looked upon as more or less fixed instruments in our domestic civilization. Also out of science from which they sprang came the internal combustion engine, which in its application to the automobile has resulted in the complete or almost complete destruction of the inter-urban railways.

Or take another case, one in the amusement field, the silent motion picture, where with the coming in from the outside of another adaptation of science the whole industry had to be shifted over from the silent operation to sound.

So whether it is for the internal protection of an industry which wants to advance in its own field or for its protection against the incursion of something from the outside, in the last analysis if that industry is based on an application of science, it behooves the industry to look keenly to its interest in organized scientific research.

In addition to these factors, which are present in any industry grounded in the application of science, there is another factor which results from the operation of the patent law which creates in many industries a very strong urge not only to conduct scientific research but likewise to cover the results of this

116

research with patents. Contrary to what I think is the common belief, patents issued by the Government on inventions do not convey an exclusive right to the patentee to do the thing described. The right to do things not otherwise prohibited is assumed to be a right common to all. What a valid patent does do is to give to the patentee the right to exclude others from employing the things covered by the patent, except as he may give permission either by license, sale or otherwise. This is a property right which the patentee cannot be forced against his will to extend to others. In such a situation there are only two things which a desiring purchaser has available; one is money, which may be useless if the patentee has no desire whatever to sell for money, or if his money price is exorbitant. The other thing is patents of a character which the patentee himself may desire and need in the operation of his affairs. As this situation often exists it becomes important to have patents for trading with or without money consideration.

The spread of applied science with consequent increasing number of patents of increasingly wide applicability has created an increasing number of situations in which both parties holding patents must have rights under the other's patents in order to operate. From this standpoint alone there is every reason why industries grounded in science should seek to conduct industrial research as the cheapest and most certain way of insuring freedom to operate and expand.

The Importance of Research in Industry

I have often thought that if I were interested in a large way in the financial aspects of industries involved in applications of science and whose future I wished to guard, I would be very much more concerned with finding out what the attitude of management was toward organized scientific research in their own field, and the way in which they carried it out, than I would in any other aspect of the business. No amount of good organization, no strength of financial structure, no amount of good salesmanship can counteract the destructive effects of something which may spring almost overnight out of some new discovery in science, or the application of old knowledge by people quite outside of one's own business. Both as regards internal growth and external protection, we have had enough proof in the last twenty or thirty years to show us that applied science research is one of the essential things in many modern businesses if they wish to live and prosper.

In a well organized industrial research establishment—and by well organized I mean one in which the quality of the men engaged in it and the way in which they are associated together is effective—findings are practically devoid of the possibility of major catastrophes. This is because the final conclusions of a train of research undertakings are the end result of a process made up of an infinitude of small mistakes, each corrected as it arises, and no one of which is vital. When therefore the stage of practical application has been reached substantially all possible technical difficulties have been unearthed and taken into account. One can then proceed with a high degree of assurance.

It is not, however, safe to stop at this point since otherwise the time may come when one's activities may be subjected to a danger from the outside. Hence one must also progress with investigation of allied arts as well as his own.

Now in all industrial research, in whatever field, there is a common factor. The productive strength of any research organization is the trained understanding of human beings associated together for teamwork and applying the scientific method in which preconceived ideas are tested experimentally, under controlled conditions, with the implements and techniques of an established proven art.

As to his ability to carry on effective work, it makes very little difference in what field of science a man has obtained his training in the fundamentals of the scientific method. It may mean of course that Bill Jones, who obtained his training in

118

the field of physics and finds himself injected into problems in the field of the chemical sciences, is at a slight disadvantage to Sam Smith who obtained the same fundamental training in chemistry. It is, however, only a temporary disadvantage which obtains only until Bill has acquainted himself with certain facts. Initially he must work a little harder to get his facts but the scientific methods and techniques with which he has become acquainted are applicable in all branches of scientific investigation.

An illustration from my own field comes to mind. Under the operation of our age retirement rule we recently retired a man who has probably produced more of outstanding value in the communication field than any other man now living. His productions were in the field of abstruse mathematical physical science but his training was that of a civil engineer. However, it was a good training and when he found himself injected into a strange field he was not lost because all he had to do to become a producer was to learn certain fundamental facts in that field and apply to them the methods he had already learned.

The Field of Research in Electrical Communication

Now to get on to the field in which I am particularly interested—electrical communication. This field of electrical communication is characterized by something which is rather unique in the whole field of industrial research. While we deal enormously with physical things, our objective in the last analysis is not primarily an interest in physical things per se. Substantially we sell nothing of a physical character. Practically every other industrial research organization I am acquainted with is engaged in creating physical things to be sold to the ultimate consumer.

In our business the thing which we sell is the most intangible thing in the world. Our vendible product is merely an ability to give to men the facility for transmitting their thoughts from one place to another. Substantially all of our work in con-

119

nection with physical things is designed to give us a better, more extensive, cheaper and so a more desirable facility.

We are, moreover, necessarily dealing at all times with an intricate past as well as a future. Everything which we do and everything which we put into use must not only be good in itself and attain its individual objective, but it cannot be used at all, no matter how good it may be inherently, if its injection into an already complex existing entity will destroy a part of what we have already accomplished.

In other words, if, for example, we design a peculiar form of telephone equipment for the city of Portland, Maine, it cannot be employed, no matter how well it may be adapted to some peculiar local situation there, if its introduction will destroy or impair the ability of the people of Portland to talk, say, with people in New York. This necessity arises from the fact that electrical communication, and particularly telephony, involves an enormous complex interrelated functioning of material things, no one of which can be altered without danger of dislocating somewhat the functioning of something else at a distant point.

The job which we industrial research people do may appear complicated to an outsider not trained as a scientist. Like all intricate things, it is complicated in a way but in another way it is a definitely straightforward kind of a job, and this for a very simple reason. I have mentioned that effective research organizations have to be equipped with properly trained, properly qualified human beings. The problems with which they deal, however, since they concern inanimate things, are not such as to involve many of the things concerned with human emotions and reactions which complicate our undertakings in many other activities. In a word, we industrial research people do not have to concern ourselves largely with human behavior reactions. In any particular investigation, whether we know it or not, the yardstick by which our undertaking will finally be judged is the yardstick of absolute truth.

Old Dame Nature sets the yardsticks and no amount of mental gymnastics or wishful thinking on our part can alter them. Whether we do a good or a bad job is therefore dependent very largely on our ability and upon our knowledge of the invariable factors which Nature puts up.

Coming now to telephony, the ultimate is a system which would enable any one anywhere, at any time he might elect, to be put in instantaneous perfect communication with anybody anywhere else in the world. This is the ideal toward which we have always striven but which in all probability we will never quite reach.

Telephony's Three Major Fields of Research

Now this ideal telephone service involves three major fields which interest us on the physical side and within which, broadly speaking, all of our problems lie. First, at the sending end, there are the instrumentalities which translate speech waves in air into those electrical impulses which we use to carry the message of the intangible thing called " thought," to some distant point, at which point there are other instrumentalities which reconvert the electrical impulses into sound waves that are substantially replicas of those issuing from the speaker's mouth. In other words, the instrumentalities of this first category are represented by the familiar telephone transmitter and receiver which you have on your desk, and the apparatus immediately associated with them. Second, there are the channels over which the electrical impulses are carried from one place to another. These channels must be efficient not only from an energy standpoint but also they must transmit that energy from one point to another without sufficient modification of form to impair intelligibility. It would be of no value to me as a telephone engineer to devise a telephone channel from here to San Francisco so efficient that it would deliver all of the originating energy or even many times that amount if the energy reached San Francisco in such a form as to prevent the production of intelligible speech. Thus in this second category we have a dual problem. On the one hand we have the same sort of problem with which power engineers have to deal, namely, one of energy efficiency, and in addition we have an intricate problem of so transmitting the energy that we do not substantially impair the intricate and rapidly varying form in which speech delivers it to us.

The third problem pertains to the means of interconnecting these channels of transmission quickly and economically to provide for the random demands of those who wish to use the telephone. At one minute you or I may wish to telephone to a man in the adjoining block and a few moments afterwards from the self-same instrument we may wish to talk to a man in London or in San Francisco. Ability to do these things to the satisfaction of our customers is dependent on our ability to switch and interconnect channels of communication with great rapidity.

These are our three major fields of interest, and I am now going to attempt to illustrate a very few of the problems with which we have to deal and the distance to which we have gone in their solution.

Time will not permit consideration of all the fields and consequently I will not bother you with anything concerned with the first category, that is, the apparatus on your desk, although the problems concerned with it are at the very heart of all we do. Let us take up, rather, the case of switching mechanism, after which, if time permits, I will go a bit farther and tell you something about the field which is most spectacular and in some ways most interesting, namely, the channels of communication.

Originally, in the earliest commercial adaptations of telephony, when the art was simple and embryonic, switching was invariably done by a piece of human apparatus—the telephone operator. To a large extent it is still done in this way. Initially and where it is still used this human switch was and is effective, despite certain obvious limitations. In some situations it is doubtful whether there can ever be any other form of switching mechanism.

As a human relay or switch the operator receives spoken orders which indicate to her that two particular channels of communication are to be connected together, and then with her hands she connects these channels together by means of flexible cords or otherwise. Originally that was all there was to the switching operation, but as telephony grew, as the number of subscribers to be taken care of increased and as the number of channels between switching centers increased, the limitations of the human relay became increasingly apparent. Obviously, a single human relay could not perform unaided any operation which was beyond the reach of her arm. Since each terminal requires a finite amount of space there was a limit to the number of channels which the operator could interconnect directly.

As soon as the number of channels exceeded this limit interconnection required the operation of two or more of these human relays in some sort of tandem operation. This necessity introduced difficulties and objections which increased with the number of relays in the tandem team. These difficulties and objections were mainly of two kinds—increasing risk of error and a slowing down in the speed with which connections could be made. Each relay in turn had to receive correctly the order given to the originating operator. Each such repetition enhances the chance of error. In the second place, since the operations of the human relay are relatively slow as compared with the time required by mechanical relays, the time required for a tandem operation, even if errorless, is appreciably longer than that required for a single operation.

Even before the time arrived when the multiplicity of channels to be interconnected had reached the point of requiring tandem operation, numerous automatic devices for doing some of the things originally required of the human relay had begun to develop as a result of scientific research. Developments along this line have proceeded steadily until today we are taking the last step and substituting an entirely automatic form of switching under the control of the originating subscriber as a means of performing all the acts required to establish connection between distant subscribers. As noted before, it may never, however, be possible or desirable completely to eliminate all the human operators from our intricate system.

Full electromechanical operation of the switching phenomenon has many advantages and some disadvantages, none of which I intend to touch upon. There is, however, one outstanding advantage in a city like New York, or other great metropolitan areas, in the fact that it makes very little if any difference in the time required to complete connections, whether the called party is in the next block or as far separated from the calling party as the uppermost parts of the Bronx are from Coney Island. In other words, it takes practically no longer to complete a connection from a Coney Island substation to one in the Bronx than it does to complete one in Coney Island. Thus in addition to an almost complete elimination of error on the part of the switching mechanism, we have also speeded up the time of completing connections.

Now, it is a curious fact in telephony that developments in the switching side of our business almost invariably find their first application in the local service, from which they spread gradually into the short and then into the longer toll services. On the other hand, advances which are made in the realm of transmission, which I am going to mention next, usually do exactly the reverse, that is, improvements destined ultimately to have wide application in the field of transmission make their first appearances in the longer circuits and, with increasing knowledge and increasing experience, spread into the shorter circuits.

While at first sight this may seem a somewhat curious effect, it is quite a natural phenomenon. It results from the fact that initial adaptations are usually more complicated and expensive than they later become, with the result that their economic field is where maximum economies or advantages exist.

THE CHANNELS OF COMMUNICATION

Passing now to channels of communication, let me tell you about a few things that have come directly and exclusively out of scientific industrial research. Initially the distances over which one could talk telephonically were very short and the number of people who wanted to use the telephone very small. The efficiency of transmitters and receivers was low and it was quite easy to make connection between stations using ordinary wires or pairs of wires whose dimensions were dictated mainly by mechanical considerations. Originally these wires were of iron, which was later superseded by copper when means were found to make copper relatively strong, because copper is a substantially better conductor than iron.

At first all the wires between central offices and the subscribers were placed on poles, much as you see them today on the poles which parallel our country roads or railroad rights of way. The individual wires, even though associated together in pairs, were separated a considerable distance from each other and were supported on insulators. As the number of channels increased, however, a limit of capacity was reached beyond which additional channels could not easily be provided by this type of arrangement. It became necessary to find some way to crowd these conducting channels closer and closer together. To make a long story short, out of this need science developed an entirely new arrangement which we call the telephone cable. You are doubtless all familiar with these cables, which have the appearance of lead pipes. In country and suburban districts they are hung from steel cables supported on poles. In cities and to some extent on country roads they are drawn into buried ducts under the streets—frequently you see them being installed in such location.

In these lead pipes are associated together vast numbers of

125

wires, each wire insulated from its neighbors by a thin wrapping of paper. All of these wires are associated together in pairs by a twisting operation and each pair constitutes a transmission channel. Electrical interference between these channels is prevented by a proper selection of twists, each pair being given a twist which is different from that of the surrounding pairs. In all of the pairs, however, the currents which flow are similar and have the same frequencies as those produced in ordinary speech. In such cables the ability to crowd many circuits together without cross-interference is obtained through a geometrical arrangement of the wires.

There is, however, an entirely different method which science has developed for crowding many channels of communication together in a small space without cross-interference. Before I tell you about this other way, let me first digress a moment and tell you something of the telephone repeater. This is an essential implement on all longer distance telephone channels.

It was long ago apparent that the limits over which commercial speech could be transmitted without some form of rejuvenation were rapidly being reached. This is because in any form of electrical transmission a certain amount of the initial energy is lost. As you progress along the channel there comes a point where the residual energy is not more than sufficient to operate the receiving apparatus commercially at its lower limit. This point marks, therefore, the limit of transmission over that particular type of channel. If one would go further some way must be found at this point or before it is reached, to add new energy to the current without, in the case of telephony, producing distortion which would render the speech unintelligible.

Out of this necessity, and again as a direct result of scientific research, came the development of the so-called telephone amplifier or repeater. With this instrument we can build up the weakened speech currents and send them on either directly to their destination or, in the case of very long circuits, to successive additional repeaters which repeat the amplifying operation.

Where transmission is of ordinary voice frequency individual repeaters have to be provided for every channel at every point where amplification is required. If you go about the country along the main roads over which long distance circuits run you will find at intervals neat brick buildings. One such building you will find just outside of Princeton on the main highway to Trenton. These are the buildings in which telephone repeaters are housed. If you step inside you will find a vast quantity of vacuum tube apparatus, all of which resembles in appearance the inside of your radio sets. You will also find some form of power plant for supplying energy. All of the telephone circuits which require amplifiers are led through the apparatus in this building and there have new energy supplied to the speech currents passing through them.

Now to come back to the entirely different mode of transmission which I mentioned a few moments ago.

THE APPLICATION OF CARRIER CURRENT SYSTEMS

With increasing scientific knowledge we have found à way, and in many situations what appears to be a better way, for carrying the intelligence of speech from one point to another over the longer distances and with many channels packed closely together.

Instead of using ordinary speech frequencies at every one of the number of parallel circuits between two points, we mix the ordinary speech current at the sending end with an artificially produced high frequency current which is above the range of audition. We can superimpose on the same conductor a considerable number of non-interfering transmissions, provided only that we use a different high frequency current for each transmission. When currents of two frequencies are thus mixed together the resultant frequency is a composite of the two, and when many of these composites are mixed together for transmission over a single conductor the resultant current in the conductor is a composite of them all. We are not, however, interested particularly in what this composite is provided only that at the distant end of a line we can separate it into its elements and finally strain out the original speech currents and deliver each one to its proper recipient.

This we know how to do but time will not permit me to attempt a detailed explanation. In a way one might liken the operation at the sending end to the association together, in a common runway, of a large number of differently colored sheep, no one of which can reach the runway except through a particular gate. Within the runway all of the sheep move forward together and at the distant end each can find egress only through his own particular gate. Anything which we do along the runway to speed up the movement of the sheep speeds them all up equally. This whole system we refer to technically as a carrier current system.

Over certain kinds of conductors enormously wide bands of high frequency can be transmitted, bands up to one million cycles or more in width, that is, bands sufficiently wide to accommodate 300 or more speech channels, since the ordinary width of speech frequency bands used in telephony is in the order of 3000 cycles.

The fact that transmission between the terminals is in the nature of a single transmission means that at each point where amplification is required only a single amplifier is needed instead of individual amplifications for each channel to be operated on. Of course this single amplifier is different from the individual amplifiers but the fact that it is single offers great opportunities for simplification. At the point where this single amplifier is inserted the current which it operates on is infinitely complex. If one had an ear that could hear or an eye that could see within the circuit at this intermediate point he would apprehend simply a veritable Choctaw of electrical currents wholly unintelligible. In a sense it would be analogous to observing the gyrations of the air particles in a crowded room where a vast number of people were talking together in pairs.

Most of you have probably seen in the papers in the last year or so reference to what is known as the coaxial cable. This cable, of which there is a trial installation at the present time under test between New York and Philadelphia, is a very simple mechanical structure. It is a small lead pipe in which there are two smaller copper tubes each about the size of a lead pencil and down the center of each of which runs a smaller copper wire which is insulated from its enclosing tube. Through each of these pipes, however, can go simultaneously hundreds of telephone messages transmitted in the general manner which I have just outlined to you. At each point where amplification is needed to revivify energy, all that is required is a single amplifier associated with each tube. At the receiving end of the circuit the separating operation is performed. This coaxial cable represents the present stage of development to which our research work in the realm of transmission has now brought us. It bids fair to open up some very considerable fields of utility.

This coaxial cable is now in the trial stage as to practical application but in the final stage as to the research and development features of its operation. It is a stage necessarily preliminary to use in a general commercial sense. This trial installation procedure is one which we follow religiously in all development work. When we have carried our research and development work as far as seems feasible in the laboratory we always supplement our work by a limited trial installation. This is necessary because there are certain things which cannot be learned within the confines of a laboratory. Such a trial in so far as it affects normal operation limits unanticipated difficulties in a way in which they could not be limited if we went directly from the laboratory to general use.

I have said that the coaxial cable development started in the

129

laboratory. Actually it started in the realm of mathematical analysis. It started back in the original work of Maxwell, Rayleigh and others, who considered mathematically the problems of transmission of electromagnetic waves in space. Gradually, through the increase in our knowledge of physics and mathematics, we came to understand that in this type of physical structure, if we could realize certain properties of matter on a commercial scale we would have a very simple form of transmission channel.

The question was, therefore, could we obtain commercially these properties which our mathematical analysis indicated to be necessary? Could we get material which would have this or that property? If so, would it act in this and that way? Considerations of this kind set the pattern, then, for the stages of laboratory development and marked out the experimental course to be followed. Taking the elements of the pattern one at a time and in proper order, we made progress gradually until we arrived finally at a stage where we could put them all together on a large scale laboratory experiment.

This coaxial cable is one of those developments which, as I indicated to you, will, when our field experiments have been completed, find its first application in the longer distances of telephony and over routes where the number of telephone channels is large. Unless past history fails to repeat itself in this case (and I have no reason to believe that it will) the distances over which we will find it economical to employ this general type of structure will tend to decrease. As time goes on and experience enlarges we are almost sure to develop better ways of doing things and better materials with which to do them.

Incidentally, this particular form of transmission channel has the unique advantage that if and when the much-talked-of television reaches the stage of wide commercial utilization it is easily adaptable to the type of transmission which will be required to carry the electric currents of television from point of origin to the points where the impulses can be distributed to the ultimate user.

If in the future coaxial cables come to be used for shorter distances than those which are now indicated, it will but repeat the history of the older and simpler types of carrier current transmission which were not originally economical for anything less than distances of four or five hundred miles and with circuits employing a particularly fine grade of open wire facilities. Through continued intensive research and development we have during the past ten or fifteen years progressively reduced these distances until we now use carrier current methods on circuits as short as ten or fifteen miles. In the other sector, during this same period, switching mechanisms which were originally applicable wholly in local areas where concentration of service was heavy, have gradually spread out until we are today employing them for establishing many of our toll connections.

Frank B. Jewett

ELL TELEPHONE QUARTERLY

TELEPHONE SECRETARIAL SERVICE

ACCIDENT PREVENTION IN THE BELL SYSTEM

JOHN J. CARTY: TELEPHONE ENGINEER

"EACH IN HIS DEAREST TONGUE"

WORLD'S TELEPHONE STATISTICS:
JANUARY 1, 1936

BELL TELEPHONE QUARTERLY

*A Medium of Suggestion
and a Record of Progress*

CONTENTS FOR JULY 1937

VOL. XVI **NO. 3**

PUBLISHED QUARTERLY FOR THE BELL SYSTEM BY THE AMERICAN
TELEPHONE AND TELEGRAPH COMPANY. SUBSCRIPTION, $1.50 PER YEAR,
IN UNITED STATES; SINGLE COPIES, 50 CENTS

Address all communications to

**INFORMATION DEPARTMENT
AMERICAN TELEPHONE AND TELEGRAPH COMPANY**

195 Broadway, New York

Contributors to This Issue

HARRY R. WHITE

Massachusetts Institute of Technology, B.S., 1901; Assistant, Engineering Laboratories, 1901–03. Commercial engineering activities, 1903–10. American Telephone and Telegraph Company, Department of Operation and Engineering, Engineering Section, Plant Extension Engineering group, 1910–18, Equipment and Building group, 1918–.

W. P. ELSTUN

Purdue University, B.S. in E.E., 1907. New York Telephone Company, Plant Department, 1907–13; District Plant Engineer, Buffalo, N. Y., 1913–15. In 1915 Mr. Elstun was transferred to the American Telephone and Telegraph Company, joining the Outside Plant section of the Engineering Department, which later became the Department of Operation and Engineering. He is now in the Plant Training group of the Plant Operation Engineering section of that Department.

FRANK B. JEWETT

Throop Polytechnic Institute (now California Institute of Technology), B.A., 1898; University of Chicago, Ph.D., 1902. Several honorary degrees. Instructor in Physics and Electrical Engineering, Massachusetts Institute of Technology, 1902–04. American Telephone and Telegraph Company, Transmission and Protection Engineer, 1904–12; Western Electric Company, Assistant Chief Engineer, Chief Engineer, Vice President, 1912–25; Vice President, American Telephone and Telegraph Company, in charge of Development and Research Department, and President, Bell Telephone Laboratories, 1925–.

R. T. BARRETT

Lafayette College, B.A., 1907; New York Law School, LL.B., 1909. Engaged in practice of law, 1909–18, and in newspaper work until 1921, when he entered the Information Department, American Telephone and Telegraph Company. Mr. Barrett is now Librarian of the American Telephone Historical Library.

K. FICK

Hellerup Gymnasium, Copenhagen, Denmark, B.A., 1916; University of Copenhagen, Cand.Ph., 1918. Danish Government Service, 1918–24. American Telephone and Telegraph Company, Chief Statistician's Division, 1925–.

Telephone Secretarial Service

TELEPHONE secretarial service is one of the many advancements that have been made in recent years for extending the use of the telephone and increasing its value to the customer. This new service is designed to supplement the ordinary telephone service of customers who desire to have their telephones answered while they are out and no one else is present in their homes or offices to answer for them. It appears to be of particular value in apartment houses, professional buildings, and office buildings catering to tenants requiring small quarters. Telephone secretarial equipment is subscribed for and operated by the building management as an added service to its tenants, or by some other agency as a commercial business. With the new secretarial arrangements subscribers need no longer feel compelled to remain near their telephones for fear of missing important calls as this service permits them to go out with the assurance that their calls will be answered. A secretarial board is employed for this service with an attendant who receives incoming calls when desired by the secretarial user.

Secretarial service is ordinarily furnished to supplement business or residence individual or two party line service although in occasional cases it may be employed to advantage in connection with P.B.X. trunks or P.B.X. stations. The prospective secretarial user applies to the telephone company in the usual way for regular telephone service and to the building management or other agency for such secretarial service as he may require. The management of the building or other agency contracts with the telephone company for the secretarial board and provides for its operation to furnish a telephone secretarial service best suited to the particular needs of the tenants or clientele concerned. Telephone secretarial service is appropriate for stations located outside the building from which the secretarial service is furnished as well as for stations on the premises. Off-premises secretarial service is particularly suitable for certain types of customers such as physicians and surgeons who may wish to be served from a secretarial bureau.

General Operating Method

Each user having this service has his direct central office line extended to the secretarial board through a secretarial line and the attendant answers calls, takes messages, and gives reports, as may be directed by the secretarial user. In addition to this secretarial line, a supplementary or house service line may be provided between the user's station and the board to permit the customer to communicate directly with the attendant and also with certain building management stations, where such stations are provided, without going through the central office. The customer uses this line, where provided, to give instructions to the attendant before leaving the premises, to inquire for messages on his return, to call the superintendent or resident manager, or to have visitors announced by the attendant. The equipment at the secretarial board, however, is arranged to prevent unauthorized usage of the service, that is, the secretarial users cannot be interconnected at or originate central office calls via the secretarial board and the attendant cannot originate calls over the users' lines. Provision is made for obtaining privacy on central office calls, that is, for preventing the attendant from listening in, if this feature is desired by the user.

General Arrangement of Equipment

Two secretarial attendant's boards have been made available for this service: one for use where one or in some cases two positions are required, and the other where two or more positions are necessary. A general view of the single position board, which employs a standard non-multiple P.B.X. section, is shown in Figure 1. The arrangements of the multi-position board are similar except that standard multiple P.B.X. sections are employed. The equipment permits a wide variety of service features, which may include any of the following:

1. *Secretarial Lines.* Used solely for the answering by the secretarial attendant of incoming calls on the secretarial users' central office lines. As indicated above, these users may be located in the same building as the secretarial board or in other buildings.
2. *P.B.X. Stations.* For the use of management and house service points.
3. *P.B.X. Trunks.* For the use of the management and house service points.
4. *House Service Lines.* Supplementary lines for direct communication between the secretarial users and the attendant, and also for intercommunication between the users and the management or house service stations.

METHODS OF HANDLING SECRETARIAL CALLS

Provision is made for two methods of arranging for the reception of incoming calls by the secretarial attendant. In one of these methods the reception of incoming calls is controlled at the board and in this case the secretarial line is multipled directly to the customer's line. With this method a customer wishing to have his calls answered at the board notifies the attendant and the removal of a dummy plug from the jack in which the secretarial line terminates causes the line lamp to light when ringing current is applied to the customer's line at the central office. In the other method, the reception of incoming calls is controlled at the secretarial user's station and the secretarial line is extended to the board through a key located at this station. In this case the secretarial line lamp will be lighted on incoming calls when the station key is in the operated position.

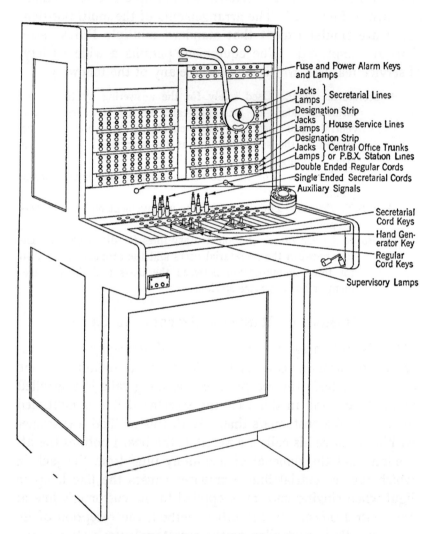

Fuse and Power Alarm Keys and Lamps

Jacks } Secretarial Lines
Lamps

Designation Strip

Jacks } House Service Lines
Lamps

Designation Strip

Jacks } Central Office Trunks
Lamps } or P.B.X. Station Lines

Double Ended Regular Cords

Single Ended Secretarial Cords

Auxiliary Signals

Secretarial Cord Keys

Hand Generator Key

Regular Cord Keys

Supervisory Lamps

FIG. 1. SINGLE POSITION SECRETARIAL BOARD.

The main features of the two methods of controlling the reception of incoming calls at the secretarial board may be summarized briefly as follows:

Control at the Secretarial Board

1. The secretarial user can at any time instruct the attendant to answer his line, regardless of whether he is on the premises or at some distant point. This feature is particularly important should the customer leave his premises and find he has not instructed the attendant to answer his line during his absence. (With control at the user's station, this would, of course, not be possible.)
2. Where it is necessary for the customer to give specific instructions to the attendant to answer his line, as is the case with control at the board, he is more likely to give her the information as to his whereabouts while off the premises than with control at the station. This is desirable from the standpoint of the calling party as well as the secretarial user.
3. This arrangement inherently gives privacy on outgoing calls. Privacy on incoming calls may be obtained through the provision of an automatic cut-off feature.
4. Secretarial service is not applicable to two-party lines with this method of control.

Control at the Secretarial User's Station

1. This arrangement gives the secretarial user complete control over the secretarial arrangement. When the user's key is thrown, all incoming calls are indicated at the secretarial board.
2. This arrangement also gives privacy at minimum cost. When the key is thrown to pick up a central office call, the line to the secretarial attendant is disconnected.
3. The secretarial user need only throw the key to receive secretarial service. The attendant does not have to set the equipment so that she can answer incoming calls or to reset the equipment when the user returns.

HOUSE SERVICE LINES

As indicated above, house service lines serve as a convenient means for communication between the secretarial users and the

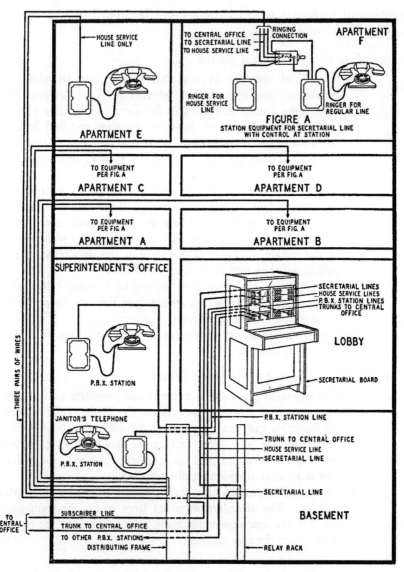

FIG. 2. CONTROL OF SECRETARIAL LINE AT STATION.

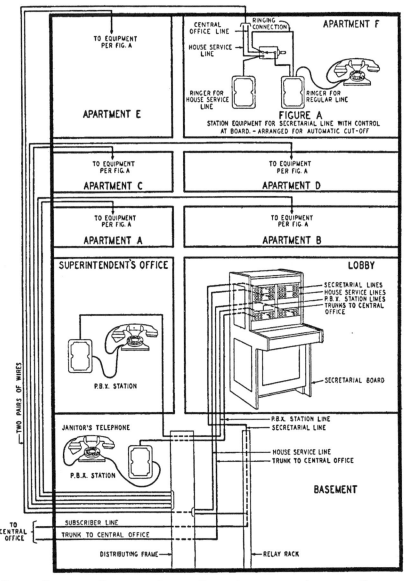

FIG. 3. CONTROL OF SECRETARIAL LINE AT BOARD, ARRANGED FOR AUTOMATIC CUT-OFF.

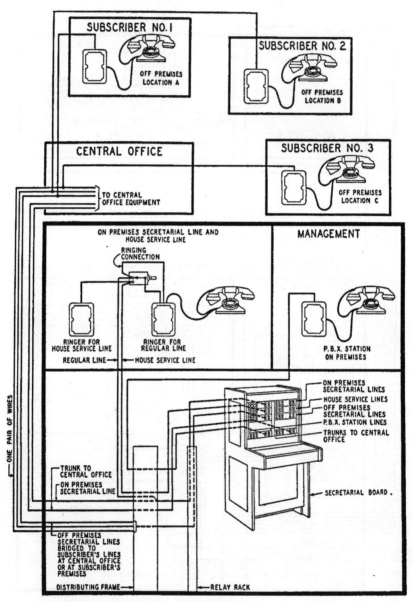

FIG. 4. CONTROL OF SECRETARIAL LINE AT BOARD, NOT ARRANGED FOR AUTOMATIC CUT-OFF.

attendant. They may be omitted, if desired, in cases where the board is so located that it is convenient for the tenants to advise the attendant verbally with regard to the reception of their incoming calls. Where these house service lines are furnished in conjunction with the arrangement for controlling the secretarial feature at the board, a key is employed at the secretarial user's station, the operation of which transfers the telephone instrument from the central office line to the house service line. Where house service lines are furnished in conjunction with the arrangement for controlling the secretarial feature at the station, the operation of the station key, in addition to connecting the central office line to the secretarial board, simultaneously transfers the telephone instrument to the house service line. These house service lines terminate at the board in a jack and lamp. House service lines are also used for intercommunicating service between secretarial users' and house service stations in apartment houses or between secretarial users' and management stations in secretarial bureaus, where management stations are provided. The lines for these latter stations are terminated at the board like regular P.B.X. extension lines. House service lines would, ordinarily, not be justified for off-premises secretarial service and are usually furnished only in cases where the secretarial lines are on-premises.

LINE, TRUNK AND CORD EQUIPMENT

Single ended cords, as shown in Figure 1, are provided at the secretarial board for answering incoming calls from the secretarial lines. As also shown in this Figure, provision is made in the secretarial board for two-way central office trunks and for double-ended cords. These double-ended cords are used for establishing connections between house service lines and regular P.B.X. station lines for intercommunication between regular P.B.X. station lines and for establishing connections between the central office trunks and regular P.B.X. station lines.

143

Typical Applications for Secretarial Service

A typical layout for secretarial service with control at the station is shown in Figure 2. In the case illustrated the service is furnished for an apartment house, all of the associated telephones being located on the same premises as the secretarial board. The distributing frame for terminating the wires and the relay rack for mounting the apparatus are located in the basement and the board is located in the lobby of the building. As will be noted from the typical arrangement shown in Apartment F, three lines are connected to the control key; the customer's central office line, the secretarial line and a house service line. Separate ringers are provided for the central office and house service lines. As the bell on the central office line will ring regardless of the position of the key, the signal for an incoming call is always obtained on the customer's premises and the customer can cut off the attendant and answer at any time.

Figures 3 and 4 cover typical layouts for secretarial service with control at the secretarial board. Figure 3 shows an arrangement for an apartment house where all of the associated telephones are on-premises and is comparable with Figure 2 illustrating control at the station. As will be noted in Figure 3, two lines are connected to the key at the station: the central office line and a house service line and, as in Figure 2, a separate ringer is provided for each of these lines. With this arrangement, also, the customer can cut off the attendant and answer his incoming calls whenever he wishes to do so. Where secretarial service is furnished by the method of control at the board, privacy on incoming as well as outgoing calls may be obtained by means of relay equipment arranged automatically to cut off the attendant whenever the secretarial user's receiver is off the switchhook.

Figure 4 illustrates a method of furnishing secretarial service for both on-premises and off-premises stations where provision is not made for automatic cut-off. With off-premises stations the use of the automatic cut-off feature is not ordinarily warranted as an additional pair of conductors is required between the central office and the customer's premises and between the central office and the secretarial board.

Advantages of Secretarial Service

In addition to having incoming calls received by an attendant when desired, the use of the secretarial equipment enables customers to obtain the advantages of direct connection to the central office and also to obtain the benefits of such incidental services of the attendant as may be desired. From the point of view of the office building or apartment house management it provides a desirable service that can be offered to tenants to supplement other office or house service features.

H. R. White

Accident Prevention in the Bell System

THE early history of the telephone industry indicates that in practically every phase of development the avoidance of accidents to the public and the employees was an inherent consideration. One of the first additions to the original telephone circuit was a substation protector, added to prevent accidents from lightning. As first installed, the protector was merely a device offering an easy path to ground for the high frequency discharge. As electric light, power, and trolley systems began to appear, additions were made to this protective device so that the circuit would be opened in the event that lines of higher voltage or greater current became crossed with the telephone circuit. At the central office, similar apparatus was placed to protect the operators, central office workmen, and the switchboard. The development of such devices to protect the subscriber and the subscriber's premises, as well as the employees and the telephone apparatus itself, has been continuous since the first use of the telephone, and in modern telephone exchanges and equipment these devices are found as perfect as human intelligence can devise them.

In the design and development of the outside plant, tools, materials and other equipment, the matter of preventing accidents has constantly been a fundamental consideration. Certainly in so far as the telephone business is concerned, the personnel of its early management unquestionably was among that group of pioneers who years ago laid the groundwork for what we know as the general safety movement of today.

This general movement evolved through a number of rather separate and distinct stages.

Industrial management at the start of the movement had been engaged in developing ways and means of establishing

146

and maintaining quantity production and distribution. Thus there had come about the development of high speed machinery, the perfection of production methods, intensive sales campaigns, etc., all having to do with the technical mechanical phases of business in contrast with the human relations aspect of business operations. The industrial managements of this country which first attacked the industrial accident problems were for the most part " technically minded." In consequence, the movement at first took the form of placing safety guards on or around machines, and this initial period of the movement might be termed the " mechanical " stage. All types of guards were developed. Some were good and survived. Others were impractical: they were too heavy and cumbersome, or difficult to use, while a few actually interfered with production. The impractical types, needless to say, were discarded. It soon became evident that, although the guarding of certain machines was desirable, something more was necessary.

The accident data which were being collected seemed to indicate that the actions of the workmen themselves were contributing to a large percentage of the accidents. Statistics were circulated claiming to show that seventy, eighty, and even ninety per cent of all industrial accidents were due to carelessness. Thus the stage was set for the second period of the evolution of the general safety movement, the " inspirational " or " emotional " stage.

Throughout the country, industry employed people to meet with the workers and to talk to them about accident prevention. The serious consequences of accidents were verbally and sometimes graphically pictured to the workman. His love of home and family were appealed to, pride of craft was stressed, economic factors were emphasized, but little or nothing was developed which would actually teach him how to prevent accidents.

Finally analysts, through a careful study of the situation, developed the basic principles underlying the industrial accident problem, and real progress began to be evidenced through the application of these principles. Thus the present or "scientific" stage of the safety movement was reached.

Accompanying these transitory stages of development of the industrial accident prevention movement there was a change in conception with relation to it.

Originally there was a tendency to view the movement as largely humanitarian, with possibly an accompanying objective of reducing the expenses incident to accidents. Coupled with these views was the thought that so-called safety measures necessarily were extensive adjuncts to operating practices and as such tended to interfere with efficient production.

However, as the analysts developed the underlying causes of industrial accidents and the preventive measures to be applied, it became increasingly apparent that those factors in industry which were producing accidents were very largely the same factors which tended to lower quantity and quality of production, and so industrial accident prevention was no longer viewed as simply a humanitarian measure but became one of the objectives of efficient managerial administration.

In the Bell System, as in many other industrial organizations, careful study was being made of the trend of events in the general safety movement, in order that the System might profit by both the successes and mistakes of the experimental measures being so generally applied.

As a result of this study together with the System's own experiences in preventing accidents, a planned, co-ordinated program of accident prevention was developed and adopted. In developing this program it was the objective to so apply the fundamental principles of accident prevention that the activities would be an integral part of the day-to-day job of every employee rather than a series of undertakings set apart from the normal functions of each employee.

Broadly, the System's accident prevention program consists of ten major features. To those associated with the System, these features are not new. Most of them were taught to the present employees, craftsmen, supervisors, and members of the management, by their predecessors in the business, not necessarily as a part of an accident prevention program but as features of an efficiently functioning organization and in consequence of good industrial management. Because, however, these features of the System's accident prevention program are so fundamental and so important if avoidable accidents in the telephone business are to be prevented, they warrant frequent repetition. Just as the repetition of the slogan of the commercial advertisement ultimately produces general acceptance of its message, so repetition of these features of the System's program has aided in producing a general acceptance, and in consequence a united purpose on the part of all employees to support and aid the program, thus helping in accomplishing the objective of preventing accidents. The ten major features of the program, briefly described, follow.

(1) *The Selection of Employees*

Every reasonable and practicable effort is made to select employees who are physically and mentally qualified to perform the tasks to which they will be assigned. They must contribute to the satisfactory functioning of the organization as a whole and not constitute a hazard to themselves, their fellow employees, or the public.

(2) *The Assignment of Employees*

Assignment is mentioned apart from selection because this feature extends far beyond the recruit's initial selection, training, and assignment to a job. The assignment responsibility of supervision begins the moment the employee enters the business, and continues until the time he leaves the service. No employee should be assigned to work alone on a task requiring more skill, knowledge, physical strength, or judgment than the particular employee possesses at the time.

149

(3) *Craft and Supervisory Training*

Craft or vocational training teaches the employee how to perform efficiently each task to which he is assigned. Standard practices, sub-divided into numerous individual items or operations, are taught in proper sequence by a competent supervisor, either in central schools or on the job.

Supervisory training in several forms is given by the Bell System. One type is intended to teach supervisors how to train the men working under their direction. Another type is that designed to impart to the supervisor an appreciation of his responsibilities as a supervisor and how best to meet these responsibilities. All of this supervisory training is directed toward the objective of developing competent supervisors who know just what they want done, and how to get it done that way.

(4) *First Aid Training*

Training in proper first aid practices has been given to large numbers of Bell System employees. A knowledge of such practices to be applied should an injury occur on the job does not transcend the necessity for knowledge of how the job should be done safely. The latter, if applied with reasonable skill and care, should prevent the occurrence of most of the injuries concerned with job operations. But experience has indicated that persons trained in first aid have a better understanding of the seriousness of injuries, and in consequence tend to be more careful workers. Furthermore, such knowledge may be used to prevent the conversion of a rather minor injury into one with more serious consequences.

Bell System plant men on their regular jobs are scattered all over the country. They may be found on the streets, in the homes and offices of the big cities, installing and repairing telephones or placing and splicing the cables. In the remote sections of the country, wherever the wire highways of the

150

nation reach, they travel on trucks and small cars. They are equipped to render service to the general public not only in the field of communication but in saving life and relieving pain. Almost daily, news accounts describe some meritorious act of first aid performed by a telephone man in aiding some injured person. Special recognition of some of the most outstanding acts of this character is found in the records of Vail Medal Awards, in those of the President's Awards of the National Safety Council, and in the records of the awards of the American National Red Cross. Certainly these acts typify a great humanitarian service of which the employees can be justly proud and, too, some reflected credit is due the Companies which made it possible for these employees to obtain this knowledge.

In all of this first aid training work done throughout the country, the Bell System has had the benefit of the assistance of the American National Red Cross.

(5) *Provision of Adequate, Competent Supervision*

This objective has been established in order to insure that each job is carefully analyzed and planned, with possible hazards recognized and guarded against, and that only pre-scribed efficient practices are followed. The Company can have the safest possible tools, the best possible standard prac-tices, and a 100 per cent safe plant, but if the men performing the operations do not continually follow prescribed safe prac-tices, occasionally something will go wrong. The first time something goes wrong, no damage may be done; the second time, possibly a tool or a piece of material may be ruined; but finally, someone will get hurt. This is the reason that in the last analysis so much of the success of the accident preven-tion effort depends on supervision. The moment that a foreman sees a workman follow an unsafe practice, he should correct that practice at once and not wait for a personal injury to focus at-tention on the fact that he has permitted improper practices in

151

his group. By and large, the supervisors of the Bell System Operating Companies have this view of their responsibilities, otherwise the System could not have made the progress in reducing accidents that it has. Probably never in the history of the business has a finer type or a more competent group constituted the supervisory personnel of the System. This fact in itself is a most important factor contributing to the success which the System has enjoyed in its accident prevention efforts.

(6) *Bell System Practices and Specifications*

Standard practices for the performance of the various work operations have been developed only after careful study and field trials. Operations possessing unusual accident possibilities are covered in more detail than most of the other operations by the use of illustrations and by additional instructions as to the methods to be used. Standard practices and specifications not only result in a standard product, but are the very essence of the craft training program making up the larger portion of text material used for plant training purposes. Supervision undoubtedly would be seriously handicapped without them.

(7) *Provision of Protective Equipment*

The standard goggles are typical examples of protective equipment furnished to telephone employees. Various types of commercial goggles were subjected to severe impact tests in the Bell Telephone Laboratories. Various designs were studied to determine which seemed to fit most comfortably the greatest variations in face contours. Possibilities as to fogging were tested. All this was done to determine the type and make of goggles best suited to the needs of telephone workers.

The carbon monoxide detector, which indicates the presence of carbon monoxide in an atmosphere down to less than six parts in 10,000, was originated in the medical department of the American Telephone and Telegraph Company and devel-

Some of the Posters Used by the Bell System Operating Companies
Referred to on Page 158.

see path from
furnace to man~
hole is *clear*

grasp hook firmly.

raise pot *clear*
of furnace.

hold *away* from
legs.

Where practicable
10 feet or more, on downhill side

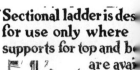

Sectional ladder is des
for use only where
supports for top and b
are avai

use on stra

to pull apa

A SAFE
WAY

to engage

to disengage

SAFETY
STRAP

1 on slippery roads ~
reduce speed.

2 use chains as speci-
fied in Bell System
Practices.

3 to slow up apply
brakes gradually
without disengaging
clutch.

Proper arrangemen
tools helps in perfo
ance of job and preve
injury to individu
and damage to prope

Carry only what you
can handle with
safety....

See

o obstructions which
may dislodge load.

Use
Flashlight

when
entering
dark places

PROVIDE ADEQUATE,
SUPPORT FOR ALL V

*makeshift supports
lead to accidents.*

SOME OF THE POSTERS USED BY THE BELL SYSTEM OPERATING COMPANIES
REFERRED TO ON PAGE 158.

oped by the Bell Telephone Laboratories. The suction gas indicator was likewise perfected to detect the presence of natural gas or an oxygen deficiency. Through the use of these two devices and proper ventilation, where required, gas sickness, which in the past occasionally occurred in connection with work in manholes, can now be prevented. These are examples of steps taken to provide adequate protective equipment.

(8) *Collection, Distribution and Analysis of Accident Data*

The sole purpose of collecting and analyzing accident data is to utilize past experiences in preventing future accidents. The proper use of these data enables the organization to continually focus attention on those phases of the job to which remedial measures might profitably be applied. It is a very important part of carrying out all the other mentioned features of the accident prevention program.

About sixteen years ago the managements of the Bell System Operating Companies decided that a concerted effort was needed to reduce accidental injuries to employees in the Plant Department. At the request of the Companies, the General Staff of the American Telephone and Telegraph Company undertook a study of the subject. The first move recommended was that a routine be established whereby each personal injury to an employee involving lost time from duties of one full day or more should be reported on a standard form. These forms were to be routed to a central point in the local Company, and from there one copy of each report was to go to the General Staff in New York. The thought behind this procedure was that the local Company would first study and analyze the case, to determine what could be done locally; then the General Staff, through summaries of data, could determine weak spots, if any, in the standard practices, tools, or equipment which had been adopted. Also, at New York, accident data and summaries could be prepared for supervisory use throughout the System. These data and summaries would make available the accident experience of each Company to all the areas. The plan was put into effect and is still in operation.

As the data began to be accumulated, it was found, among other things, that safety straps worn by linemen and other employees while aloft occasionally failed in service. When the subject was studied, it was further found that some Companies provided body belts and safety straps for employees while in other Companies the employee purchased these himself. Naturally, the employee would shop around to buy the tool as cheaply as he could, sometimes sacrificing quality. The matter was referred to the Companies, and they decided that, as rapidly as possible, the policy should be generally established that all tools on which the employee's safety directly depends would be supplied by the Company. The adoption of this policy had two major benefits from the standpoint of accident prevention. First, it insured the supply of an article of good quality, and second, it permitted the withdrawal of the item from service, when, through normal wear or damage, its condition appeared hazardous. But the problem was not so simple as all that. It was necessary to insure that every belt and strap supplied was a safe and reliable product, and so a very thorough study of body belts and safety straps was undertaken.

Skilled craftsmen, such as experienced linesmen, have certain tools with which they have become accustomed to work. This long experience with a particular type of tool has inevitably developed in their minds a preference. When for years a large group of workmen have themselves been purchasing and using various types of tools of this nature, it is quite difficult to obtain complete agreement on the part of all concerned on a particular type of tool for standardization. It took time and discussion all over the country to harmonize the views of all those concerned and finally arrive at a reasonably uniform view as to the details of the belt and strap to be standardized.

Thus, through the accident data and other studies, a lot was learned about belts and straps. For example, the leather from portions of the hide other than the back tends to stretch and its tensile strength will at times be questionable. It is, therefore, essential to see that only the best quality back leather is used in the standard safety straps.

The metal " Dee " rings, buckles, and snaps, the hardware on the belt and strap, are all drop forgings because of the greater reliability of this type of processing. The snap hook of the strap has been especially designed to permit of readily engaging in the Dee ring and yet to be so constructed that it cannot be easily disengaged inadvertently. Samples of each manufactured lot of Dee rings and snap hooks are tested to destruction to insure that every one of these items in the completed straps will not fail in use. Finally, each completed strap is given a thorough visual inspection to determine that the high quality of workmanship that has been prescribed is being really followed.

It was also found desirable to insulate the rivets in the standard body belt to prevent interference with service and to avoid slight shocks from ringing current on the telephone lines. This is a comparatively minor feature, but it illustrates the detail of care and thought given in an endeavor to make the tool just as safe as it is practical to make it.

The development of the standard lineman's climbers is another illustration of the way the accident data were used to further perfect a tool. A number of years ago, the accident data indicated that some difficulty was being experienced with the breaking of gaffs on certain commercial climbers. It was decided to propose specifications for climbers and have them made under these specifications. Special heat treatment of the entire climber was required in order to insure a uniform structure in the steel throughout. Some excellent work was done by the experts in the Laboratories in developing a much safer and more uniform climber. In addition, the Western Electric inspection department put samples of each manufactured lot through rigid tests and inspections.

155

The accident data were also useful in pointing out the need for improved standardized goggles, gas detectors, and many other items.

But it is not always a tool item that the accident data show should have further attention. A number of years ago there were accidents involving the unloading of poles from flat cars. Bell engineers thereupon developed a safe practice for unloading poles. Severe accidents in connection with this job need not occur now.

However, studies of accident data do not always indicate that modifications of practices or changes in tools or material are required. These cases are exceptions rather than the rule. As one situation after another is cleared up, the need for modifications of practices or changes in tools or materials becomes increasingly rare. Usually the data indicate a lack of analysis in the planning of the job or a need for further training in the actual work operation being performed. Probably the reason why the plant managements of the Bell System Operating Companies take the accident reports so seriously and study them so carefully is because they know that the report is an indication of inefficiencies occurring on the job. They are reasonably sure that a number of like inefficiencies occurred before one finally resulted in the personal injury which produced the report. Usually a whole chain of waste, involving damaged tools and material and lost effort, has preceded the personal injury. If these occurrences can be stopped, the accidents will not occur.

(9) *The Provision of Safe Tools, Materials and Equipment*

In the discussion of the use of the accident data, the care taken to provide certain safe tools has already been outlined. It should be emphasized that effort is made to provide all tools, materials, and equipment which are safe when used with reasonable skill and care. In the Bell System, a considerable proportion of the tools, materials, and equipment used are manufactured under specially prepared specifications, in the development of which safety is always given major consideration. Samples of each manufactured lot are inspected and tested to insure that the finished product meets the requirements of the specification. Such items as rubber gloves, body belts and safety straps, lineman's climbers and the like—items on which the employees' safety may directly depend,—are given special treatment. The development of the present standard belt and safety strap, which has been described, illustrates the precautions followed in manufacture and later inspection and test of tools, materials, and equipment to insure a safe product.

The installation of the new coaxial cable recently placed for experimental purposes between New York and Philadelphia is a typical example of the effort of telephone management to provide safe tools and materials. The manufacture, installation, and subsequent maintenance of this cable and its associated equipment introduced new problems, and some of these problems concern accident prevention. The point to be emphasized is the thoroughness with which the new undertaking was studied and planned. Every possibility of an accident was considered in advance and every reasonable effort was made to safeguard against such an occurrence. Not only were safe practices developed for the various operations incident to the installation and maintenance of the cable and equipment, but safeguards were incorporated as an integral part of the design of the equipment. Each man who worked on this new type job was given special training. Supervisors for the job were carefully selected and trained. All of these are fundamental accident prevention measures, and the case is cited as another illustration of how the Bell System endeavors to prevent accidents in connection with telephone work.

(10) *The Establishment of Incentives*

These incentives result from the efforts of the Bell System Operating Companies to engender and maintain interest in the accident prevention activity. These efforts include the publication of comparative accident data, in order that there may be a friendly contest to reduce accidents which will arouse Companies, areas, divisions and districts to constantly endeavor to improve their past records and to better those of the other operating groups. There is also the wide group discussion of published information on current accidents in order to call attention to accident possibilities and develop the ways and means of meeting such possibilities without the occurrence of an accident. And there is the general use of posters which graphically depict methods and practices that experience has proved to be right and safe.

Such activities as these help to keep alive interest and desire to work the safe way. And underlying them all is the enlightened recognition of the problem's importance by the supervisory forces, and the co-operation and support of the men and women in the organization.

This review of the Bell System's accident prevention program merely outlines the program and its application. The provision of safe tools, protective equipment, adequate, competent supervision and the uses of accident data have been stressed to some extent. But such matters as the proper selection and assignment of employees, craft and supervisory training, first aid training and the development and use of standard practices and specifications could each be the subject of separate articles, such is their interest and importance.

Any account, however brief, of the Bell System's accident prevention program and its application, would be glaringly incomplete if it did not include a tribute to the employees of the Operating Companies for the way they have met the problem and are helping in its solution. Industrial accident prevention is a co-operative undertaking, with certain definite responsi-bilities allocated to management and supervision and others to the individual craftsman and office worker. It has only been possible to gain such a measure of success as the System has enjoyed through the co-operation of every employee. Fur-ther progress must inevitably be predicated upon maintaining and improving this co-operation.

W. P. ELSTUN

John J. Carty: Telephone Engineer

(The following biographical memoir of General John J. Carty, formerly Vice President of the American Telephone and Telegraph Company, who died December 27, 1932, was written by his associate and successor, Dr. Frank B. Jewett, at the request of the National Academy of Sciences, for permanent preservation in the Academy's Archives.)

HENRY CARTY, the father of John J(oseph), emigrated to America in 1825, when eighteen years of age. He landed at Eastport, Maine, and after trying work on a nearby farm, moved on, finally reaching Cambridge, Massachusetts, where he settled and learned the machinist's trade. Here he married Elizabeth O'Malley who, like himself, was of Irish lineage. It is reported that fortune smiled rather genially upon the couple and that they became respected and comfortably well-to-do citizens of their adopted city.

John J., the fourth child of the union of Henry and Elizabeth, was born in Cambridge, April 14, 1861. During Carty's boyhood, his father operated a bell foundry. It does not appear that he evinced more interest in his father's profession than might have been shown by any normal youngster, but he did give evidence of being strongly attracted by Physics, and in particular by Electrical Science, which was then quite in its infancy. His first schooling was in the Allston Grammar School, where he had the good fortune to come under the tutelage of a G. W. Roberts, the master of the school. Viewing his youthful days in retrospect, Carty once said affectionately, almost reverently: "People like 'Donkey' Roberts don't exist nowadays; ours is the era of the chain-store fellows."

From the Allston Grammar School, Carty passed to the Cambridge Latin School, with the intention after graduation to carry out his parents' wishes by entering Harvard College and then finishing with a course in the Law School. But the plans for making a lawyer of John J. Carty never reached fruition, although in view of the qualities of intellect he later disclosed there can be little doubt that he would have made a most brilliant and able barrister. At a critical moment, trouble developed in his eyes and became so acute that for a time he was compelled to discontinue all study. Rather than graduate behind his old classmates, Carty, then seventeen years of age, decided to seek employment. Following his natural bent, the first job was in a shop devoted to the sale of, as the phrase then went, philosophical apparatus and of which the proprietor was one Thomas Hall. Although the atmosphere of the shop quite satisfied his youthful curiosity, his employment there was short-lived and terminated abruptly when he electroplated some old bits of brass to make them appear like gold and left them for Mr. Hall to discover.

From the scientific shop, Carty seems to have wandered quite by chance to the office of the Boston Telephone Despatch Company, where E. T. Holmes was operating a small telephone exchange as an adjunct to an already established burglar alarm system. This exchange included a switchboard for interconnecting telephone lines. After an interview with the superintendent, Carty was hired at twice his former wage to serve as one of the boy operators. Thus began his lifelong connection with the telephone business. Years afterward, speaking of the boy operators, he said that they made very poor precursors to the girls; "They were not old enough to be talked to like men, and they were not young enough to be spanked like children."

Carty's service with the Boston Telephone Despatch Company and with the New England Telephone and Telegraph Company continued from 1879 to 1887. He soon passed from the ranks of the boy operators to work involving design, construction and maintenance, and he early showed facility at finding ways to improve the primitive, almost naïve, apparatus

161

and methods which characterized the earliest years of the telephone art. One of his outstanding contributions, made in 1881, was the application to commercial use of the full metallic circuit instead of the single grounded wire which had been previously used and which had been borrowed from the telegraph art as it then existed. It was also at this time that Carty laid the foundation of what was later to become the common battery telephone system. This momentous development required several years to perfect, however, and his most valuable inventions pertaining to it did not arise for another decade.

A complete list of Carty's patents comprises twenty-four in all, which were issued in the period between 1883 and 1896. There were other inventors whose contributions to the telephone art were more numerous than Carty's, but no contemporary excelled him in the importance of his inventions; for example, his common battery switchboard, his bridging bell and his transformer or repeating coil type of phantom circuit are as fundamental to the telephone art of today as they were forty years ago.

In 1887, Carty left Boston and the New England Telephone and Telegraph Company to take charge of the telephone cable department of the Western Electric Company with headquarters in New York. His genius appears to have been too many-sided, however, for him to remain long in this rather specialized work. From the cable department he passed to the switchboard department and then, in November of 1889, was appointed "Electrician" of the Metropolitan Telephone and Telegraph Company, now the New York Telephone Company. Thus, in his twenty-eighth year, he stood as the technical chief of what was then the greatest telephone system in any city in the world.

Had Carty's contributions to the communications art extended no further than the inventions and developments just noted, he would have lived and been remembered today as one of the greatest of telephone engineers, but his genius was as

162

remarkable for its power to visualize the needs and possibilities of the future as to solve particular problems once they had arisen in concrete form. He not only foresaw that the business was destined to be an extremely technical one but had the courage to act upon this vision and build up a scientific department years in advance of the time when it became the practice of the industry to employ trained scientists and investigators. More than this, he conceived one of the functions of his engineering department to be that of a training school for the men who would later become officials of the Company. Carty was, therefore, one of the early initiators of industrial research and one of its most ardent advocates. During his long career as Chief Engineer of the American Telephone and Telegraph Company and later as Vice President, he brought into being what is thus far the world's largest industrial research organization, an organization which through his wise leadership rapidly placed the United States as the foremost nation in matters telephonic.

In reviewing the outstanding activities of Carty's life, one is tempted to say that they all sprang from a single guiding principle or motif, namely, a passionate belief in the value of the communion of mind with mind and the smooth collectivity of action which would in time arise therefrom. Such a motif accounts, of course, for the fact that he dedicated himself without reserve to the telephone and its future. It accounts equally for the type of research organization which he built up to insure the materialization of the future of which he dreamed. Even from the days of his earliest association with it, he seems to have entertained a firm conviction that the telephone was destined to make possible a nation-wide transmission of speech. To his maturer mind, such a far-flung network of telephone lines became more than an arrangement for exchanging conversations. He thought of it as a national nervous system, binding the people and the geographical units of the country

163

together and serving indispensably that collectivity of action which is the ultimate goal of super-organic evolution.

In the importance which Carty attached to human coöperation, he was a true disciple of Herbert Spencer. He knew that in human society, the whole is much greater than the sum of its parts; that individuals by themselves could never reach the same high level of output, either intellectually or materially, that could characterize the group under harmonious coöperation. It was from this standpoint that he appraised the research organization he had brought into existence. To him it was more than a group of individuals—it was a sort of collective mind which, made up of experts in many fields who collaborated continually with one another, could arrive quickly at the solutions of problems so intricate in their ramifications as to require years of single-handed effort, if indeed they could be solved at all single-handed. Such research organizations Carty constantly advocated in his public addresses as one of the most important contributions of our age to the progress of mankind. He in turn seemed to obtain a double satisfaction from the fact that the laboratory—the collective research mind —whose work he directed was developing a nervous system for the nation as a whole, so that it in turn might function more smoothly as a well-integrated organism and reach that higher goal which represents perfectly coördinated coöperative effort.

This is the theme which Carty promised himself he would elaborate after retirement from active service. Unfortunately, an untimely death prevented. As matters stand, it finds scant place in any of his writings, for these were usually directed to an immediate end, and the pressure of his life was such that he economized words on every occasion. A few brief paragraphs taken from his address, "Science and the Social Organism," delivered in celebration of the twenty-fifth anniversary of the Cold Spring Harbor Laboratory of the Carnegie Institution, are, however, worth noting here.

" The awful spectacle of the increasing numbers of the mentally sick, the prevalence of nervous diseases, and the generally disturbed condition of the nations, have caused many to believe that we are headed in the wrong direction, and that our ideals should be those of the so-called simple life, or that we should seek to attain to the static condition of ancient China. Were it not for my faith in the ultimate success of such researches as you are conducting in this institution, I believe that I, too, would share these views and be inclined to the opinion that in merely material progress we had gone far enough—perhaps too far, or too fast.

" While I have frequently asserted that human behavior presents the most important and the most formidable problem of all the ages, I believe that its solution can be achieved. . . .

" To me, this celebration today is an event of the deepest significance, for it indicates the beginning of a new era of social development. As Trotter * so well puts it:

" ' The method of leaving the development of society to the confused welter of forces which prevail within it is now at last reduced to absurdity by the unmistakable teaching of events. The conscious direction of man's destiny is plainly indicated by Nature as the only mechanism by which the social life of so complex an animal can be guaranteed against disaster and brought to yield its full possibilities.

" ' A gregarious unit informed by conscious direction represents a biological mechanism of a wholly new type, a stage of advance in the evolutionary process capable of consolidating the supremacy of man and carrying to its full extent the development of his social instincts.'

" Human progress need no longer be left solely to chance. By the aid of science, it can be brought under our conscious control.

" In concluding, let me say that if we rightly interpret the work of these scientists which we are briefly to examine today, we shall find that it is directed ultimately to the overcoming of the defects both of body and mind which are found in the individual man, and which now prevent him from properly performing his function as a member of society. We shall also, I think, be made to feel that in the great plan of creation, the highest part has been assigned to man; for he must direct the development of that

* W. Trotter—Instincts of the Herd in Peace and War.

social organism which has been foreshadowed ' with its million-minded knowledge and power, to which no barrier will be insurmountable, no gulf impassable and no task too great.' "

For some years after Carty assumed administrative work, he still found time to indulge his strong natural bent for original investigation. It was in this period that he carried on his fundamental researches regarding the nature of the electrical induction between parallel circuits which, in telephone parlance, gives rise to "crosstalk," i.e., to the transfer of part of the speech energy from one circuit to another parallel to it. It had been commonly supposed that the induction was largely electromagnetic. Carty was able to prove that it was, on the contrary, largely electrostatic. In 1889 he published an account of this work, pointing out that " there is in the telephone line a particular point at which, if a telephone instrument be inserted, no crosstalk will be overheard." He gives directions for determining the location of this neutral point, and goes on to develop the ideas of electrical balance and the transposing of circuits—two operations which are of fundamental importance in the art today. From this period there also came his contribution of the bridging bell, a circuit which he was forced to evolve to meet an embarrassing contract into which his Company had entered with the New York Central Railroad to supply them with a multiparty private line, but which rapidly found widespread use in a multitude of rural lines all over the country.

It is an interesting side-light on Carty's fecundity of mind that during this strenuous period, when he was guiding the engineering and research activities of an adolescent telephone industry and organizing and building up the nucleus of what was later to become the Bell Telephone Laboratories, and was indeed personally leading the attack on many problems, he found time to write regularly for *Electrical Review*. These contributions were known as "The Prophet's Column" and appear to have supplied him a sort of mental relaxation—he seldom, if ever, resorted to physical exercise as a means of relaxation. His discussions were usually in the lighter vein and offered the opportunity of mixing mild doses of scientific information with a leavening of humor, for, true to his Irish ancestry, he had an inexhaustible store of the latter continually bubbling up for release. A single quotation will serve by way of illustration.

> " The man who could have bought Bell Telephone stock at $10 a share and didn't is now becoming extinct. His favorite haunt was the smoking compartment of a Pullman car, where he was wont to repeat the oft-told tale of the grocer who did and got it in payment of a bad debt at that. In his place we have another specimen quite as easy to recognize. After some of the strange tales of electrical science have been discussed, he is sure to gravely remark, as though it had never been uttered before, ' Well, electricity is in its infancy,' and quickly add the inevitable corollary, ' but it's the coming power, though.'
>
> " Just watch this man. You will be surprised to see how many there are of him. He is the Public. You must study his moods and lead him aright. The marvelous products of electrical science have so charmed his mind that no story of its newly discovered powers can be so much at variance with the laws of nature as not to be received by him with ready belief."

In 1893, Carty was elected an Honorary Fellow of the American Electrotherapeutic Association, in recognition of his success in the self-imposed task of rationalizing the electrical terminology of the medical profession of that day. He inveighed strongly against such puzzling and nonsensical terms as Faradism, Franklinism and Galvanism and a host of others, submitting to medical men an earnest plea for the revision of their electrical nomenclature in accordance with the language of Physics. Thus we see again clear evidence of Carty's insistence on clarity of thought.

As the prime requirement of a leader is accuracy of thought and clearness of vision, it is worth quoting at some length from Carty's paper of 1906 entitled " Telephone Engineering," delivered before the American Institute of Electrical Engineers. It is a lucid exposition of the responsibilities of the telephone engineer or, with proper changes in terminology, of the engineer in general.   In closing this paper, he said:

" From beginning to end, the engineer is thus placed in a position to exercise a veto power upon any adverse methods which might otherwise be allowed to creep in. . . .

" The importance of this coördinating function cannot be overestimated and it is only at some central point that such function can be exercised.   Being judged from the maintenance point of view, a piece of apparatus might have qualities of a high order; but when considered with reference to its effect upon the traffic, difficulties might be discovered which would entirely overweigh the maintenance advantages.   In such a case the conflicting claims with respect to the apparatus must be judiciously considered by the engineer, and his decision must be rendered with a view to producing the best net result.

" Again, systems might be proposed which, considered solely from the maintenance, construction and traffic points of view, might seem to possess all of the advantages of an ideal arrangement; but when considered from the standpoint of the efficiency of transmission might be found to involve an impairment of transmission on one hand or such increase in cable and line costs on the other hand as to render its use out of the question.

" In order to exercise proper coördinating functions, it is essential that the engineer should be placed and should maintain himself in such relations with all of the departments of the telephone organization that he may get from them and fairly consider all of the projects and ideas pertaining to the design, operation, construction and maintenance of the plant which naturally originate in such departments when they are conducted with proper efficiency.

" Viewed from this standpoint, it will be seen that while the function of the engineer with relation to the plant is of the utmost importance, nevertheless the work of the traffic, maintenance, construction and other departments has such an important bearing upon the whole question, that the successful engineering of a telephone system must be regarded not only as the work of the engineer himself but as the work of all the other departments concerned. Not only this, but what is still more important, the successful engineering of a telephone plant depends upon proper business management, as I have indicated by several striking examples. Without an intelligent, progressive and broad-gauged business management, there cannot be good telephone engineering."

In 1908, Carty, who had become Chief Engineer of the American Telephone and Telegraph Company in 1907, visited the Pacific coast to assist the local telephone officials in formulating plans for rebuilding and enlarging the telephone plant. He was accompanied by some of his assistants and was joined later by T. N. Vail, then President of the American Telephone and Telegraph Company. San Francisco was in the initial stages of cleaning up the debris of earthquake and fire preparatory to building a new city and of christening it with a great international exposition!

The hardihood and daring of the program appealed to both Vail and Carty, as did the urgent demand of the citizens that the Pacific and Atlantic coasts be linked telephonically by the time the job was done. To Carty, accustomed as he was to daily talks with associates even though hundreds of miles away, the sense of remoteness caused by this western trip was oppressive. As he observed, with a twinkle in his eye, to a native son of Califronia, he " was greatly impressed with the isolation of the rest of the country."

However, to promise meant to fulfill, and how was more than three thousand miles of distance to be spanned telephonically when the existing art had conquered even poorly but half that distance? Night after night, for weeks on end, after hard days on current problems, Carty and two or three of his associates spent evenings in their hotel among the ruins analysing the possibilities of an unconquered future. Finally the chances of success were established to Carty's satisfaction and the promise was given—to be sealed irrevocably next morning by glaring newspaper headlines.

Carty returned to New York to put the necessary machinery in motion for this gamble with Fate. Six years later saw the opening of the first transcontinental wire line, and a few months afterward, using very nearly the same instrumentalities, he was able to announce the first successful transmission of the voice by radio telephone across the Atlantic and also across the American continent and as far out into the Pacific as Honolulu. During these six years, Carty was at the apex of his powers. He drove himself and his associates with a force that was untiring and unsparing. Sleep and relaxation in small doses were grudgingly accorded. For the rest, it was unceasing labor, with the success of the organization, which was his life, and the good of the nation he loved, as the goal.

Both the opening of the transcontinental telephone line and the first transmission of speech by radio to Paris occurred in 1915, after the outbreak of the World War. The military importance of the enormous extension of the scope of telephony which these two events signalized led General McComb, President of the Army War College, to invite Carty to deliver a confidential lecture before that body on " The Organization, Plant and Personnel of the Bell System." This lecture was repeated a few weeks later before the Naval War College. From these two appearances there followed a series of events leading up to the subsequent extensive utilization of the facilities of the Bell System by the Army and Navy. There was springing up in high places a very definite realization of the military importance of the latest telephone developments, and a belief that the research facilities of the Bell Telephone organization could probably contribute still other new devices of value in the national defense, in case the United States were forced into the hostilities. The Honorable Josephus Daniels, Secretary of the Navy, wrote to T. N. Vail, President of the American Telephone and Telegraph Company, "appealing to the patriotic sense of this Company" and inquiring whether it was in a position to give the Navy Department " a demonstration of what could be accomplished in the way of communication, particularly in long distance telephony and telegraphy, which would bring the offices of the Department and the Navy Yards and Stations within the limits of the United States proper into that close touch which the exigencies of war might demand."

"In order that this mobilization of forces of communication may be complete, and recalling the close coöperation of officials of the Department in the past with the officials of your Company in the development of the wireless telephone, it is confidently hoped that its use as a means of communication with a ship at sea could also be demonstrated at the same time under such conditions as might be mutually agreed upon." The Secretary added, "Congress provides no funds whereby the expense of such a demonstration could be borne by the Government and thereby recognizes that whatever is done by your Company will have to be free of all expense to the Department."

The coöperation of Carty and his research staff to this request and similar ones from the Signal Corps of the Army was immediately forthcoming, and among other contributions there should be mentioned particularly a sturdy radio telephone outfit that was extensively used on aircraft and on destroyers and submarine chasers. The American Army, of all those in the field, alone was able to avail itself of the aid of radio telephony.

But Carty, ever mindful of the personnel side of every situation, realized that physical things alone would not suffice. To be effective they must be in the hands of a properly qualified operating organization. Thus, while on the one hand he brought to the administration at Washington a realization of what the telephone art and the telephone organization could offer, he also arranged a complete plan of action with the executives of the Bell organization. Addressing a conference of Presidents of the companies comprising the Bell System, he said:

" Our plans contemplate two classes of Signal Corps officers to be recruited from the Bell System. One of these is to consist of engineers and executives who will remain in their offices,—representing the War Department and taking their orders direct from Washington. Their duty will be to direct the highest possible military utilization of the Bell System plant and personnel, without at the same time crippling the service as a whole.

" The other group will consist also of executives and engineers, who will select and organize the trained personnel of the Bell System into companies and battalions, for such field service as occasion may require. I cannot, of course, take final steps in this vital programme without your support. I now ask that support. We must act as a unit."

Again Carty's foresight and his forceful call to action were vindicated. When war was declared with Germany, the entire Signal Corps personnel, including men in the field as well as a small group at headquarters, consisted of 55 officers and 1,570 men. Within a few months, this nuclear organization was swelled by 4,525 persons taken out of the Bell System alone.

Then the question arose as to how to equip the Army shortly to depart for France. The military type of telephone and telegraph apparatus theretofore employed was simple in design, sturdy in construction, and not easily put out of order, but its capabilities were extremely limited in comparison with the latest results which the commercial system in the United States was obtaining. The new apparatus was complicated and delicate, and the unfavorable conditions of warfare would tax it in a manner never experienced before. Should Carty, to whom the Army had turned for guidance, recommend that our Army be provided with such a modern communication system capable of furnishing a service virtually unlimited both as to message carrying capacity and as to distance, or should he recommend the traditional Army equipment? It was a vital decision. He had confidence that the men he would send to France could make a success of the system employing the newly developed telephonic repeaters and utilizing the latest type of multiplex printing telegraph apparatus. Weighing the factors involved, he concluded that the advantages of modern equipment were too great to be disregarded, and with what success the following quotations will indicate. Speaking after the war was over, before the Committee on Military Affairs of the House of Representatives, he said:

> " There had been preparations made for war in the European terrain for forty years. When the war broke it was not possible for any of the European nations to provide a communication system adequate for the conduct of the war. It remained for the Signal Corps of the U. S. Army in nine months to construct a long distance telegraph and telephone system which the Governments of Europe had failed to do in forty years."

For the first time, it became possible to talk from Paris to Rome, and from Marseilles in the south to Le Havre, and even across the Channel to London and Liverpool. And, following the Armistice, Colonel (later General) Saltzman, Acting Chief Signal Officer of the Army, wrote Carty, saying:

> " In the operations in France, our Army has enjoyed a wonderful system of communication of an efficiency and capacity never before contemplated in the history of warfare. In considering the initial conception and the successful operation of this system, the Signal Corps will ever remember your splendid foresight and the technical efficiency of the thousands of trained men that you brought into the service. It would be very difficult to place a value on the service which you have rendered to our country in this connection alone."

In recognition of his service during the war, Carty was on October 23, 1921, created a Brigadier General in the Officers' Reserve Corps.

Following the cessation of hostilities, Carty again returned to the commercial and social aspects of the telephone. Always in the background of his thoughts was the idea of adapting the telephone more and more fully and intimately to the needs of the country, so that to the greatest extent possible it could play its part in facilitating harmony of action. A memorable instance of this occurred at the burial of the Unknown Soldier in Arlington Cemetery, November 11, 1921. Realizing the dramatic possibilities inherent in the ceremony, he offered to the administration in Washington the nation-wide use of the public address system which had but recently emanated from the telephone laboratories. His offer was accepted and circuits, amplifiers, and loud speakers were so arranged that thousands of people in New York and San Francisco as well as in Washington heard and participated in the entire service— the invocation of the chaplain, the words of the commitment— and finally, at the close, joined with the President in reciting the Lord's Prayer.

So rapidly have events moved in the field of electrical communication that it is difficult now to realize that at that time, scarcely fifteen years ago, radio broadcasting was an unknown development. At the burial ceremony, the entire transmission was by wire telephone lines, and the multitudes who heard were of necessity gathered within earshot of powerful loud speakers—in Madison Square and Madison Square Garden in New York and in the great Civic Plaza in San Francisco. In a very real sense, as we look back upon this outstanding occasion, it may be said that Carty was the father of broadcasting. Today, the local distribution of programs takes place by radio while, as in that occurrence, the broadcasting stations themselves are tied together by long distance telephone circuits. Radio stations, together with receiving sets in the hands of the public, have displaced Carty's powerful loud speakers but not the nation-wide network of long distance wire lines. On a somewhat similar occasion in February, 1924, after radio broadcasting had appeared, Carty connected seven large broadcasting stations by a telephone circuit extending from San Francisco to Havana, a distance of more than five thousand miles. This constituted a forerunner of chain broadcasting as we know it today, and newspapers at the time estimated that no less than fifty million radio listeners heard the program, which comprised portions originating at several points along the route. Carty himself remarked:

> "We are only just beginning to appreciate how fundamental are electrical communications in the organization of society. We are as yet unable to appreciate how vital they are to the ultimate welfare of mankind. I believe that some day we will build up a great world telephone system, . . . which will join all the people of the earth into one brotherhood."

This was the goal for which he worked unremittingly and the later years of his life enabled him in large measure to provide the material accessories necessary to the realization of his vision.

Just fifty years after the invention of the telephone, the first two-way conversation was heard across the Atlantic Ocean, and the year following, regular commercial service with England was begun. Beginning with this single overseas circuit, progress became so rapid that now it is possible for any telephone anywhere in the United States to be connected with about ninety-three per cent of all the telephones in the world

For some years, of course, Carty had made no technical contributions to this epic of progress, but his was the vision and the generalship which, on the one hand, created an engineering and scientific organization capable of solving the countless problems involved, and on the other convinced those who held the purse-strings that the financial risk they were taking was one which some day they would be very grateful for having taken.

In the case of one who was as firm a believer in the value of scientific research, both fundamental and applied, and who was so successful in inspiring it as Carty was, it is not surprising that his counsel was frequently sought by others and that he undertook a considerable amount of proselytizing. Most of the addresses which he gave during the later years of his life were devoted to pointing out the benefits which the world had reaped by the industrial application of science and to evaluating these benefits both in terms of human comfort and conveniences and in terms of money. These addresses contain characteristic phrases and similes. Carty always took delight in coining a new one, but the old ones were seldom discarded. Thus, "Science and the Industries," which was given before the National Research Council, February 6, 1920, contains an allusion to the North American Indian. Referring to the rapid strides which science had been making in recent decades, he pictured "future generations looking back upon us with our present limited knowledge of the forces of Nature as we now regard the North American Indian who, cold and shivering in his scanty clothing, was ignorant of the coal at his feet with its stores of warmth and power." To this Indian Carty frequently and jocularly referred as his "star performer."

In many other ways, Carty fostered the interests of science, both at home and throughout the world. In 1923, he was elected to the Board of Trustees of the Carnegie Corporation. He was a Trustee of the Carnegie Institution of Washington; an Associate of the Council of New York University; a Fellow of the American Academy of Arts and Sciences; and a member of the National Academy of Sciences and of the National Research Council.

Carty's intense devotion to the National Academy of Sciences and the National Research Council was typical both of his broad interests and of his penetrating understanding of the power existing in institutions founded solidly on a broad base properly related to its surroundings. That he enjoyed the intellectual and personal contacts which these associations afforded was self-evident. They were, however, secondary to his interest in the continuing constructive influence which the Academy and Council could exert on the proper development of the nation. He gloried in the simple national charter of the Academy because he saw in it an instrument of great power. He was disdainful of all that savored of making the Academy merely a home for established scientific reputations—it could hardly escape being that,—but in his eyes it must be a tool by which science could aid the nation to a better way of living.

With the passing of Dr. John J. Carty on December 27, 1932, the telephone industry lost its foremost artificer and seer, the engineering fraternity one of its keenest minded members, and the American nation a most devoted patriot and champion. The far-flung and highly developed telephone service of the United States today is in large measure the outward embodiment of the imagination and creative power of Carty's mind.

The following honorary degrees had been conferred upon him:

DOCTOR OF ENGINEERING: *New York University*
Stevens Institute of Technology
DOCTOR OF LAWS: *McGill University*
University of Pennsylvania
DOCTOR OF SCIENCES: *Bowdoin College*
Princeton University
Tufts College
University of Chicago
Yale University.

For the active part which he took in assisting the U. S. Signal Corps during the war, he was awarded the Distinguished Service Medal. He also received the Edison Medal of the American Institute of Electrical Engineers; the Franklin Medal of the Franklin Institute; the John Fritz Medal; and the Edward Longstreth Medal.

FRANK B. JEWETT

(Editor's Note: The appendix to this memoir, listing General Carty's published writings and addresses, is omitted here for lack of space.)

177

"Each in His Dearest Tongue"

MORE than twenty years ago Dr. John H. Finley wrote a poem that was prophetic. A meeting of the American Institute of Electrical Engineers had been conducted by telephone, as if the participants were in the same room, though some of them were separated by thousands of miles. At this meeting the late John J. Carty presided. Stirred by this dramatic event, Dr. Finley composed "Carty's Hall," now recognized as one of the classics of telephone literature.

"Carty's Hall," the writer declared, was the United States. Its walls have since been pushed outward until it is world-wide in its extent, as Dr. Finley predicted in these striking lines:

> 'Tis prophesied that all the quick and dead,
> From Boston to Bombay and back again,
> Shall at one moment hear the selfsame sound,
> The stirring sound of Gabriel's final trump;
> But long before that day shall come, perchance,
> A Carty, or his scientific heir,
> Will make the universe his "Carty's Hall"
> Wherein each earth-encircling day shall be
> A pentecost of speech, and men shall hear,
> Each in his dearest tongue, his neighbor's voice
> Tho' separate by half the globe.

"*Each in his dearest tongue*"—striking words, these, to describe the inclusiveness of telephone service. Not less remarkable than the extent of the reach of this man-serving instrumentality, measured in miles, is the marvel of its adaptability to the transmission of the spoken word, regardless of what language the telephone user may chance to speak.

This adaptability of the telephone to the needs of the world's polyglot population has been so long a demonstrated fact that it is now recognized as a commonplace. But there was a time

178

when the telephone had transmitted only a single language, and when its inventor was asked, in all seriousness, whether it could "talk anything but English."

The visit of Dr. E. H. Colpitts, who recently retired as Vice President of the Bell Telephone Laboratories, to Japan, early in the present year, where he delivered what are known as the Iwadare Lectures and was signally honored by the Japanese government, makes it appropriate to recall at this time that Japanese was the first language, other than English, to be transmitted by telephone.

A Sixtieth Anniversary

This incident took place sixty years ago. It has been briefly described in the writings and public addresses of Alexander Graham Bell, inventor of the telephone, and of his assistant, Thomas A. Watson. These sources of information have been supplemented, for the purpose of preparing the present article, by valuable data collected in 1929 by William Chauncy Langdon, then Historical Librarian of the American Telephone and Telegraph Company. The latter information has never before been made public.

During the months immediately following the invention of the telephone, Professor Bell was conducting classes for instructors of the deaf, and for the improvement of speech, in connection with Boston University. In one of his classes was a young Japanese named Shuji Isawa, who was a student at Harvard and who had come to Bell, the inventor later declared, for the purpose of studying Visible Speech as a means of enabling him to perfect his pronunciation of English. Visible Speech was, it will be remembered, a system of symbols, invented by Bell's father, Alexander Melville Bell, by which the proper positions of the lips, tongue, teeth and other vocal organs used in the production of speech sounds might be represented in graphic form.

Bell and his young pupil became friendly and when the

179

Japanese learned about the telephone he was intensely interested.

"Mr. Bell, will this thing talk Japanese?" he asked, when Bell exhibited his invention to him.

"Certainly," replied the inventor, "it will transmit any language."

PUT TO A TEST

The young Oriental expressed a desire to put the instrument to a test, and Bell had him go to one end of the circuit while he stood at the other. His visitor talked Japanese, and Bell reported the result to him, no doubt admitting, as he did in later years, in describing the incident, that the telephone talked Japanese but that he "couldn't quite understand it."

The visitor was apparently impressed, but not entirely convinced. He asked Bell for permission to bring to the latter's rooms, at 5 Exeter Place, some of his countrymen who were also students at Harvard. This permission was graciously granted and later this first two-way conversation in a foreign tongue took place. On January 21, 1877, Bell wrote a letter to his parents, in Canada, in the course of which he said: "Last night two Japanese gentlemen conversed in Japanese, through the telephone, with success." There is a fair presumption that this was the first occasion on which such a conversation was held and that the first telephone conversation in a language other than English took place on January 20, 1877.

In the account of Bell's first telephone demonstration, in which he transmitted speech from Salem to Boston, on February 12, 1877, as published in the *Boston Globe* of the next day, the reporter states "Mr. Shaje Zsawa was recognized, Mr. Watson being perfectly familiar with his tones." It would appear that, although the spelling is erroneous, the person here referred to was Isawa.

In addition to Isawa, three Japanese students appear to have participated in these early telephone experiments: Jutaro

Komura, Shinichiro Kurino, and Kentaro Kaneko. All three of these became prominent in the field of statesmanship in Japan, and Isawa himself held a position of leadership in the development of modern education in his native country, as will appear from brief biographical notes to be included later in the present article.

Isawa and Komura have been dead for some years. Kurino is still living, according to the most recent issue of "Who's Who in Japan," but efforts to get in touch with him for the purpose of obtaining his personal recollections of his part in these experiments have thus far been unavailing.

COUNT KANEKO'S NARRATIVE

Such an account has, however, been provided for the archives of the American Telephone Historical Library by Count Kaneko, who responded to a request by Mr. Langdon with a description of his part in these experiments, painstakingly set down in his own handwriting and in English which, considering his long absence from America, is remarkable alike for its preciseness and for the clarity of the picture which it presents.

After recounting his introduction to Bell by his friend Isawa and describing Bell's bedroom "in one of those boarding houses behind the State House," Count Kaneko gives this graphic narrative of the event:

> " After explaining the discovery and invention of the telephone, he took us into the next room—the same size as his bed room. This room was used for his experimental purpose, where was a pile of coiled wires on one side, and on the opposite side, the same kind of wires was piled up, and two piles were connected by one line of wire. Pointing to these piles, he told that they are the same length as the submarine cable between New York and Liverpool."

INTERCOMMUNICATION PREDICTED

It may be of interest to note that, in an interview published in the *New York Sun* of February 23, 1877, Thomas A. Wat-

181

son, Professor Bell's assistant, is quoted as declaring: "We have, in fact, talked through a wire arranged to give an artificial resistance equal to 40,000 ohms, which is more resistance than the Atlantic cable would offer." In the then state of knowledge of the flow of electric currents, it probably was not generally known that, although it was possible to talk through such an artificial resistance, it would not have been possible to talk through an Atlantic cable, because of its capacitance and other electrical characteristics.

It was doubtless to such an experiment that Bell referred in his conversation with the young Japanese student. This supposition gives point to the inventor's words as further reported by Count Kaneko:

> " Giving me a receiver in one corner, he went to the other, and spoke with speaking tube [evidently the transmitter] in a very low voice, but I heard every word distinctly. Turning to me, he said: ' There we speak across the Atlantic.' Then he explained his project for organizing a telephone company in following plan—the following words are as nearly as he said at that time:
>
> " ' In the center of Boston, we establish a main office, from which a separate wire is connected with the State House, the City Hall, hotels, banks, stores, factories, schools, newspaper offices, private residences and others. Then to show the usefulness: a person, waking up in the morning, calls up the main office and asks to connect with grocery store; when connected, he tells to bring a bread, butter, fresh milk for breakfast at 7 o'clock; then again he calls up the main office to connect with the stable, and he tells to send a carriage to his house at 8; and after then in the same way, he calls up his office boy and tells him to send a telephone to Mr. A. to come to his office at 8.30 and Mr. B. at 9 and Mr. C. at 9.30, to dispatch business. Is it not convenient? ' "

This description which Bell gave of his vision of the future of the telephone service, as recounted by Count Kaneko, is of historic interest for the reason that it clearly shows that the inventor then had in mind a service of intercommunication, such as was later predicted in his better known prospectus issued in

London, and which first became a reality with the opening of the first commercial telephone central office in the world, at New Haven, Conn., within a few days of a full year after his talk with the young Japanese student.

COMMERCIAL DEVELOPMENT

Practically-minded, even as a youth, Count Kaneko at once brought up the question of the commercial development of the telephone. His account continues:

> " Thereupon I asked Mr. Bell whether he consulted to organize a company with business men and capitalists. He said: ' Yes! but they will not take up my project; therefore I am going to appeal to the public by a lecture, showing the wires, machines and the working process, and explain the usefulness.' "

The first of these public lectures, to which reference has already been made, was held at the Essex Institute, Salem, Mass., on February 12, 1877. Of a subsequent lecture and demonstration, Count Kaneko writes:

> " A few weeks after, he gave a public lecture on the telephone in the Tremont Temple, Boston. I went and found a tolerably good audience. After the lecture, as we were going away, I overhead a group of men and women, in my front, saying: ' Bell's invention is very ingenious and interesting, but to form a company and invest the money is another question.' "

It would appear to have been the practice of these early students from Japan to call the attention of their government in Tokio, or its representatives in Washington, to anything with which they came in contact while in the United States that they believed might be of service in the development of their native country. There is circumstantial evidence, though no direct reference to the matter in Count Kaneko's account or in other data in the possession of the American Telephone Historical Library, that it was these young students who first described the telephone to the Japanese authorities. Such an assumption seems well founded, for Isawa, Kaneko, Kurino and Komura were unquestionably young men of unusual alertness and were filled with a desire to be of service to their country, as their later careers clearly demonstrate. It seems entirely natural to suppose, therefore, that they did not delay in advising their government of this remarkable invention which, by a curious coincidence, it had been their privilege to view at first hand, before its general introduction to the public.

THE TELEPHONE REACHES JAPAN

Be that as it may, the evidence is clear that the news of the invention was not long in reaching Japan, and that actual telephone apparatus, for experimental purposes, soon followed. Among the interesting and significant data unearthed in the course of research in connection with this first foreign-language telephone conversation is a letter, in the files of the Department of State at Washington, of which the following is a copy:

" No. 724

United States Legation
Japan
Tokio, February 1, 1878

" Hon. William M. Evarts,
  Secretary of State
        Washington, D. C.
" Sir:

It is a pleasure to note that this Government has already put the telephone into practical use, thereby giving another assurance of its purpose to employ as soon as possible for the advancement of this people all the agencies of our Western civilization.

" His Excellency Mr. Iwakura, the Junior Prime Minister, some days since informed me of the experiments recently made in this capital with the telephone, and said that the experiments were entirely satisfactory.

" I have the honor to be,
      Sir,
      Your obedient servant
      WM. A. BINGHAM "

184

Count Kaneko was graduated from the Harvard Law School in 1878 and thereafter returned to Japan. Of his subsequent part in the introduction of Bell's invention into the Japanese Empire, he writes:

" When the telephone was brought to Japan for adoption, our Government took it up as the government work, for the similar works, such as the mail and telegraphy are already managed by the Government. When asked, I told the Government what I saw in Boston and of all I knew of Mr. Bell's plan."

The first practical use of the telephone in Japan appears to have been by the Police Department of Osaka, where circuits as long as thirty miles were constructed. As many as ten instruments were connected with a single iron wire circuit. In 1883 a private company was formed to develop the telephone commercially, but little progress was made until 1889, when the government decided, as Count Kaneko states, to take over the telephone business as a government monopoly.

The Students' Subsequent Careers

The subsequent careers of the students who played parts in this first foreign-language telephone conversation are of interest, as indicating the type of young men they must have been while in America. This biographical material has been supplied through the courtesy of the Consulate General of Japan in New York.

Marquis Jutaro Komura, upon returning to Japan after his studies at Harvard, entered the diplomatic service and held various posts in Korea and in China, his fame as a diplomat having been established by the judgment shown by him as minister to China during the Boxer incident in Peking. He became Minister of Foreign Affairs in 1901, at which time he was created baronet. He was Japan's chief delegate to the Russo-Japanese Peace Conference. He was promoted to a viscountship, became Privy Councilor and Ambassador to London. He held the post of Minister of Foreign Affairs between

185

1907 and 1911. He was raised to the rank of marquis in recognition of his successful diplomatic efforts and of the peaceful arrangement for the future of Korea.

The career of Viscount Kurino was similarly distinguished. He also played an important part in the settlement of Korean affairs, became Minister to the United States in 1894 and later held the same office in Italy and in France. Not the least interesting item in his biography, as published in "Who's Who in Japan," is the brief note, "well known as the father of the telephone administration in Japan."—an interest which, it may well be, dated back to his early associations with the inventor of the telephone in his student days at Harvard. It appears that soon after his return to Japan from Harvard he became private secretary to the Japanese Minister of Communications and for a time served as Principal of the Tokio Postal-Telegraph School and as head of the Research Bureau of the Foreign Office. He was created baron at the close of the Japanese War and was made Ambassador to France in 1906.

MEET AFTER MANY YEARS

In "Prehistoric Telephone Days" by Alexander Graham Bell, published in the National Geographic Magazine for March, 1922, the inventor, after describing his associations with the young Japanese students in Harvard, wrote:

"A great many years afterward, I was in Yokohama when the American residents there were entertaining a new Japanese minister who was about to start for Washington. I attended the banquet and was about to be presented to the minister, when he came forward and said there was no necessity for introducing him to Mr. Bell, as he knew me years and years ago, when he was a student in Harvard College. He turned out to be one of Mr. Isawa's friends who had been present when Japanese was first used over the telephone. This was the celebrated Baron Kurino."

Count Kaneko, whose career led him also into the diplomatic service and into other fields of political endeavor in Japan,

186

recounts another incident of what appears to have been the same visit of Bell to Japan. He says:

> "While Col. Buck was the U. S. Minister in Japan, Mr. and Mrs. Bell came to Tokio. The American Minister and Mrs. Buck invited the Cabinet Ministers and many important persons to a large dinner party to introduce the world's renowned inventor. I was the Minister of Justice and was invited, but I had not seen Mr. Bell for 23 years. In the reception room, the American Minister and Mrs. Buck were standing with Mr. and Mrs. Bell. As I crossed a threshold of the anteroom, Mr. Bell suddenly rushed to me and grabbed my hand, saying ' This friend I came to Japan to see! ' And he took me by the arm and went back to his former position and introduced me to the American minister and Mrs. Buck, who were both at loss for the moment."

Count Kaneko was the chief advisor to Marquis Komura at the time of the Russo-Japanese Peace Conference at Portsmouth, and at that time and subsequently he played an important part in promoting cordiality between Japan and the United States. He later served as Privy Councilor. He writes that when he went to Washington during the Russo-Japanese War Dr. Bell "gave a large dinner at his house to introduce me to many influential persons—official, political and social—and in an after-dinner speech he told of our first acquaintance in Boston and second and recent meeting in Tokio, and in conclusion he remarked of the Japanese language being the first foreign language spoken through the telephone; therefore Japanese and Bell's telephone will be always associated together and remembered with a happy historical recollection."

ISAWA'S EDUCATIONAL CAREER

Distinguished though the careers of Komura, Kurino and Kaneko were in the realm of statesmanship, it is not difficult to imagine that for Alexander Graham Bell, who throughout his life never lost his keen interest in work for the deaf, there was perhaps as great satisfaction in the accomplishments of the first of his Japanese friends, Shuji Isawa. He had worked in the Japanese Department of Education before coming to America to study, and upon his return to Japan was, in succession, President of the Tokio Musical College, the principal of the School for the Deaf and Dumb, Councilor of the Department of Education, Director of the Bureau of Education of Taiwan (Formosa), President of the Tokio Higher Normal School and Vice President of the Council for Higher Education.

During Bell's visit to Japan, to which reference has already been made, he was a guest at the Tokio School for the Deaf and Dumb and was photographed with Mr. Isawa, Mr. Konishi, the principal of the school, and a number of its pupils. Particularly significant, in view of the fact that Bell and his father and grandfather before him had been engaged in the teaching of proper articulation and the remedying of defects of speech, is it that in 1903 Dr. Isawa established Rakuseki Gakuin, which is an institution for stammerers.

Prophecy Fulfilled

Fittingly enough, Japan is one of the countries reached by the Bell System's radio telephone facilities, the service having been officially opened on December 7, 1934. It is now possible for every Bell System telephone to be connected with about 35,000,000 other telephones, or about 93 per cent of all the telephones in the world. Of these, about 16,000,000 telephones are in foreign lands. There are about 1,200,000 telephones in Japan, of which about 600,000 may be reached through the Bell System's overseas service.

Over a world-wide network of wire and radio circuits the races of mankind are brought into direct and personal contact through the spoken word—a veritable fulfillment of the prophecy of a "Pentecost of Speech" toward which four young Japanese students led the way when, sixty years ago, they found themselves, to their astonishment, conversing over a wire, "each in his dearest tongue."

R. T. Barrett

World's Telephone Statistics

January 1, 1936

THE latest of the annual statistical surveys of wire communication systems undertaken by the Chief Statistician of the American Telephone and Telegraph Company has just been published in the form of a pamphlet entitled " Telephone and Telegraph Statistics of the World, January 1, 1936." This compilation reveals that the total number of telephones in service throughout the world was at that date within one per cent

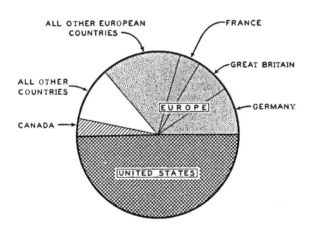

DISTRIBUTION OF THE WORLD'S TELEPHONES
January 1, 1936

of the peak reached in the beginning of 1931: 35,028,682 on January 1, 1936 as compared with 35,336,467 five years earlier. In view of recent rates of growth as indicated by incomplete data, the total number of telephones in the world at the present time is estimated to be at least two million greater than at the beginning of 1936. In the following paragraphs some of the outstanding facts shown by the tables and charts contained in the pamphlet are summarized, all figures referring to the beginning of 1936 or, in the case of traffic data, to the year 1935.

COMPARATIVE TELEPHONE DEVELOPMENT BY COUNTRIES

With only six per cent of the world's population of slightly more than two billion people, the United States had one-half of

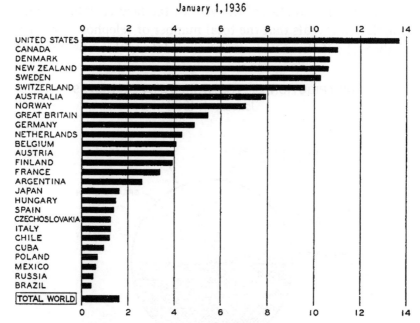

TELEPHONES PER 100 POPULATION
January 1, 1936

Telephones per 100 Population

the world's telephones. This number, 17,423,871, is far in excess of the number of telephones in service in any other country of the world, the next highest number being 3,269,952 in Germany, followed by 2,551,117 in Great Britain, 1,441,273 in France, 1,208,815 in Canada and 1,131,748 in Japan. These countries alone account for 77.65 per cent of all the telephones in the world.

A more significant measure of the comparative extent of telephone facilities, however, is the number of telephones in relation to the population served. This relationship of telephones to population is shown in the table " Telephone Development of the World, by Countries" and in the accompanying chart entitled " Telephones per 100 Population." As in previous years, the United States also exceeds all other countries in terms of this measure, having 13.69 telephones for each 100 of its population, or about six times the corresponding ratio for Europe. Canada remains in second position with 10.99 telephones per 100 population, closely followed by Denmark with 10.64, New Zealand with 10.59, and Sweden with 10.28. These, incidentally, were the only other countries in the world with more than one telephone for every 10 inhabitants. The major European countries ranked considerably lower in telephone development, e.g., Great Britain had 5.44 telephones per 100 population, Germany 4.87, France 3.38, Italy 1.25, and Russia 0.49. Among non-European countries Japan has the largest system in Asia, with 1,131,748 telephones; this number, however, is equivalent to only 1.62 per cent of the population. In South America, Argentina leads with 327,149 telephones, the equivalent of 2.64 per cent of the population. The average telephone development of the world outside the United States is only 0.87 telephones per 100 population, or about one-sixteenth of the development in the United States.

Nearly 61 per cent of all the telephones in the world are operated by privately owned systems; the remaining 39 per cent are operated by government administrations. Not only are the majority of all telephones under private operation, but the best developed countries in the world, in point of telephone facilities, are those in which the service is in the hands of private companies, either completely or to a predominating extent. Thus, the United States, which leads the world in telephone standards, has never known other than private operation of its communication facilities. In Canada, second in respect

TELEPHONE DEVELOPMENT OF THE WORLD, BY COUNTRIES
January 1, 1936

Countries	Government Systems	Private Companies	Total	Percent of Total World	Telephones Per 100 Population
NORTH AMERICA:					
United States............	—	17,423,871	17,423,871	49.74%	13.69
Canada..................	192,220	1,016,595	1,208,815	3.95%	10.99
Central America.........	12,356	13,571	25,927	.07%	0.36
Mexico.................	1,337	112,949	114,286	.33%	0.61
West Indies—					
Cuba...............	600	38,794	39,394	.11%	0.93
Puerto Rico.........	537	13,076	13,613	.04%	0.79
Other W. I. Places...	7,580	15,705	23,285	.07%	0.34
Other No. Am. Places...	—	12,936	12,936	.04%	3.66
Total............	214,630	18,647,497	18,862,127	53.85%	10.63
EUROPE:					
Austria.................	272,139	—	272,139	.78%	4.00
Belgium**..............	339,592	—	339,592	.97%	4.09
Bulgaria................	22,267	—	22,267	.06%	0.36
Czechoslovakia.........	190,098	—	190,098	.54%	1.25
Denmark‡..............	16,911	376,616	393,527	1.12%	10.64
Finland.................	4,093	145,176	149,269	.43%	3.94
France.................	1,441,273	—	1,441,273	4.11%	3.38
Germany‡..............	3,269,952	—	3,269,952	9.34%	4.87
Great Britain and No. Ireland.	2,551,117	—	2,551,117	7.28%	5.44
Greece.................	8,467	23,986	32,453	.09%	0.48
Hungary...............	130,472	739	131,211	.38%	1.47
Irish Free State‡.......	36,093	—	36,093	.10%	1.19
Italy...................	—	543,835	543,835	1.55%	1.25
Jugo-Slavia............	47,298	1,663	48,961	.14%	0.33
Latvia‡................	68,488	—	68,488	.20%	3.49
Netherlands............	366,325	—	366,325	1.05%	4.32
Norway*...............	123,987	79,406	203,393	.58%	7.05
Poland.................	126,517	104,337	230,854	.66%	0.68
Portugal...............	15,137	41,240	56,377	.16%	0.78
Roumania..............	—	63,092	63,092	.18%	0.33
Russia ¶...............	861,181	—	861,181	2.46%	0.49
Spain..................	—	341,390	341,390	.98%	1.38
Sweden................	641,179	1,415	642,594	1.83%	10.28
Switzerland	399,532	—	399,532	1.14%	9.59
Other Places in Europe..	89,530	12,740	102,270	.29%	1.32
Total............	11,021,648	1,735,635	12,757,283	36.42%	2.24

SOUTH AMERICA:					
Argentina	—	327,149	327,149	.93%	2.64
Bolivia	—	2,367	2,367	.01%	0.07
Brazil	1,924	196,982	198,906	.57%	0.41
Chile	—	55,161	55,161	.16%	1.21
Colombia	7,964	29,592	37,556	.11%	0.39
Ecuador	3,499	2,954	6,453	.02%	0.26
Paraguay	—	2,974	2,974	.01%	0.33
Peru	—	22,272	22,272	.06%	0.34
Uruguay	20,000	13,000	33,000	.09%	1.62
Venezuela	700	19,000	19,700	.05%	0.58
Other So. Am. Places	2,861	—	2,861	.01%	0.52
Total	36,948	671,451	708,399	2.02%	0.76
ASIA:					
British India‡	25,952	43,364	69,316	.20%	0.02
China	80,000	90,000	170,000	.49%	0.04
Japan‡	1,131,748	—	1,131,748	3.23%	1.62
Other Places in Asia	153,322	79,132	232,454	.66%	0.14
Total	1,391,022	212,496	1,603,518	4.58%	0.15
AFRICA:					
Egypt	52,740	—	52,740	.15%	0.24
Union of South Africa	150,000	—	150,000	.43%	1.73
Other Places in Africa	95,623	1,978	97,601	.28%	0.08
Total	298,363	1,978	300,341	.86%	0.20
OCEANIA:					
Australia*	532,377	—	532,377	1.52%	7.92
Hawaii	—	25,560	25,560	.07%	6.55
Netherlands East Indies	37,302	3,688	40,990	.12%	0.06
New Zealand‡	166,565	—	166,565	.47%	10.59
Philippine Islands	6,000	21,342	27,342	.08%	0.20
Other Places in Oceania	3,852	328	4,180	.01%	0.18
Total	746,096	50,918	797,014	2.27%	0.86
TOTAL WORLD	13,708,707	21,319,975	35,028,682§	100.00%	1.63

* June 30, 1935.
** February 29, 1936.
# March 31, 1936.
¶ U.S.S.R., including Siberia and Associated Republics.
§ Includes approximately 16,700,000 automatic or "Dial" telephones. of which about 44% are in the United States.

of telephone development, 84 per cent of the telephones are owned and operated by private companies, while 96 per cent are so operated in Denmark, telephonically the best developed country in Europe. On the other hand, the telephone development of Great Britain, Germany and France, where the service is a government monopoly, is only 25 to 40 per cent of that achieved in the United States.

TELEPHONES IN LARGE CITIES

There are four times as many people living in France, Germany and Great Britain as in the largest 53 cities in the United

OWNERSHIP OF THE WORLD'S TELEPHONES
January 1, 1936

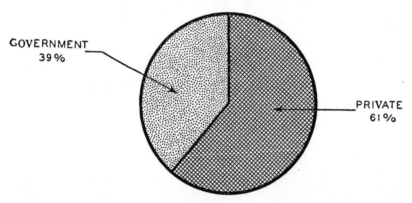

GOVERNMENT 39%

PRIVATE 61%

States, but there are half a million more telephones in these United States cities than there are in the three European countries combined. Three other countries, China, British India and Russia, account for half the population of the world, but have only three-fourths the number of telephones serving the City of New York alone. The British Empire has a population equivalent to every fourth person on earth, but 12 United States cities have in the aggregate more telephones than that Empire. These examples reflect the high telephone development prevailing in American cities. In fact, the American

194

WORLD'S TELEPHONE STATISTICS

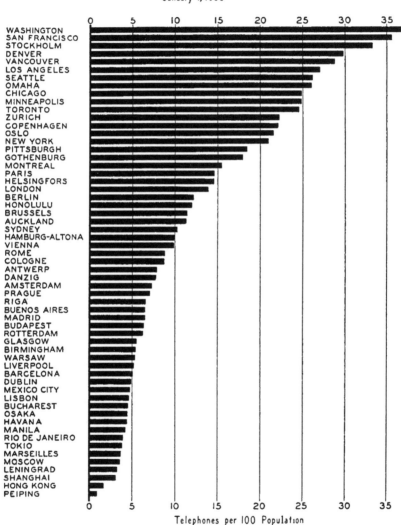

TELEPHONES PER 100 POPULATION
OF LARGE CITIES

January 1, 1936

Telephones per 100 Population

195

Country and City (or Exchange Area)	Population (City or Exchange Area)	Number of Telephones	Telephones per 100 Population
ARGENTINA:			
Buenos Aires..................	3,000,000	195,715	6.52
AUSTRALIA:			
Adelaide.....................	315,000	30,445	9.67
Brisbane.....................	306,000	29,126	9.52
Melbourne...................	1,008,000	111,622	11.07
Sydney......................	1,255,000	128,628	10.25
AUSTRIA:			
Graz........................	153,000	11,223	7.34
Vienna......................	1,876,000	184,840	9.85
BELGIUM:**			
Antwerp.....................	527,000	41,404	7.86
Brussels.....................	976,000	111,059	11.38
Liege.......................	422,000	24,825	5.88
BRAZIL:			
Rio de Janeiro...............	1,820,000	70,746	3.89
CANADA:			
Montreal.....	1,070,000	165,231	15.44
Ottawa	186,100	36,453	19.59
Toronto.....................	778,200	191,545	24.61
Vancouver...................	187,500	53,978	28.79
CHINA:			
Canton......................	1,070,000	8,600	0.80
Hong Kong..................	860,000	14,549	1.69
Peiping.....................	1,560,000	12,483	0.80
Shanghai††	1,660,000	51,190	3.08
CUBA:			
Havana.....................	704,000	30,688	4.36
CZECHOSLOVAKIA:			
Prague......................	928,000	65,537	7.06
DANZIG:			
Free City of Danzig........	230,000	17,843	7.76
DENMARK:			
Copenhagen..................	825,000	182,946	22.18
FINLAND:			
Helsingfors..................	270,000	39,193	14.52
FRANCE:			
Bordeaux....................	269,000	20,972	7.80
Lille........................	202,000	17,471	8.65
Lyons.......................	672,000	36,321	5.40
Marseilles...................	970,000	35,627	3.67
Paris........................	2,910,000	422,755	14.53
GERMANY:#			
Berlin....	4,225,000	513,610	12.16
Breslau.....................	628,000	43,571	6.94
Cologne.....................	762,000	66,581	8.74
Dresden.....................	789,000	65,436	8.29
Dortmund...................	581,000	24,938	4.29
Essen.......................	672,000	31,420	4.68
Frankfort-on-Main............	649,000	62,723	9.66
Hamburg-Altona.............	1,627,000	161,387	9.92
Leipzig......................	761,000	66,565	8.75
Munich......................	832,000	82,835	9.96
GREAT BRITAIN AND NO. IRELAND:#			
Belfast......................	415,000	20,252	4.88
Birmingham..................	1,220,000	65,876	5.40
Bristol......................	418,000	24,664	5.90
Edinburgh...................	445,000	37,055	8.33
Glasgow.....................	1,200,000	65,897	5.49
Leeds.......................	517,000	27,748	5.37
Liverpool....................	1,205,000	62,663	5.20
London—			
(Telecommunications Region)	9,450,000	960,709	10.17
(City and County of London)	4,472,000	617,213	13.80
Manchester..................	1,106,000	70,085	6.34
Newcastle...................	472,000	21,665	4.59
Sheffield....................	522,000	22,803	4.37
HAWAII:			
Honolulu....................	145,000	17,263	11.91
HUNGARY:			
Budapest....................	1,387,000	88,627	6.39
Szeged......................	139,000	2,065	1.49
IRISH FREE STATE:#			
Dublin......................	430,000	21,065	4.90

Rome.................	1,050,000	91,869	8.75
JAPAN:#			
Kobe.................	925,000	37,636	4.07
Kyoto.................	1,100,000	44,745	4.07
Nagoya.................	1,100,000	37,391	3.40
Osaka.............	3,050,000	135,098	4.43
Tokio.................	5,970,000	226,028	3.79
LATVIA:#			
Riga.................	387,000	25,654	6.63
MEXICO:			
Mexico City...............	1,390,000	65,731	4.73
NETHERLANDS:			
Amsterdam................	790,000	58,028	7.35
Haarlem.................	164,000	13,178	8.04
Rotterdam................	620,000	38,950	6.28
The Hague................	520,000	49,949	9.61
NEW ZEALAND:#			
Auckland.................	207,000	23,427	11.32
NORWAY:*			
Oslo....................	250,000	53,825	21.53
PHILIPPINE ISLANDS:			
Manila....................	425,000	18,023	4.24
POLAND:			
Lodz.....................	930,000	16,044	1.73
Warsaw..................	1,290,000	68,461	5.31
PORTUGAL:			
Lisbon....................	660,000	30,248	4.58
ROUMANIA:			
Bucharest..................	646,000	29,209	4.52
RUSSIA:			
Leningrad.................	3,100,000	99,463	3.21
Moscow..................	4,100,000	144,669	3.53
SPAIN:			
Barcelona.................	1,110,000	55,569	5.01
Madrid..................	1,015,000	66,148	6.52
SWEDEN:			
Gothenburg................	258,000	46,269	17.93
Malmö....................	141,000	22,639	16.06
Stockholm.................	446,000	148,433	33.28
SWITZERLAND:			
Basel.....................	152,000	34,003	22.37
Berne....................	114,000	26,284	23.06
Geneva...................	148,000	27,870	18.83
Zurich...................	273,000	60,705	22.24
UNITED STATES: (See Note)			
New York.................	7,178,000	1,503,712	20.95
Chicago..................	3,410,000	849,889	24.92
Los Angeles...............	1,335,000	360,506	27.00
Pittsburgh................	1,023,900	188,871	18.45
Total 10 cities over 1,000,000 Population..............	22,023,000	4,546,669	20.65
Milwaukee.................	772,000	139,960	18.13
San Francisco...............	699,500	248,652	35.55
Washington...............	550,000	201,884	36.71
Minneapolis................	508,000	126,342	24.87
Total 10 cities with 500,000 to 1,000,000 Population......	6,586,600	1,371,979	20.83
Seattle....................	418,500	109,296	26.12
Denver....................	305,000	90,902	29.80
Omaha....................	241,000	62,676	26.01
Hartford..................	239,000	55,862	23.37
Total 33 cities with 200,000 to 500,000 Population........	10,106,800	1,847,598	18.28
Total 53 cities with more than 200,000 Population........	38,716,400	7,766,246	20.06

NOTE: There are shown, for purposes of comparison with cities in other countries, the total development of all cities in the United States in certain population groups, and the development of certain representative cities within each of such groups.
* June 30, 1935.   ** February 29, 1936.   # March 31, 1936.
†† International Settlement and French Concession.

TELEPHONE DEVELOPMENT OF LARGE AND SMALL COMMUNITIES
January 1, 1936

Country	Service Operated by (See Note)	Number of Telephones		Telephones Per 100 Population	
		In Communities of 50,000 Population and Over	In Communities of less than 50,000 Population	In Communities of 50,000 Population and Over	In Communities of less than 50,000 Population
Australia*	G.	316,900	215,477	9.75	6.20
Austria	G.	210,600	61,539	9.56	1.34
Belgium**	G.	239,336	100,256	6.78	2.10
Canada	P.G.	665,786	543,029	18.78	7.28
Czechoslovakia	G.	96,928	93,170	5.56	0.69
Denmark	P.	206,892	182,608	19.50	6.95
Finland	P.	55,608	93,661	11.30	2.84
France	G.	770,448	670,825	8.66	1.99
Germany#	G.	2,120,098	1,149,854	7.56	3.27
Great Britain and No. Ireland#	G.	1,865,560	744,440	7.01	3.67
Hungary	G.	99,843	31,368	4.79	0.46
Japan#	G.	759,026	372,722	3.53	0.77
Netherlands	G.	239,357	126,968	6.82	2.56
New Zealand#	G.	67,342	99,223	11.92	9.84
Norway*	P.G.	80,718	122,675	19.88	4.95
Poland	P.G.	137,830	93,024	2.70	0.32
Spain	P.	211,528	129,862	4.07	0.66
Sweden	G.	250,329	392,265	23.64	7.56
Switzerland	G.	182,001	217,531	20.52	6.64
Union of South Africa#	G.	90,271	61,900	7.83	0.82
United States	P.	9,929,998	7,493,873	19.32	9.87

Note: P. indicates that the telephone service is wholly or predominantly operated by private companies, G. wholly or predominantly by the Government, and P. G. by both private companies and the Government. See first table.
* June 30, 1935.
** February 29, 1936.
# March 31, 1936.

capital, Washington, D. C., leads all large cities of the world, with 36.71 telephones for each 100 inhabitants; San Francisco is next with 35.55. Stockholm, Sweden, ranks third with 33.28, a telephone development which is found to be exceptional among European cities. Berne, Switzerland, comes next in respect of urban telephone development in Europe, with 23.06 telephones per 100 population. Greater London, with more people than New York City, had only 960,709 telephones compared with 1,503,712 in New York; the development of the latter city was 20.95 telephones per 100 population or twice as high as that in London (10.17). Berlin, similarly, is some 25 per cent larger than Chicago in point of population, but it had only 513,610 telephones compared with 849,889 in Chicago, the corresponding relative developments being 12.16 and 24.92. Paris had 422,755 telephones, but this number was equivalent to only 14.53 per cent of its population. By way of contrast, the telephone development of Los Angeles (27.00) was nearly twice as high.

Telephones in Large and Small Communities

The extent to which telephone service is available in all communities in the United States, regardless of size, may be seen from the following figures:

	Telephones per 100 Population
Communities with over 1,000,000 population................	20.65
Communities with 500,000 to 1,000,000 population...........	20.83
Communities with 200,000 to 500,000 population............	18.28
Communities with 50,000 to 200,000 population.............	17.08
Communities with less than 50,000 population..............	9.87

Particular interest attaches to the last figure, which represents the telephone development in the smaller towns and more sparsely settled areas of the United States. Although naturally lower than the development characteristic of the larger cities in the United States, this figure of 9.87 nevertheless exceeds the overall telephone development of all but two European countries and even surpasses the average telephone development of cities with more than 50,000 population in such countries as Belgium, France, Germany, Great Britain, Hungary, Italy, Poland, Russia and many more. In comparing the relative telephone development of smaller with that of larger communities, it will in fact be seen that the general tendency abroad, with few exceptions, is toward concentration of telephone facilities in the larger towns and cities. No city in this country contains as much as nine per cent of the total number of telephones in the United States, but Greater London has more than one-third of all the telephones in Great Britain and Northern Ireland. The telephone development of the more sparsely settled areas in Great Britain, those with less than 50,000 inhabitants, is 3.67 or only about one-third of the corresponding development in the United States. Nearly 29 per cent of all telephones in France are in the city of Paris, while the smaller French communities average less than two telephones for every 100 inhabitants—only a fifth of the corresponding American development.

TELEPHONE TRAFFIC

On January 1, 1936, the world's telephone facilities included a total of 158,871,500 miles of wire conductors; and overseas radio connections make it possible for a telephone user in this country to reach any one of 93 per cent of the telephones in the world, including some 18 million telephones located in other countries. Available statistics indicate that the world total of telephone conversations during the year 1935 amounted to 50 billion. This corresponds to an average of nearly 1,600 conversations per second and 23 conversations per average capita. In the United States the telephone calling rate per average capita was 197.0 for the year 1935, compared with an annual calling rate of 12.5 for the rest of the world. Not only are telephone facilities much more abundant in the United States, but the use of these facilities is far greater than elsewhere.

K. FICK

Notes on Recent Occurrences

OPENING OF TELEPHONE SERVICE WITH CHINA BRINGS 70TH COUNTRY WITHIN VOICE REACH OF THE BELL SYSTEM

CHINA is the most recent addition to the list of foreign countries to be brought within voice reach of this continent by means of the transoceanic radio telephone circuits of the American Telephone and Telegraph Company. Conversations formally opening the new service took place on May 19, when the speakers talked from the office of the Secretary of State in Washington, D. C., and the Palace Hotel in Shanghai. The time at the American end of the 9,400 mile radio and telephone circuit was 10:00 A.M., E. S. T., while the clocks along the Bund registered 11:00 P.M.

In addition to conversations engaged in by Secretary of State Cordell Hull, Dr. Wang Chung-hui, Minister for Foreign Affairs for China, and other high government officials in the two countries, the ceremonies were made especially interesting by chats between leading women of the West and the East. In this connection, Mrs. Franklin D. Roosevelt talked with Mme. Chiang Kai-shek, wife of China's Generalissimo and President of that country's Executive Yuan. Later, Mrs. Roosevelt exchanged greetings with Mme. H. H. Kung, wife of the Chinese Minister of Finance and Vice-President of the Executive Yuan; and Mme. Kung spoke with Mme. Sao-Ke Alfred Sze, wife of the Chinese Ambassador to the United States. Both Mesdames Chiang and Kung, incidentally, are graduates of American colleges.

The ceremonies began with a conversation between T. G. Miller, Vice President of the American Telephone and Telegraph Company and master of ceremonies, and Dr. Yu-ching Wen, Director General of Tele-communications for the Chinese Government. Following these greetings, Secretary of State Hull, while speaking with Dr. Wang, recalled that the first American ship to visit China with a cargo of merchandise arrived there in 1784. The voyage from New York to Canton occupied more than six months, he said. But "today," he added, "I am exchanging greetings with you half-way around the world in approximately the same time as would be required were we talking by telephone from different points in the same city."

In reply, Dr. Wang pointed to Confucius' ideal of universal brotherhood and remarked that scientific achievements "have gradually led human beings, whatever their race, religion and political creed, to live, think, and act like members of one great family."

Secretary Hull and Minister of Foreign Affairs Wang then turned their telephones over to others who engaged in additional conversations. Among these were Chinese Ambassador Sze and Nelson T. Johnson, American Ambassador to China; Anning S. Prall, Chairman of the Federal Communications Commission; General Yu Fei-peng, Minister of Communications in China; and other well-known persons in the two countries.

The extension of service to China, the seventieth country to be brought within reach of the Bell System, leaves but two large telephone systems—those in Russia and New Zealand—yet to be connected with the United States. The new service is available to about 57,000 telephones in Greater Shanghai and to Bell and Bell-connected telephones in the United States, Canada, Cuba and Mexico. The short wave circuit connecting radio stations near San Francisco and Shanghai is more than 6,000 miles long.

NEW RADIO TELEPHONE SERVICE WITH ALASKA BRINGS LAST MAJOR U. S. TERRITORY INTO VOICE CONTACT WITH THE CONTINENT

Radio telephone service between Continental United States and the Territory of Alaska was formally inaugurated on July 8 over a radio telephone channel between Juneau, Alaska, and Seattle, Wash., the installation of which had recently been completed by the Signal Corps of the United States Army in co-operation with the American Telephone and Telegraph Company. Arrangements have been effected between the War Department and the A. T. & T. Co. for interconnecting the wire network of the Bell System with the Signal Corps' radio telephone channel at Seattle, thus making possible conversations between telephones in Juneau and Bell and Bell-connecting telephones in this country.

Ceremonies opening the new radio telephone channel to Alaska were held in Washington, D. C., and Juneau, the conversations taking place over a circuit 3906 miles long. Of this, 3021 miles were Bell System land lines between Washington and Seattle, and 885 miles were the Signal Corps' radio telephone channel between Seattle and Juneau. Taking part in the conversations between the two cities were government and civic officials, Signal Corps and other Army officers, and representatives of the American Telephone and Telegraph Company. Because of the difference in time between the National and Territorial Capitals, words spoken in Washington at 2 P.M. were heard, practically instantaneously, at 10 A.M. in Juneau, and vice versa.

Establishment and operation by the Signal Corps of the radio telephone circuit between Seattle and Juneau is the latest step in the Army's program of development of communication with Alaska. The Signal Corps has operated the Alaska Communication System since 1900, when the War Department was authorized to establish an electrical communication system primarily for military use in affording communication between the various Army garrisons stationed in the Territory and secondarily for commercial use. First established as land telegraph lines between important points, the system was supplemented between 1900 and 1904 with short lengths of submarine cable. In the latter year a submarine cable was laid between Seattle, Valdez, and Seward, providing the first direct communication between Alaska and the United States. This submarine cable was supplanted in 1931 by a network of radio telegraph stations for communication within and to and from the Territory. This network represents the principal means of communication for the Territory of Alaska and has been an important factor in its commercial development. The Signal Corps' new radio telephone channel constitutes an additional means of communication between Alaska and Continental United States.

The opening of service with Alaska took place within a few days of the seventieth anniversary of the acquisition of this northern Territory by the United States, the treaty ratifying the purchase of Alaska from Russia having been proclaimed on June 20, 1867. Alaska is the last of this country's major Territories and Dependencies to be brought within voice range of the mainland, since radio telephone service was opened by the American Telephone and Telegraph Company with Hawaii in 1931, with the Philippines in 1933, with the Canal Zone in 1933, and with Puerto Rico in 1936.

KARL W. WATERSON ELECTED A VICE PRESIDENT

A T their meeting on May 19, the Directors of the American Telephone and Telegraph Company elected Karl W. Waterson a Vice President of the Company. He succeeds Edwin F. Carter, who retired last May, as Vice President in charge of Personnel Relations.

Mr. Waterson was born at Chelsea, Vt., on March 9, 1876. He was graduated from the Lowell, Mass., High School, and, in 1898, from Massachusetts Institute of Technology, with the degree of Bachelor of Science in Electrical Engineering. On June 13, 1898, he entered the service of the Bell System at Boston. In September, 1901, he was placed in charge of Central Office Engineering and, in January of 1905, of Traffic Engineering. In 1907, in which year Bell System head-quarters were transferred to New York, Mr. Waterson was made Assistant Chief Engineer. In 1927 he was appointed Assistant Vice President in charge of Plant Operation, Traffic and General Operating Results in the Department of Operation and Engineering.

W. H. HARRISON ELECTED PRESIDENT OF A. I. E. E. FOR COMING YEAR

WILLIAM H. HARRISON, Assistant Vice President, Department of Operation and Engineering, American Telephone and Telegraph Company, was elected President of the American Institute of Electrical Engineers for the year beginning August 1, 1937, it was announced at the annual meeting of the Institute, held in Milwaukee, Wis.

BELL TELEPHONE

QUARTERLY

)L. XVI   OCTOBER, 1937   NO. 4

"TWX"—ITS GROWING IMPORTANCE TO THE
NATION'S BUSINESS

THE PUBLIC HEALTH ASPECT OF THE TELEPHONE

THE ORIGIN AND DEVELOPMENT OF
RADIO TELEPHONY

SOUTHWEST PASSAGE

THE INTERNATIONAL RADIO MEETING OF 1937

BELL TELEPHONE

QUARTERLY

*A Medium of Suggestion
and a Record of Progress*

CONTENTS FOR OCTOBER 1937

VOL. XVI   NO. 4

PUBLISHED QUARTERLY FOR THE BELL SYSTEM BY THE AMERICAN
TELEPHONE AND TELEGRAPH COMPANY. SUBSCRIPTION, $1.50 PER YEAR,
IN UNITED STATES; SINGLE COPIES, 50 CENTS

Address all communications to

INFORMATION DEPARTMENT
AMERICAN TELEPHONE AND TELEGRAPH COMPANY
195 Broadway, New York

Contributors to This Issue

R. E. PIERCE

Cornell University, 1913, A.B. and M.E. American Telephone and Telegraph Company, Engineering Department, 1913-19; Department of Operation and Engineering, 1919-. Mr. Pierce has been engaged in work on telegraph matters and during the period with the Department of Operation and Engineering has been in charge of telegraph engineering.

JOSEPH V. DUNN

Sheffield Scientific School, Yale University, Ph.B., 1921. American Telephone and Telegraph Company, Department of Operation and Engineering, Plant Engineering Division, Transmission Section, 1921-31; Commercial Engineering Division, 1931-.

W. H. MARTIN

Johns Hopkins University, A.B., 1909; Massachusetts Institute of Technology, S.B., 1911; American Telephone and Telegraph Company, Engineering Department, 1911-19; Department of Development and Research, 1919-34; Bell Telephone Laboratories, 1934-. Mr. Martin, who is at present Switching Research Director of the Laboratories, for a number of years has been associated with the development of station apparatus.

LLOYD ESPENSCHIED

Pratt Institute, 1909. Engineering Department, American Telephone and Telegraph Company, 1910; Department of Development and Research, 1919-34; Bell Telephone Laboratories, Inc., 1934-. Mr. Espenschied, now Research Consultant of the Laboratories, first became acquainted with radio as an amateur wireless telegraphist, was associated with the founding of the Institute of Radio Engineers and has represented the Bell System at various international radio conferences.

GEORGE G. BREED

U. S. Naval Academy, 1918. U. S. Navy, 1917-23 (Lieutenant). Reporter, *Springfield Republican*, 1924-25; *Newark Evening News*, 1925-27. Publicity Department, Long Lines Department, American Telephone and Telegraph Company, 1927-.

THE BUSY HOURS AT THE TELETYPEWRITER EXCHANGE SWITCHBOARD REQUIRE AN OPERATOR AT EVERY POSITION IN ORDER TO HANDLE ALL REQUESTS FOR SERVICE WITHOUT DELAY.

"TWX"—Its Growing Importance to the Nation's Business

IN 1931 the Bell System offered a nationwide teletypewriter exchange service on a basis somewhat similar to telephone service. Today the directory for TWX, as this new service is called, lists more than 12,000 subscribers representing a good cross-section of modern financial and industrial business as well as governmental agencies. This growth has been rapid, substantial increases in stations being realized in practically every section of the country. It is true that the " private line " teletypewriter service of the Bell System with its rapid, direct, two way features has been available for more than 20 years, but this new service, which allows any subscriber to be connected with any other subscriber, greatly extends the benefits of this form of communication.

The inauguration of this new service involved many new problems; but the perfection of the teletypewriter, experience with switchboards for private line teletypewriter installations and the marked improvements in circuit stability and transmission characteristics, coupled with the general background of more than fifty years of experience in handling switching problems, gave assurance that such a service would be a success. The fact that the service was needed and has been satisfactory is demonstrated by the ever increasing group of users who have made this new communication service an integral part of their business. There has been developed and put into use a nationwide system of teletypewriter stations, circuits and switchboards with trained operating and maintenance personnel, which has no parallel. Switchboards are now in service in 160 centers with positions for 650 operators. These switchboards are interconnected by facilities providing 700,000 miles of teletypewriter channels. The largest circuit group is between the switchboard in New York and the switchboard in Chicago with a total of 27 circuits. The longest circuit group is 3400 miles with 8 circuits between New York and Los Angeles. This vast network of circuits may be interconnected at the switchboards so that a connection may be built up on an instant's notice between any two subscribers.

THE TELETYPEWRITER STATION

TWX subscribers are furnished a complete sending and receiving teletypewriter set. The sending is done from a keyboard very similar to that of a typewriter, and messages are received on a letter size page form. If the customer prefers, machines for typing on a continuous tape are available. For those having considerable traffic, a teletypewriter set is available which allows the message to be typed and stored in a perforated tape before the call is actually placed for the distant station. With this arrangement the messages may be prepared and checked in advance so that when the connection is established the transmission can go ahead at maximum speed (60 words per minute) without any interruption. For those who have need for typing on printed forms, an arrangement is provided for feeding the paper through the machine in accurately spaced steps by means of feed holes in the paper and sprocket pins on the paper platen. Also, as many as 6 or 7 carbon copies can be made when desired.

The subscriber's station is connected to a switchboard over a local loop as in the case of the telephone, and the trunk circuits of the system interconnect these switchboards. The subscriber calls an operator by operating a switch and the operator answers by typing "OPR" over the connecting loop. The subscriber then types the number of the called station, the operator proceeds to establish the connection, and the distant subscriber is called to his machine. This entire operation takes on the average about 1.3 minutes from the signal of the calling subscriber to the answer of the called subscriber.

In those cases where a subscriber desires to receive messages in his absence the station is arranged for unattended service. In this case the switchboard operator starts the subscriber's machine for the reception of a message and stops it when the transmission is completed. This feature is especially useful when there is a large difference in time between two points such as between the Atlantic and Pacific Coasts.

The charge to a subscriber for a connection depends on the distance between stations and the duration of communication as is the case with toll telephone service. For example, a 3 minute connection costs 30 cents for 50 miles, 90 cents for 500 miles and $2.20 for 2500 miles.

SWITCHING THE WRITTEN WORD

Teletypewriter switchboards are much like telephone switchboards. They consist essentially of terminations for subscriber lines and intertoll trunks and the switching and communicating facilities used by the operator in conversing with the subscriber and with other operators and in interconnecting the line terminations. The one outstanding difference at once apparent is that in the case of the telephone the operator communicates by talking while in the TWX switchboards she communicates by typing. Various arrangements of these switching facilities have been made to meet the various conditions arising principally from the size of the subscriber group to be served. For example, the switchboard in New York has 1900 stations connected, 55 operating positions and 18 more positions being engineered. There are 330 toll lines terminated on this switchboard. This office has handled as many as 3700 outward calls in a single day.

One of the latest developments in TWX switching facilities is an automatic concentrator for mechanically switching a group of subscribers in one locality over a group of trunks to a manual switchboard in another area. Such an automatic arrangement is installed at Norfolk, Virginia, connecting the TWX subscribers in that area over five trunks with the manual switchboard at Richmond, Virginia.

When the Norfolk subscriber turns on his machine to place a call, his loop is automatically connected to an idle trunk to Richmond and the operator there receives the calling signal. From that point on the call is handled in the usual manner. On incoming calls for Norfolk subscribers the Richmond operator plugs into an idle trunk to Norfolk, and types the called subscriber's number. This automatically connects the called station, the operator rings and the through connection is thereby established.

COMMUNICATION CHANNELS TOTALLING 700,000 MILES

The circuits which comprise the nationwide network of communication paths for the TWX service are the result of many years of development. Since they are the product of the same organization which has brought the telephone to its present stage of perfection in this country, much of the same technique is employed in both types of facilities. For example, the trunk lines of the TWX system are largely operated on telephone circuits by the carrier system. This allows the operation of 12 teletypewriter circuits at one time over a single telephone circuit. These carrier circuits and the methods of adjusting and maintaining them have been developed to a point where they can be interconnected at will and the transmission characteristics of the overall circuit accurately predicted. This flexibility and reliability is necessary in a switched service where each circuit must function perfectly whether it be made up of a single section of circuit or built up of several sections.

The fundamental plan on which the switching system is based involves Regional Centers and Routing Centers so interconnected with circuits that most connections can be established without any intermediate switches and so that in no case will more than five trunks and four switches be involved in any connection between two stations. In all cases the transmission design must be such as to provide adequate margins of operation between two stations.

In transmitting the electrical impulses which represent the characters in the teletypewriter service, there is always a certain amount of deformation or distortion. This must be kept below certain limits in order for the transmission to be letter perfect. A repeater has been designed which is capable of receiving distorted signals and retransmitting perfect signals. This is called a regenerative repeater. Such repeaters are installed at strategic points so that they may be connected into any circuit where the overall makeup is such that the transmission might not be satisfactory without corrective measures. From a transmission standpoint, the regenerative repeater makes the long circuit equivalent to a shorter circuit.

SERVICE ORGANIZATION BEHIND THE LINES

The fact has been stressed that TWX service has been made possible by the high degree of perfection which has been attained in the station apparatus, line circuit and switching facilities. In the operation of the TWX business, as previously mentioned, a large corps of operators is required to establish the connections. In many respects their work is much like that of the telephone operator and involves similar problems of recruiting, training and development. Mention should also be made of the maintenance organization which keeps all the intricate parts properly coordinated and in satisfactory working condition. Some of these maintenance groups are special for the teletypewriter service while others are engaged in telephone maintenance as well, but in all cases they have the broad background of training and experience which is necessary for the proper maintenance of modern communication facilities. For the stations there are installers, station repairmen and overhauling shops. For the switchboards there are the various groups of central office repairmen and power plant attendants and for the circuits there are repeater attendants, testboard men, linemen and repair gangs. To make their work accurate and effective the men are provided with tools, meters, testing sets, transmission measuring sets and trouble locators, all designed for the particular job to be done.

BUILDING UP THE TWX CONNECTION

As an illustration of how a connection is built up for a TWX call, consider that a subscriber in New York is calling for a subscriber in Amarillo, Texas. The N. Y. subscriber turns on his machine.—The N. Y. operator plugs into the loop and types "OPR."—The subscriber types "AMAR 5."—The N. Y. operator determines from her rate and route guide that the route is through Dallas and that a repeater is required at Dallas.—She plugs in and rings on a Dallas trunk.—The Dallas operator answers and then the N. Y. operator types "AMAR REP."—The Dallas operator inserts the repeater, plugs in and rings on an Amarillo circuit.—When Amarillo answers, the number is passed by the N. Y. operator and Amarillo rings the subscriber. The N. Y. operator waits until he answers and then retires from the circuit.

TRAINING OF CUSTOMER'S ATTENDANTS

The operation of the teletypewriter is quite similar to that of the ordinary typewriter and a competent typist can easily learn to operate it. However, in order to assure maximum proficiency in the operation of the service, the Telephone Companies of the Bell System offer to train customer attendants. At the convenience of the customers, this training is performed either on their own premises or in Telephone Company classrooms especially designed for this work. Adequate training usually takes from one to several days and covers operation of

Bakersfield, Cal.

Armour & Co meat pckrs 1427 Chester av .BKFD 20
Bakersfield Garage & Auto Supply Co
                      1701 20th BKFD 25
Barnett-Lee Tractor Co
                2130 Chester av .BKFD 19
Boss Jack auto eqpmnt 1720 'K' ....BKFD 17
Chanslor & Lyon Stores Inc auto supls
                2415 Chester av .BKFD 14
Hayward Lumber Co 1431 'H' ....BKFD 15
K E R N radio sta Elks bldg. ....BKFD 21
§Mohawk Petroleum Co Rosedale Hway ...BKFD 18
Natl Supply Co of Calif oil well eqpmnt
                3401 Chester av .BKFD 16
Pacific Tel & Tel Co traf dept 1520 20th .BKFD 9101
Pioneer Mercantile Co 1532 20th .....BKFD 12
Southern Auto Supply Co 1201 18th.....BKFD 23
Sunland Refining Corp 5th ....BKFD 22

Baltimore, Md.

Anchor Post Fence Co Eastern av & Kane .BALT 98
Armour & Co pckrs Pratt & Howard ...BALT 181
Atlantic & Gulf Stevedores Inc Amer bldg .BALT 391
Baker Watts & Co inv bnkrs
                  U S F & G bldg .BALT 395
Baltimore & Carolina Line Inc
                Pier 5 Pratt .BALT 180
Baltimore Transfer Co
        Guilford av & Monument .BALT 285
Bethlehem Steel Co Mercantile Trust bldg .BALT 291
Brown Alex & Sons inv sec
             Balto & Calvert BALT 383
Bull A H & Co SS agts Pier 5 Pratt... .BALT 180
Cahn Frank B & Co bnkrs Equitable bldg .BALT 390
Campbell Metal Window Corp
            Bush & Hamburg BALT 284
Chesapeake & Potomac Tel Co of Balt Cy 5 Light
§Genl Sales Mgr. ....BALT 9103
   Traf Training Dept. ....BALT 9104
Chevrolet Motor Co 2122 Broening Hwy. .BALT 199

              113 W North av BALT 197
Murphy G M P & Co bank & ins stks
              Calvert bldg BALT 191
Obrecht P Fredk & Son feeds 423 W Pratt BALT 399
Owens Illinois Glass Co glass containers
          Standard Oil bldg BALT 87
Revere Copper & Brass Inc Baltimore div
           1301 Wicomico. BALT 388
Roosevelt SS Co Baltimore Trust bldg ... BALT 80
Schluderberg Wm-T J Kurdle Co pckrs
          3800 E Baltimore .BALT 188
Schoeneman J Inc mfrs mens clothg
          412 W Redwood .BALT 280
Shirtcraft Co Horner Div Curtain av...BALT 190
Sitnek Fuel Co Munsey bldg. ....BALT 283
Smelkinson Bros Corp comm mchts
         109 W Camden .BALT 392
Standard Sanitary Mfg Co plbg fixts
         5315 Holabird av .BALT 294
Stein Bros & Boyce inv bnkrs 6SCalvert .BALT 393
Steiner-Liberty Corp nightwr 416 Light. .BALT 86
Sun Papers Editorial Dept Sun sq. .....BALT 282
Tri-City Freight Lines Inc 146 W West.. .BALT 84
Truscon Steel Co 330 W 24th. ....BALT 384
U S Industrial Alcohol Co Curtis Bay. ..BALT 286
W B A L radio sta Lexington bldg. .....BALT 92
W C A O radio sta 811 W Lanvale. ....BALT 287
W F B R radio sta 7 St Paul. ....BALT 189
Washburn Crosby Co Inc flour
          Whitaker bldg BALT 96
Western Elect Co Inc 2500 Broening Highway
         Point Breeze BALT 95
Westheimer & Co inv sec 211 E Redwood .BALT 292
Whinney's Express 418 S Hanover. ...BALT 290

Bangor, Me.

Eastern Mfg Co S Main Brewer. ....BANG 13
Maine Broadcasting Co Studio 100 Main. BANG 12
New England Tel & Tel Co dist hdqrs
         59 Park. BANG 9101
Pierce White & Drummond Inc invs 6 State. BANG 14

---

§ Unattended Service Available
(see Alphabetical Directory page 2)

Teletypewriter Classified Directory

Abrasives
(See Machinery & Machine Parts)

Accountants

Utility Accountants & Tax Consultants
New York N Y .... N Y 1-2360

Acids

Hardesty W C Co Inc
  Dover O .... DOVER O 29
  New York N Y .... N Y 1-1884

Adhesives
(See Paints, Colors, Varnishes & Enamels)

Advertising Service

Albert Frank-Guenther Law Inc
  Boston Mass .... BOS 35
  Chicago Ill .... CGO 732
  New York N Y .... N Y 1-1387
  Philadelphia Pa .... PHLA 74
  San Francisco Cal .... S F 128
Ayer N W & Son Inc
  Chicago Ill .... CGO 592
  Detroit Mich .... DET 276
  New York N Y .... N Y 1-693
  Philadelphia Pa

Advertising Service
—Continued

Globe Advertising Agcy
  Laredo Tex .... LAREDO TEX 65
Igelstroem John Co
  Massillon O .... MSLN 8
  New York N Y .... N Y 1-1754
Izzard Co
  Seattle Wash .... SEAT 122
Katz Jos Co
  Baltimore Md .... BALT 281
  New York N Y .... N Y 1-986
Kudner Arthur Inc
  Detroit Mich .... DET 485
  New York N Y .... N Y 1-181
Livermore & Knight Co
  Boston Mass .... BOS 59
  New York N Y .... N Y 1-1448
  Providence R I .... PROV 196
Lord & Thomas
  §Los Angeles .... L A 590
  §New York N Y .... N Y 1-1861
McCann-Erickson Inc
  Chicago Ill .... CGO 1048
  Cleveland O .... CLEV 185
  Detroit Mich .... DET 294
  New York N Y .... N Y 1-38
News Features Inc
  New York N Y ....N Y 1-657
Petry Edward & Co

Advertising Service
—Continued

Young & Rubicam Inc—Cont'd
  §Los Angeles Cal .... L A 217
  §New York N Y .... N Y 1-1549

Air Conditioning Equipment

York Ice Machy Corp
  Philadelphia Pa .... PHLA 524
  Washington D C ......:.. WASH 188

Air Transportation

Amer Airlines Inc
  Camden N J .... CAMDEN N J 460
  Chicago Ill .... CGO 308
  Cincinnati O .... CIN 83
  Cleveland O .... CLEV 91
  Indianapolis Ind .... IPLS 398
  Louisville Ky .... LSVL 185
  New Haven Conn .... N HN 186
  New York N Y .... N Y 1-1681
  Newark N J .... NWRK 366
  Philadelphia Pa .... PHLA 379
  Port Columbus O .... COLS 92
  Rochester N Y .... ROCH N Y 460
  South Bend Ind .... S BD IND 20
  Tucson Ariz .... TSN 3
  Williamsville N Y .... WMSV 119
Pan Amer Airways Inc

PAGES FROM THE TWX DIRECTORY. THIS DIRECTORY IS NATIONAL IN SCOPE AND THE LISTINGS ARE A REPRESENTATIVE CROSS SECTION OF MODERN FINANCIAL, INDUSTRIAL AND GOVERNMENTAL UNITS. THE FIRST SECTION LISTS CUSTOMERS ALPHABETICALLY BY CITIES ALSO ALPHABETICALLY ARRANGED. THE SECOND SECTION LISTS CUSTOMERS BY LINES OF BUSINESS

The No. 3A Switchboard, Such as This One at Pittsburgh, Provides Capacity of an Ultimate of 1200 Subscribers' Lines and 240 Intertoll Trunks. The Mounting of the Teletypewriters on a Separate Table Below the Sloping Keyshelf Allows the Space Allotted to Any One Operator to Include Any Number of Cords.

READY TO CONNECT ANY ONE OF 1900 SUBSCRIBERS IN GREATER NEW YORK WITH ANY OF 330 TOLL LINES, ALL OF WHICH ARE TERMINATED ON JACKS WITHIN HER REACH.

This Automatic Concentrator Acts as the Switching Medium Between the Norfolk Subscribers and the Trunks to the Manual Switchboard at Richmond, Va.

the service, methods for setting up and organizing messages most effectively, etc.

How Business Uses TWX

That business firms are recognizing the benefits to be derived from the use of TWX service for meeting their written communication problems effectively is evidenced not only by the rapid growth in the number of subscribers but by an equally rapid expansion in the use made of the service by these subscribers. Teletypewriter connections are being established at the present time at a rate of well over five million per year.

Furthermore, the appeal of this new communication service is not confined to any particular line of business or size or type of concern. Numbered among its subscribers are the older concerns in well established lines of business and the newer concerns in more recent forms of business endeavor. It appeals in like manner to the larger business concerns with widespread interests as well as to the smaller businesses.

For the most part, especially in the beginning, TWX service has been used by subscribers primarily for communication between specific points, i.e., between various scattered units of the same firm or closely associated concerns, or between firms in different cities having a common interest or business relationship requiring more or less steady communication. In other words, the use of the service was principally on a "point-to-point" basis. This was a natural situation in that initially the relatively small number of subscribers made it somewhat difficult for individual concerns to visualize opportunities to use the service to other than the comparatively few fixed points with which they regularly did business. But as the number of subscribers grew in an ever increasing number of different lines of business, subscribers began to extend their range of calling beyond their regular "points." Use of the service was made to firms or points with whom they had need to communicate only occasionally but where speed and the two-way, written features were important. Thus slowly and steadily the "random" use of the service is being built up.

This early growth of TWX service is somewhat analogous to the early development of telephone service. Initially the telephone "outlets" for the early telephone subscribers were principally to certain other particular individuals in their own local communities. As the number of telephone subscribers in each locality increased, the usage of the service made by individual subscribers increased accordingly, eventually growing beyond their own localities to others nearby or thousands of miles distant through the vast interconnection of these localities by toll circuits. An interesting difference in the early developments of these two services was that whereas telephone service expanded initially as a local service, TWX has grown principally as a toll service.

The fast, two-way, written record features of teletypewriter exchange service—its almost instantaneous speed of connection and transmission, the ability to "talk in writing" back and forth on the same connection and the identical typed copies at both ends—are the fundamental advantages which make it adaptable to the exacting requirements of today's business methods. Prompt handling of orders often necessitating the delivery of all orders the day received, intimate supervision of widespread activities, close coordination of production and sales, up-to-the-minute accurate reports of distant operations, the planning and organizing of each day's needs for maximum efficiency—are only a few of these exacting requirements. TWX service offers a new communication medium designed to meet these needs economically, quickly and with maximum assurance of accuracy.

Its unique and exclusive features provide a type of communication service not previously available. Its use is therefore not just a substitute for older forms of written or oral communication, although this may be the case in some instances. It opens new fields for new uses of fast communication in doing business. It often enables business to carry on functions or to do things better and more economically than was possible previously. The economy is derived sometimes in lower communication costs but more often in other ways— the less tangible but definite benefits resulting from speeding up operations, improving service to customers, smoothing out routines, saving time in shipments, permitting better control and regulation of production, shipping, traffic, distribution, administration, etc. For example, by speeding up the handling of orders between sales offices and production units by using TWX, many firms are achieving overall economy through more closely coordinated production and by reducing warehousing costs by shipping direct to customers. Also, the communication time saved makes it possible in many instances to increase substantially the number of orders shipped the same day, thus materially bettering competitive positions and, through improved service, to attract new business.

Some business firms have found that TWX service enables them to handle some things by fast written communication which could not be so handled in the past. In some cases in the past these things were handled orally, by telephone or personal visit. In other cases they were not done at all because there were no economical and satisfactory ways of handling them by fast communication means. For example, a large shoe concern is now teletyping orders on specially designed order forms from sales offices direct to plants. Thus, one teletyping of an order at a sales office will produce sufficient copies locally for its use, including invoice copies, customer acknowledgments, etc., and, at the same time, the necessary copies at the plants to enable production to start immediately. This new arrangement, in addition to effecting overall economies, will save one or more days over its former methods. Furthermore, all the people involved will have complete details regarding each order almost as soon as it is received

217

at the sales offices, and thus close supervision and coordinated attention can be given to all orders.

The limitations of this article do not permit a detailed discussion of the large number of uses which business concerns are effectively making of TWX service and the benefits being derived from such usages. However, in the following paragraphs, typical illustrations of the use made of certain of the more important features of the service are briefly highspotted.

RAPID TWO-WAY WRITTEN COMMUNICATION

Of the many unique features of TWX service perhaps the one most appreciated by subscribers and extensively used is the ability to communicate back and forth—alternately but not simultaneously—on the same connection. One common application of this feature is to carry on a written communication of the question and answer type in which the reply to a specific request is given and discussed on the same connection. This may involve any of the usual details of the every day business transaction—"How soon can we ship this order?" "What price can we quote on carload lots?" "When will production of such and such an order start?" "Should we hold for further credit check?" etc.

In analyzing the value of the two-way feature, consideration might be given to its usefulness in meeting one of the simpler requirements for fast written communication found in almost any business—the transmission of orders to production points, warehouses or sources of supply. Although the actual transmission of orders might be handled in many cases by fast one-way communication service, there is frequently the need for an immediate or subsequent discussion between office and plant regarding individual orders. The plant, for example, may have recently discontinued manfacture of a specific pattern or size and may wish to obtain approval to substitute or to get suggestions from the sales office. Due to low stock, it may be impracticable for the plant to meet the shipping dates re-

quested and assurance is desired that delayed shipments would
be acceptable, or that new dates be set up.   Again, more precise manufacturing instructions, engineering specifications,
shipping information, etc., may be needed by the plant prior
to completing the order.   These typical factors tend to make

```
SUPERIOR PAPER CO  CGO

PEORIA CALLING    REF LISKA INQUIRY ON G ROD AND BLUE FOLIO 16


OUR STOCK IS OK     GRAIN 22 INCH WAY

SHALL WE SHIP

GO

OK SHIP     IS IT MILL 16

GA

MIN PLS

NO NOT MIDWEST

GO

WE DO NOT WANT A WATERMARKED SHEET     THAT IS WHY WE ASKED

GA

THIS ISNT WATERMARKED

OK SHIP

END

END
```

ILLUSTRATING THE VALUE OF THE TWO-WAY FEATURE OF TWX IN REACHING QUICK
DECISIONS. SYMBOLS "GO" AND "GA" ARE INTERMEDIATE CLOSURES INDICATING
OTHER PARTY MAY TYPE.

the problem of adequate and prompt order handling more
difficult unless the two-way interexchange of information can
be handled quickly.   Furthermore, customers frequently inquire at sales offices as to the status of orders, the probable
shipping dates, and other specific queries regarding orders already in process.   Many businesses feel that the two-way

219

feature of TWX service is necessary in order to obtain this information from the production and shipping points as soon as practicable, and is important to them in maintaining good customer service and good-will.

Other businesses find that the two-way feature of TWX helps them in their every day purchasing problems, especially when rush items or special supplies must be obtained quickly. Frequently on the one TWX connection orders can be placed and prices and deliveries agreed to—the whole transaction completed. Furthermore, they can use it to "shop around" for best prices and deliveries, particularly important when the usual sources do not have the desired supplies or can not ship them in time.

For handling credit matters, many TWX users find the two-way feature especially helpful since it permits answers to credit inquiries on the same connection, affords ample opportunity to discuss individual credit matters in greater detail or to suggest special action or treatment, and enables misunderstandings and misinterpretations to be discussed and straightened out at once. An interesting example of this usage is that made by branch retail stores of a large mail order firm to obtain the amounts of credit which can be extended on certain accounts. This firm is attempting to build up its business by offering a special purchasing arrangement on a time payment basis. Precautionary measures are, however, necessary to assure adequate protection against losses, due to poor risks, large outstanding accounts, etc. Out-of-town branches refer specially large orders to a centralized credit department at the main office for credit approval. The latter point maintains extensive records of all customer accounts and has TWX machines located in close proximity to them. In practically all cases they are able to give replies on the same connection, often within a minute or so. Delays in turning over merchandise to customers are thereby minimized and business which otherwise might be lost is saved.

General business firms find the two-way feature equally valuable for discussing matters of administrative policy with distant units, for giving or receiving comments on sales and other special reports, for obtaining quotations and bids,—for almost any of the myriad of problems which arise daily in the operation of business. Specialized businesses find it helpful also,

```
JOHNSON CARTAGE    DECATUR    MAY 26
BLOOMINGTON CALLING


WILL YOU HAVE A TRUCK COME THRU HERE.    WE HAVE A LITTLE FREIGHT
LEFT OVER FOR CHICAGO AND SOME OF IT IS PERISHABLE.      GA


I WILL NOT HAVE ANY ROOM LEFT AND WILL HAVE FREIGHT LEFT OVER.    IF
WE CAN SCRAPE UP A TRUCK WE WILL HAVE HIM COME THRU.      GA


123 IS COMING THERE FROM SPRINGFIELD.    WILL HE HAVE ANY ROOM FOR US.
HE HAS FRT FOR YOU.      GA


IF HE HAS FREIGHT FOR US WE WILL SEND HIM THRU TO TAKE CARE OF YOU.
WE WILL NOT HAVE TO LOAD ANYTHING ON HIM THAT WE KNOW OF.
END


OK   THANKS      END
```

QUICK EXCHANGE OF INFORMATION PROMOTES GREATER EFFICIENCY.

e.g.—airlines, railroads, motor transportation and steamship lines use it regularly for dispatching, arranging for freight and cargo space, making reservations, assigning relief schedules and locating delayed shipments; radio companies use it for coordinating programs and arranging for special broadcasts and pickups; newspapers and news agencies use it for getting the latest flashes on political, financial or general news; banks use it for arranging for transfers of funds; and law enforcement

221

agencies for exchanging information on law violations and criminals.

```
J D CARPENTER CO CALLING       PEORIA   6-30-36


1.  REFER DWG. F-6196 - WHY CANT SCOTT MACHINE SURFACES DOWN TO BE
    PERFECTLY FLUSH WITH TOPS OF PYRAMIDS WHICH YOU SPECIFY 3/4"
    THICK.  WITH THEIR PAPER THEY MUST AVOID ANY RECESS.
2.  WATKINS CLAIM 20" LEAD PRICE MUCH HIGHER THAN EUROPEAN COMPETITION.
    PLS ADVISE DID YOU FIGURE THIS SPECIAL BEING AN EXPORT JOB.  ALSO
    HAVE YOU PATTERNS FOR 20".  IF NOT WOULD IT NOT BE CHEAPER TO
    FIGURE 18".
3.  LITTLE WANT PRICE 150 SCREWS FOR BRONZE MACHINES LIKE FURNISHED
    LAST ORDER BUT MADE OF SPECIAL METAL MANUFACTURED BY NASH.
    GUSTAFSON.
END
1.  THEY CAN MACHINE THESE DOWN JUST AS THIN AS THEY WANT TO.  BUT
    GENERALLY THE SURFACE OF THE PYRAMIDS IS NOT PARALLEL TO THE
    PACKING SURFACE - IN OTHER WORDS YOU WOULD RUN INTO THE PYRAMIDS
    ON ONE CORNER AND NOT TOUCH THEM ON ANOTHER.  WE ALWAYS MAKE AN
    ALLOWANCE FOR THIS.
2.  YES, WE FIGURED THIS SPECIAL.  WE ALSO HAVE 20" PATTERN AND FIND
    IT FIGURES MORE EXPENSIVE IN THE 18".
3.  WILL WIRE AS SOON AS CAN GET PRICES.
END
1.  BRYAN TELEPHONED AND RAISED THE POINT BECAUSE SOME OTHER MACHINES
    AT THEIR REFINERY WITH WHICH THEY CHECKED HAD OUTER SURFACES
    PERFECTLY FLUSH AND UNIFORM THRUOUT.  I WILL THEREFORE TELL THEM
    THEY CAN MACHINE DOWN TO 3/4" OR TO THE HIGHEST PYRAMIDS.  DO YOU
    AGREE.    END
1.  YES     END
```

DIRECT, TWO-WAY TWX CONNECTIONS HELP SMOOTH OUT PRODUCTION PROBLEMS.

It has been previously pointed out that the small as well as the large business derives desirable benefits from the use of TWX service. The communication problems, however, of the

TELEPHONE COMPANY INSTRUCTORS ARE PROVIDED FOR ASSISTING TELETYPEWRITER ATTENDANTS TO B
PROFICIENT IN THE HANDLING OF TWX COMMUNICATIONS. WELL EQUIPPED TRAINING BUREAU
AVAILABLE AT THE CONVENIENCE OF THE ATTENDANTS FOR PRACTICE AND INSTRUCTION

A TYPICAL TWX CUSTOMER'S STATION EQUIPPED FOR DIRECT KEYBOARD PAGE SENDING AND RECEIVING. THE ATTENDANT HAS AT HER RIGHT THE CONTROLS FOR SIGNALLING THE TWX CENTRAL OFFICE OPERATOR.

THE HOME OFFICE OF A NATIONWIDE PRODUCE MARKETING AGENCY USES AUTOMATIC TRANSMISSION FOR DAILY CONFERENCE CONNECTIONS TO BROKERS AND BRANCH OFFICES IN DISTANT CITIES. THE TELEPHONE, CONVENIENTLY LOCATED, ENABLES LAST MINUTE QUOTATIONS AND MARKET NEWS TO BE GATHERED LOCALLY AND SENT ON THESE CONNECTIONS.

Some Large Concerns Have Need for a Group of Machines in Their "Key" Communication Centers to Handle Their Teletypewriter Traffic to Widespread Suppliers, Factories, Branch Offices, Customers, etc   (above) As Many as 1600 Messages in a Single Day, Some of Them Pages in Length, Are Handled in This Eastern Office of a Large Manufacturer   (below) A Steel Concern Keeps Up a Continuous Flow of Communications to Its Widely Scattered Units Through This Centralized Teletypewriter Communication Room.

HUNDREDS OF INVESTMENT HOUSES, LIKE THE ONE ILLUSTRATED ABOVE, FIND TWX A NECESSITY IN THE EFFICIENT HANDLING OF THEIR TRADING OPERATIONS.

TYPICAL OF THE MANY BUSINESS OFFICES WHICH USE THE DIRECT, TWO-WAY CONTACT OF TWX FOR TRANSMITTING ORDERS, REPORTS, INSTRUCTIONS, ETC, TO DISTANT PLANTS AND OFFICES

larger industrial concerns, particularly where operations are "spread out" over a wider territory, are often apt to be much more complex and require careful study and planning to determine the most satisfactory and economical methods of employing the service. The activity of each individual department or unit must be properly coordinated with that of each other department or unit so that maximum efficiency may be realized. Lack of speed or carelessness in adequately coordinating information between departments may mean costly delays, less efficient production, late shipments, lost orders, etc. Cooperative reviews by Bell System representatives with business concerns to determine how the handling of their communication problems can be improved, often develop the need for better organization, orderliness and control. It has also been demonstrated that adequate organization and supervision of communications is often as important to the smooth functioning of a concern as that of other operations of the business.

Many of these large concerns have found that the two-way feature of TWX service has been the "key" to their ability to organize their communications efficiently. Their two-way usage is not wholly the immediate "question and answer" form described earlier but the interchange during each connection of all communications on hand at each point. These communications may involve any or all departments of the business and, during any one connection, may be sometimes unrelated. Requests for information sent on one connection may be answered on the next or succeeding connections. For example, during one connection between an office and a plant, the office may send details of all new orders received and the plant send back shipping information on all orders shipped since the last connection. This form of two-way usage is particularly effective where there are fairly large volumes of routine communications not requiring instant speed. To avoid "holding up" urgent communications, additional "in-between" connections are established or those communications are sent by other means—telephone or telegraph.

Effective communication supervision and organization of course requires efficient office management. For example, the setting up of a suitably organized plan for control of communications generally includes establishing a centralized point for concentrating communications where the sending and receiving of messages may be controlled, setting up methods of collecting and distributing individual communications from this central communication point to the various departments, units and individuals involved and coordinating this distribution with shipping schedules, office routines, plant production, etc. It also frequently involves working out definite schedules of connections to specific points at those times during the day when the volume of communications between these points and their nature and urgency warrant so that all communications may be sent, received, distributed or relayed with clocklike precision.

Business firms report that this better organization has not only added to the volume of business matters handled by fast communication but has also, among other things, facilitated inquiry and reply, speeded up internal administration, simplified and expedited order distribution, and enabled closer supervision of shipping, production, purchasing, etc. These advantages arise from the fact that under organized communication plans all departments know when to expect communications and can plan their actions accordingly. Communications thus become not an adjunct to the operations of the business but are made an integral part of them. These firms also report that when intelligently worked out, organized plans of usage permit ready supervision of the flow and direction of all communications and thus assure getting the maximum value for the communication dollar spent.

COMMUNICATING SIMULTANEOUSLY WITH SEVERAL POINTS

Many business firms have need, either regularly or occasionally, to communicate with a number of points at one time. This may be, for example, to get information or instructions to several points quickly and accurately, to receive comments or reports from all points promptly, or to permit these points as a group to exchange ideas and views on important matters. Service arrangements which permit the simultaneous connection of three or more stations are available to accomplish this. This feature of TWX service is known as " conference service."

A large copper and brass company with headquarters in the east and sales branches throughout the country uses conference connections as occasions arise to get important price changes to all points quickly. The speed of this service feature is particularly helpful to them in protecting against further orders at the former prices and the simultaneous coverage assures that the new prices will become effective at all points at the same time.

Another excellent illustration of the value of this feature in meeting business requirements of this type is the use made by a large marketing agency that distributes throughout the country a general line of fresh fruits and vegetables for the account of growers. Several times daily the home office uses TWX conference calls to furnish about 35 brokers and branch offices last minute reports on quotations and market data. This large and fast coverage gives better assurance that quotations will reach markets where prices and demand are greatest. It provides the brokers and branch offices with a greater amount of produce to sell and, through furnishing them with firm quotations, enables them to complete transactions with no further need for confirmation. This latter factor alone saves them several hours daily.

One of the most interesting uses of TWX conference service is that made by the Federal Bureau of Investigation of the

U. S. Department of Justice. The headquarters in Washington may wish to disseminate quickly to all field offices throughout the country special information or instructions regarding a new administrative routine, a robbery, a kidnapping, a "manhunt" or any one of hundreds of law enforcement activities

```
V  OPR  CONF 812  OKV  READY ON CONFERENCE 812  OK


8.13 AM EST ANCE PITB CALLING 9-1-37

ALL QTNS SUBJ TO CONFMN FOB SHPG PT UNLESS OTHERWISE SPECIFIED


LOS ANGELES - CITRUS
USUALLY CAN DEPEND HIGHER PRICES VALS IMMED FOLLOWING LABOR DAY WHEN
VACATIONERS RETURN SCHOOLS REOPEN LOCAL PRODUCTS BEG CLEANUP  WIDE RANGE
PRICES ACCORDING QUAL INDIVIDUAL CARS

SUBJ UNSOLD  5.00-150S LGR  5.35-176/288S  MIMIC  .15 HIGHER KANSAS CITY
   MERCY   5.85 SAME DISCOUNTS ROLLING CGO  MORAL  MOUTH

FINISHED VAL SHPMTS THIS YR WITH LAST FRUIT SHIPT YEST AT BOTH POMONA
GLENDORA  EXPECT START SHPG BLUEBOW RUBIDOUX PACKS FROM RIVERSIDE
LAST THIS WK


TOKAYS
FLORIN SHIPT 29TH   910 GOOSE 28-LB NET DISPLAY LUGS 1.05 PFE 70882
IMMED SHIPT 1.00

MODESTO SHPMT 30TH GOOSE MIXT  5 SDLS .722  62 TOKS .95  843 RED MALS
.85  RD 21953

IMMED SHPMT REEDLEY GIRDLED SDLS 28-LB NET DISPLAY LUGS CELLOPHANE
CURTAIN CUSHION PACK GOOSE  .722

BARTS
LAKE CO COLD STGE  SANTAROSA  SIGNAL LABEL  MOSTLY 150S SMLR 1.85
PLACER CO BALLOON LABEL 180S LGR HVY 150S LGR  IMMED SHPMT 1.50
PLACERVILLE STGE SACTO 180S LGR  HVY 165S LGR RYMAN LABEL /.80 GOLDEN
AGE LABEL 1.65

BOSC
PLACER CO 180S LGR HVY 135S LGR USONE PROMPT SHPMT /.25
SANTA CLARA VALLEY SAME 1.50
```

START OF TYPICAL CONFERENCE CONNECTION. HOME OFFICE IS ADVISING DISTANT UNITS OF LAST MINUTE MARKET NEWS, QUOTATIONS, BIDS, ETC.

involving the G-men. In a surprisingly short time, teletypewriters in as many as 44 field offices are simultaneously typing out the message.

AFTER-BUSINESS-HOURS COMMUNICATIONS

Some customers wish to receive communications during the night or other hours when their offices are closed, or during the attendant's absence. This need can be met by the special "unattended" feature arrangement mentioned earlier in this article.

Typical of the specific uses some concerns are making of this feature of TWX service is that of a motor freight transportation company which receives communications during the night from its branches as to shipments to be picked up the following morning. The "unattended" messages received during the night are ready for immediate attention the first thing in the morning, assuring minimum delay in getting truck shipments under way.

Often, differences in time between the calling and called station may play an important part in determining how any particular firm may best organize its use of TWX service to obtain the most benefit. For example, concerns with offices on both the East and West Coasts operate under a three hours difference in normal working hours. These time differences have the effect of narrowing the business day and restricting the use of two-way communications. In fact to insure that communications are exchanged during working hours at both ends, TWX connections would have to be established between 12 noon and 5 P.M. E.S.T. with two more hours out if machines are not covered during lunch hours. Some firms with branches on both coasts have found that these time differences can often be effectively overcome by using the unattended service feature. As an illustration, a large clothing concern specializing in women's wear with several branch stores on the Pacific Coast and buying headquarters in New York send all its eastbound communications involving buying requirements, price and style inquiries, etc., which arise after 2 P.M. and before 5 P.M. "Pacific Time" in one or more connections on an unattended basis. This permits the buying headquarters in New York to work on these requirements the first thing the following morning, several hours before the opening of business on the Pacific Coast. Subsequently the New York headquarters may

227

in turn establish one or more unattended connections—between 9 and 12 noon E.S.T.—and have all replies, new inquiries, prices and data regarding merchandise purchased, advice concerning new style trends, etc., at the Pacific Coast offices at the opening of their business day. Thus—no business time at either end has been lost. Although this example has cited coast-to-coast usage, the same benefits in some degree are being obtained by other firms between any points in different time zones.

Calling Anyone for Written Communication

As mentioned earlier, many firms use TWX service for the less frequent, or perhaps only occasional, communications with other concerns where the speed, two-way and written record features of the service are important, i.e., on a "random" basis. The use of the service by brokers and investment dealers for trading in non-listed securities is quite illustrative of this type of usage. Since there is no central exchange or clearing house through which operations for securities might be centered, the first problem of a dealer commissioned to buy some is to locate a supply which could be purchased at the desired price.

The use of TWX by these dealers now makes it possible for them to call other dealers one after another, anywhere in the country, in order to locate adequate sources. The speed of TWX service enables many potential sources to be reached in short order, so much more rapidly than previously that sending out several inquiries at once is no longer necessary. The two-way feature makes it possible to find out immediately whether and how soon these distant dealers can furnish the desired securities and at what price. In this way a quick job can be done and any unnecessary effort avoided which may arise when several firms reply offering securities simultaneously. Furthermore, experience indicates that the communication cost is relatively low, such as to keep the cost of doing business low enough to be attractive.

A large steel fabricating concern occasionally receives orders specifying special items or parts not normally made or stocked by that concern. It is often important in placing orders for these items with outside suppliers that deliveries be arranged so that all parts are coordinated properly in final assembly. TWX is used for this purpose since its speed assures a prompt placing of orders and its two-way feature is helpful in reaching quick agreement as to suitable delivery dates.

From such varied usage as is described above, it is evident that American business has found, in TWX, a remarkably efficient and adaptable agency both for routine and emergency interchange of written information. That 12,000 subscribers are already listed in the TWX directory, after only six years of the service's availability, is proof that the Bell System, in developing the service, has met a great need. And, from the six year record of progress, it may safely be inferred that TWX is destined to serve the nation in still greater measure.

R. E. PIERCE

J. V. DUNN

The Public Health Aspect of the Telephone

SINCE the discovery of the role of bacteria in disease much attention has been directed to the manner in which they may get from one person to another. Preventive medicine has fostered many sanitary codes in the fight to prevent these minute organisms from entering our bodies through drinking water, milk and food. Sterilization of the doctor's implements has materially reduced the hazards of surgery. Disinfection of our cuts and scratches has become common practice. We are conscious that when we touch doorknobs, stair rails, handles in public conveyances, money and the many objects which others have touched, there is a chance that germs may be deposited on our hands. And now recent research has shown that droplets from the mouth and nose may remain suspended in the air and so be borne to us.

The idea of germs everywhere may lead an unduly timorous person to an attempted avoidance of all the many objects with which our manner of living brings us into frequent contact. The more rational people, drawing upon their experience of general freedom from disease, realize that such an avoidance is futile and unnecessary. They feel, however, that under our complex conditions of living, certain sanitary practices are justified, particularly those applying to our supply of water, milk, and food and to the disposal of garbage and sewage. As to the extent to which it is reasonable to go in preventive measures, they want the guidance of unbiased experts in the field of hygiene and public health.

The fact that the user of the telephone brings the instrument to the head, and particularly near the mouth, has naturally raised the question as to whether this practice plays any appreciable part in the spread of communicable diseases.

230

Especially has this question been directed at the public telephone with its succession of different users. This matter has engaged the interest of the medical profession, bacteriologists and workers in the field of public health, both in this country and abroad. It has also been the subject of much attention by those responsible for supplying telephone service, both at home and abroad. Information about the experiences and practices regarding this matter has been exchanged between the telephone administrations of Europe and the Bell System. These organizations have sponsored investigations by medical authorities and sought advice from public health experts on this matter.

This combined attention, both inside and outside the telephone business, and the experience with millions of telephones used each day for tens of millions of conversations, have not produced one authenticated case of disease transmission by the use of the telephone. While it is doubtless difficult to prove such a transference, it seems reasonable to assume that the billions and billions of chances would have revealed some cases if it were at all likely to occur.

There has also been a third group who have been at times vigorously concerned with this matter in their own financial interests. There are those who have proposed some device which they claimed was required to make the telephone sanitary. There have been others who have had a formula for some solution which if sprayed or otherwise applied to the telephone would temporarily disinfect it and it has been claimed that some of them would keep the telephone sterile for a considerable period of time by killing the germs which reached it. Others in this group have offered a service of having attendants visit telephone stations and disinfect the telephones—for a monthly fee.

Many of these devices—and there have been many—proposed for attachment to the telephone and designated as "antiseptic" or "sanitary" would interfere with the use of

231

the telephone without serving any useful purpose. Some of these devices and some of the designated "antiseptic" or "germicidal" solutions have apparently been based on the idea of creating around the telephone instrument a strong odor which presumably would make the user think the telephone had been disinfected and was sterile as long as the odor remained. Some of the solutions proposed would corrode or otherwise damage the instrument. Doubtless their proponents have thought they were trying to sell something beneficial and worth while.

Others unfortunately have tried to reach the potential market of the millions of telephone users by attempting to arouse fear of all the diseases which they claimed might be picked up by the use of the telephone. In some cases attempts have been made to supplement such a campaign of fear by agitating for legislation requiring disinfection of telephones. Their proposals have not been supported by the authorities responsible for public health who generally have been interested in determining whether the suggested regulations would benefit public health and have been guided by the opinions of experts in that field.

With such agitation and with advertisements in the daily papers trying to support a sales campaign by arousing fear of infection in the use of the telephone, it is not surprising that from time to time many queries come to the Bell System asking for its ideas regarding the possibility of disease being spread by the use of the telephone and the matter of disinfection. One such question in 1933 from a member of the public health staff of a large city was answered as follows—stating the conclusions which had been reached from the previous studies and experience—by Dr. C. H. Watson, Medical Director of the American Telephone and Telegraph Company:

> We are familiar with the article of Saelhof and also some researches of still earlier dates. As you have stated . . ., some of the Companies still make limited use of the formalin solution

at public telephone stations. In most of the Companies, this has been succeeded by a regime providing for reasonable cleanliness. We arrived at this conclusion in view of the growing scepticism on the part of the medical profession to so-called safe germicides when used in concentrations necessary to insure sterility. Furthermore, a high degree of bacterial cleanliness would involve a germicidal procedure after each telephone conversation. It has been felt that institution of cleaning routines should depend on the conditions and particularly apply to the public telephones and pay stations. The use of a clean moist cloth to remove mucous debris, organisms and accumulated dust from the exterior surfaces of the transmitter, particularly those portions liable to come in contact with the face, is considered good practice. It is particularly important, however, that no free moisture be allowed to reach the inner parts of the instrument.

From the Saelhof experiment and those of others, it is apparent that the viability of the pathogenic bacteria largely depends on the presence of such human residues as mucous, moisture, etc., deposited in the act of talking. On the other hand, we feel and the facts seem to bear us out, that the telephone transmitter, even when used improperly, is a relatively insignificant source of contamination. As a matter of fact, the organisms must be transferred by contact from a transmitter surface, to the surface of the individual's face, and because of the diameter of the transmitter aperture, this area must include surfaces close to nose, mouth, lips and cheeks. Again from such points, the organisms must be introduced into nasal passages and mouth by secondary contacts, namely, individual's hands and whatever other means are brought into play during the usual activities. The organisms found by Saelhof are the usual pathogens which constitute a large part of the every-day bacterial flora of the upper air passages. Likewise, these same organisms, together with those of the lower bowel tract, are commonly found on the hands of most of the population, and many of the objects of day to day use with which they come in contact, such as paper money, door-knobs, straps, hand rails, etc. Many of these bacterial contact opportunities are of an equal or greater potentiality than the telephone mouthpiece, particularly those which are associated with hand to mouth, and hand to nose, transmission. Furthermore, we have yet to learn of an authentic instance in

233

all our telephone experience, of an actual case of infection from a telephone transmitter. It would seem that after the many years of telephone use and the millions of exposures, many of which, from what we know, should have been of the most extremely hazardous types, have never brought forth, so far as our records are concerned, an authentic instance of infection.

For that reason, we base our cleanliness procedure on the same reasonable approach which prompts the washing of the hands, the wiping down of hand-rails and other objects with which the community members, particularly in the larger metropolitan districts, are so frequently in contact.

The above statement is a generalization of our feeling in this matter.

A similar statement by Dr. H. E. McSweeny, Medical Director of the New York Telephone Company was published in the New York Times on July 11, 1934.

Investigations by medical and health authorities and the experience of the telephone company indicate that the telephone transmitter is not to be considered as a source of infection. The use of the telephone is not attended by even the slight risk encountered in the case of many objects of daily use with which a person comes in contact.

Germs which may be deposited on such exposed surfaces are generally short-lived. Further, such organisms must be transferred by actual contact from these surfaces to such places as the face and hands of the user and then introduced by further action into the nasal passages or mouth.

If it is desired to clean the telephone mouthpiece, wiping with a cloth is usually adequate and, if necessary, the cloth may be damp. The cloth should not be sufficiently wet to introduce moisture into the transmitter since this may interfere with the operation of the telephone.

Although these conclusions appeared to be well founded by previous investigations and experience, because of the importance of this matter, arrangements were made in 1934 to get further information. It was decided to have two independent investigations by, competent authorities who could bring to this matter the best bacteriological techniques and would represent the expert opinions in the field of public health. On the advice of outstanding authorities in medical research, arrangements were therefore made to have such investigations carried out under the direction of the late Dr. E. O. Jordan,* then Distinguished Service Professor of Bacteriology in the Department of Hygiene and Bacteriology, University of Chicago, and of Dr. Haven Emerson,* Professor of Public Health Practice in the Institute of Public Health, College of Physicians and Surgeons, Columbia University.

Both Dr. Jordan and Dr. Emerson were asked to have carried out under their direction whatever work they considered necessary to enable them to arrive at conclusions as to the possibility of disease transmission in the use of the telephone. One investigation was made in Chicago and the other in New York. Participation of the operating telephone companies in the two localities was limited to arranging access to the telephones which the investigators selected to visit and providing the facilities which they needed.

The bacteriological work under Dr. Jordan was carried out by Dr. S. A. Koser, Associate Professor of Bacteriology, and Dr. J. M. Birkeland, then on the staff of the Department of Hygiene and Bacteriology and since Assistant Professor of Bacteriology at Ohio State University. The independent investigation at Columbia University was undertaken in the De Lamar Institute of Public Health by Dr. C. B. Coulter and Dr. Florence N. Stone.

These two investigations have now been completed and reports made of the bacteriological studies. Those directing the investigations have also made statements as to their conclusions regarding the public health aspects. The report of the Columbia University work has been published in the American Journal of Public Health, October 1937. The report of the University of Chicago work has not as yet been published.

* Brief records of these two men, distinguished in public health and allied fields, are to be found in the 1936–1937 issue of Who's Who in America.

In both studies the general procedure was the same. A bacteriologist went to each of the telephone instruments which he had selected, wiped a sterile moistened swab over the mouthpiece of the telephone transmitter and then in the laboratory made cultures from the swab to determine the kind of bacteria present. In the Chicago study 100 public telephones were so examined in a general search for various kinds of bacteria and 100 additional telephones in a specific search for the presence of tubercle bacilli. In the New York study 246 telephones, most of them public telephones, were so visited and examined. Tests were also made in the laboratories to cover other phases of the problem.

In both studies harmless bacteria were found on many instruments and certain types of disease-causing or pathogenic bacteria were found on some instruments. In the Chicago study no diphtheria, pneumonia or tuberculosis bacteria were found. In the New York study no diphtheria bacteria were found, but some pneumonia types were revealed in the winter and spring months.

In the Chicago study, for the 100 telephone locations included in the general survey, swabbings were made not only from the transmitter mouthpiece but also from the receiver earpiece, the receiver shell and the handle of the door of the booth. The purpose of taking cultures from these four surfaces was to determine the occurrence of bacteria on a surface exposed to the mouth while talking, relative to the occurrence on other surfaces with which contact was made by hand, ear, or other parts of the body. The earpiece surface showed slightly more than the transmitter mouthpiece, while the receiver shell and the door handle which were about equal, showed somewhat less. This would indicate that objects exposed to the mouth when talking are in the same range as repositories for bacteria as objects with which contact is made by other parts of the body.

Also in the Chicago study an investigation was made of the longevity of bacteria deposited on the transmitter mouthpieces. It was found that in general 90 per cent of most kinds of bacteria were dead within one hour and nearly as many within the first 15 minutes. This is supported in the New York study by the finding that "since the number of bacteria which may be recovered from a telephone in constant use is often no greater than the number which may be deposited in a single conversation, it is evident that there is no tendency toward the accumulation of living bacteria on the transmitter." There is also some indication in these studies that the exposure of pathogenic bacteria on the transmitter mouthpiece, causes a material loss in their potency. In the New York study some of the potentially pathogenic streptococci obtained from the surface of the telephone instruments were found in fact to be non-pathogenic for laboratory animals.

In laboratory studies it was found that types of bacteria which were known to be in the mouths and nasal passages of a talker could subsequently appear on the transmitter mouthpiece surface, but this was not always the case.

It was also shown by both groups of investigators that there was relatively small chance of bacteria on the mouthpiece of a transmitter being removed by talking into it or of being picked up by the talker.

The public health conclusions as derived from these studies are best expressed by quoting from letters of Dr. Jordan and Dr. Emerson to Dr. F. B. Jewett, Vice President of the American Telephone and Telegraph Company.

Dr. Jordan's letter of July 31, 1935 reads as follows:

> I am transmitting herewith the report of Professor S. A. Koser and Dr. J. M. Birkeland relating to the possible role of telephones in spreading communicable disease.
>
> Briefly the results of the work are as follows:
>
> I. Bacterial examination of the mouthpieces of frequently used public telephones in various parts of the city of Chicago

showed, as might be expected, the presence of bacteria. These belonged chiefly to the types commonly found in air and dust, and, as appears in Table 1 (page 6), were not noticeably different in kind from those present on the door knobs of the telephone booths. Although intensive search was made for diphtheria bacilli and pneumococci, these microörganisms were never found. No tubercle bacilli were found, either by cultural methods or by animal inoculation. The reason for what may appear the rather surprising scarcity of respiratory tract organisms is explained in the following sections.

II. Laboratory experiments were devised to determine the longevity of bacteria smeared in large numbers directly on the mouthpiece. These observations showed that the common pathogenic organisms perish quickly under these conditions, over 90 per cent of most kinds dying within one hour and nearly as many within the first 15 minutes. This is in accord with general bacteriological experience that the life of most disease germs outside the animal body is very brief. The tubercle bacillus is well known to be more resistant to drying than many other bacteria, but even as regards this organism it is evident that considerable reduction in numbers takes place early. In all such experiments it is well known that a few especially resistant cells may survive for a number of days. It need hardly be pointed out that the bacterial contamination of the mouthpieces in these experiments is far greater than would be likely to occur in the practical daily use of any public telephone. The rapid death of respiratory tract bacteria outside the body is undoubtedly one reason why few of these organisms are found on telephone mouthpieces in constant use.

III. The possibility of transferring bacteria from mouth or throat to telephone mouthpieces in the course of conversation was tested in a variety of ways with the result that occasional transfer could be readily demonstrated. It was of particular interest, however, that with large numbers of test organisms in the mouth and throat and with telephone conversations lasting three minutes and sometimes longer, immediate examination of the mouthpieces frequently failed to reveal the transfer of any of the test organisms. After the use of the telephones for a conversation of two minutes by a demonstrated carrier of diphtheria bacilli no diphtheria bacilli were recovered from the mouthpiece.

238

IV. Experiments to determine the possibility of transfer of bacteria from telephone mouthpieces to the mouth of persons using the telephones showed that when the lips, cheek or fingers did not come into direct contact with the freshly inoculated mouthpiece no transfer of the test organisms occurred.

The conclusions that may be legitimately drawn from the experiments by Professor Koser and Dr. Birkeland, just summarized, together with previous experiments on this and similar problems, are as follows:

1. Numerous opportunities exist for picking up bacteria, including some disease germs, from our surroundings. Every city-dweller is likely to come in actual contact many times a day with bacteria on such objects as door knobs, chair arms, books, coins and paper money, playing cards, street car straps and the like, as well as on telephones. Some of these germs may be from the human alimentary tract or respiratory tract. It is practically impossible to avoid all or most of these contacts. Practice of personal hygiene, such as handwashing before meals and the avoidance of contacts between fingers and nose or mouth, seems the only effective way of protection against this possibility of disease transmission.

2. It is well recognized by sanitarians that whatever may be the danger of disease transmission from inanimate objects it is far less than from the living human carrier of infection. The role of paper money, of public library books, of articles of furniture in rooms used by diphtheria or scarlet fever patients, in spreading infection has been studied by a number of workers and has never been shown to be very important. Routine terminal disinfection or fumigation after all cases of infectious disease has now been quite generally abandoned by health authorities since it has not been found effective in reducing the amount of new infection. In Providence, R. I., for example, the records show that the number of new diphtheria cases occurring among 1457 families in which fumigation was practised after a case of diphtheria was 1.71 per cent, while in 3000 families without fumigation the proportion of new cases was almost exactly the same (1.8 per cent).

3. With respect to the particular danger from telephone instruments, the infectious hazard seems no greater than from scores of other objects. Bacteria from the mouth that may be

deposited occasionally on the telephone mouthpiece are of course not dislodged by air currents. While direct contact with lips or fingers may remove bacteria from any surface, this occurrence is entirely under individual control.

Taking into consideration the relatively small numbers of bacteria transmitted from the mouth to the telephone mouthpieces and their short life in this situation, and also the evidence that disease germs on the mouthpieces of much used public telephones are certainly not common and probably exceedingly rare, and having in mind the fact that contact with fingers, lips or tongue is a matter within the control of the individual as completely as the tongue-moistening of postage stamps, it is my belief that routine disinfection of all public telephones would not be a justifiable public health requirement. To be of any conceivable practical value such disinfection would have to be carried out after each use of the instrument. Even so there would remain so many other sources of contact for every active city-dweller that the effect of such disinfection on the spread of disease would in my opinion be negligible.

This is supplemented by a subsequent statement from Dr. Jordan's letter of April 20, 1936.

The bacteria found on the telephone receiver do not seem to me important from the public health standpoint. They are obviously mainly rubbed off from the skin or hair and are probably protected somewhat against drying by a slight oiliness. My conclusion that routine disinfection of public telephones would not be a justifiable public health requirement applies to the receiver as well as to the transmitter.

The following statement is taken from the letter of September 23, 1937 written by Dr. Haven Emerson:

Now that the publication of the report by Drs. Coulter and Stone on their bacteriological studies on the public telephone is assured in the American Journal of Public Health for October, you will, I trust, permit me to express on behalf of our staff as well as for myself individually, our appreciation of the conditions under which you made the grant for this work available.

The entire independence of those engaged in the studies both in the manner and content of the work and in the deductions drawn from it has been at all times assured by your request that the matter be approached with scientific objectivity.

It will appear, I believe, to any one trained in sanitary science and epidemiology, as it does to all of us here, that the findings of the bacteriologists amply confirm the generally held belief that the occasional contact by ear, hand and mouth, with one or other part of the telephone receiver or transmitter adds no hazard or risk of infection to the user or to the community, which does not exist in a multitude of other more direct, frequent and widely spread exposures due to usual human activity and relationships.

Fresh and dried discharges from the upper respiratory tract may spread various of the communicable diseases, but the chance of such conveyance of disease by healthy carriers, or by unrecognized or incipient or convalescent spreaders of pathogenic organisms through the use of the public telephone appears too remote to justify personal or official action in the interest of health protection, other than the usual precautions of ordinary cleanliness and a proper consideration of public decency.

As a result of conferences and staff discussions following the presentation of the Coulter-Stone report and with the study by Dr. Jordan's colleagues, Dr. J. M. Birkeland and Professor S. A. Koser in hand, my associates here, Professor Earle B. Phelps and Dr. M. L. Isaacs of the Department of Sanitary Sciences and I have expressed our combined opinion on the matter at issue as follows:

Health officers of some of the larger cities and of some states in North Eastern United States have within recent years been subject to pressure of a commercial and political nature, to persuade them to initiate official control of the public telephone instrument as if it were a substantial sanitary hazard contributing to the spread of those communicable diseases transmitted by discharges of the nose and throat.

Critical analysis of the evidence for and against the existence of such a hazard has been lacking until now because of the inadequacy of the bacteriological information offered and the uncertainty as to the reliability of the technical procedures used in discovery of the kinds and numbers of bacteria obtained from either the receiver or transmitter apparatus of the telephone instrument.

241

The painstaking studies reported by Coulter and Stone, and Koser and Birkeland, represent an important advance in our knowledge of the situation which may be summarized briefly as follows:

Bacteria of wide variety are to be found on the telephone mouthpieces with but little relation to the frequency and conditions of use of the instruments. Among these the saprophytes ordinarily found on all articles exposed to general air circulation predominate. Cocci of numerous pneumococcus and a streptococcus varieties are also found. Some of these are recognized as being pathogenic and might give rise to human infection if inhaled or removed by lip contact in sufficiently large doses by persons with a relatively low resistance to the particular strains in question.

Some of the potential streptococcus pathogens obtained from the surface of telephone instruments were found in fact to be non-pathogenic for laboratory animals.

The process of talking in a telephone mouthpiece removes but very few of the bacteria which may have been recently deposited by a previous use of the instrument.

Until the requirement and technique of our ordinary conduct of life has gone far beyond any present common practice, the telephone mouthpiece will continue to create no greater sanitary hazard than that of the hand rail, the door knob, and articles in frequent contact with human hands and exposed to airborne dust.

No sanitary code authority and no time, money or personnel of health departments should be applied in a vain hope that communicable disease will be to any extent reduced by some theoretically possible but practically futile compulsory anti-bacterial measure intended to make the telephone instrument even occasionally or intermittently sterile.

With the bacteriologist's facts and resources available to us, and no epidemiological evidence running counter to their conclusions, it ought not to be possible for legislatures, city councils, or boards of health to be forced into injudicious and profitless sanitary regulation of the public telephone.

These conclusions of Dr. Jordan and Dr. Emerson that the telephone is unimportant from the standpoint of public health are of interest to many—to the large telephone using public and also to those responsible for providing telephone service. To the latter, it is gratifying to know that the current bacteriological and public health findings confirm the past opinions and experience that the telephone instrument has no greater potentiality in transmitting disease than the many other objects of daily use. To the telephone users, and particularly those to whom this may have been a matter of concern, it should be reassuring to have authoritative advice that, as regards the possibility of transmitting disease, they can treat the telephone as they do other objects with which they come in daily contact. Furthermore it is well recognized that such inanimate objects are far less important in public health considerations than exposure to and contact with human carriers of infection.

W. H. MARTIN

The Origin and Development of Radiotelephony

(A paper presented before the Institute of Radio Engineers, May 10, 1937)

UPON this, the Silver Anniversary of the Institute of Radio Engineers, it is appropriate to recall how there came into being the art of radiotelephony and, in turn, such services as overseas telephony and broadcasting. The Institute has seen the entire evolution within its relatively short life, with radiotelephony an unsolved problem in 1912 and today an accomplished fact of world-wide application.

The pages of the Institute Proceedings testify to much of the building of the art, but nowhere has there been given a unified account of the structure as a whole and the relation of its technical substance to electric communications generally. To do this objectively and while the development is still fresh in mind is the purpose of the present paper. Naturally, the story is limited by space and by the information available to the writer. Most of the account pertains to America. If the contributions of other countries are not adequately presented, it is because the limitations of time, space and language have not yet been entirely overcome.

BACKGROUND IN THE PHYSICAL SCIENCES

It is well to acknowledge, in the first place, the debt which radio owes to the more fundamental contributions from the physical sciences, the more pertinent ones of which, underlying as they do the entire art of electric communications, may be epitomized as three major waves of advance:

The great transition which occurred in the early 1800's from the electrostatic to the electric current and electromagnetic state of electrical science, which led to the telegraph and later to the telephone (to say nothing of electric power).

The conception and demonstration of electromagnetic wave propagation and electric oscillations, notably by Maxwell and Hertz. This advance applied to guided as well as un-guided wave propagation, and is the basis of the transmission art of both wire and wireless communication.

The proof of the corpuscular nature of electricity and its identity with matter, the basis of twentieth century physics and of electronics.

EARLY EXPERIMENTS

It happens that an early attempt at transmitting speech without wires was made by the inventor of the telephone himself, Alexander Graham Bell. Back in the 1880's he sent speech over a beam of light, using reflectors in much the same way that ultra-short waves are directed today. He called the system the "photophone." Mercardier rechristened it the "radio-phone" because it employed frequencies not limited to the visible range, and here we have the earliest use of the word "radio" in the sense employed today.

Of course, the more direct forerunners of radiotelephony were wire telephony and wireless telegraphy. The transmission side of both these arts came out of the early work of Maxwell and Hertz, but they developed for many years quite independently, because of the great difference in the transmission frequencies involved. Early attempts at carrier-current telephony and telegraphy over wires, involving frequencies of tens of thousands of cycles and utilizing modulation, frequency-selecting circuits and detection, were unsuccessful because of the lack of suitable technique even for those frequencies, and were in general unknown to later wireless telegraph experimenters. The devices with which Marconi initiated practical wireless telegraphy were adapted to frequencies of the order of a million cycles, generated discontinuously by means of sparks. In time wireless telegraphy evolved toward the use of continuous waves and, by such means as the high-frequency alternator and the oscillating arc, bridged the gap between the radio and the wire frequency ranges.

In the period of 1906–1912 radiotelephony was an experimental fact but a practical non-reality. Many were the early experimenters who had succeeded in transmitting speech over distances of some miles, notably Fessenden and De Forest in America, and Majorana, Vanni and Poulsen in Europe. In 1911 General Squier, of the U. S. Signal Corps, brought widespread attention to the possible application of the then wireless instrumentalities to high-frequency transmission over wires.

But radiotelephony remained for the radio experimenter a golden goal of attainment, for there were wanting practicable means for generating the high-frequency currents, for controlling them in accordance with the relatively weak waves of speech and for renewing at the receiving end the waves so greatly weakened in transit. The story which follows of the successful meeting of these problems, principally by means of the vacuum tube, is broken by the incidence of the Great War into three periods.

THE FORMATIVE PERIOD OF 1912–1916

In retrospect, it is now apparent that by about the time of the formation of the Institute the general front of technical advance had reached the point of almost inevitably yielding the solution of the radiotelephone problem. The two-element and three-element vacuum tubes existed, knowledge of thermionics and means for attaining higher vacuua were accumulating, coupled tuned circuits were well known, and in wire telephony the basis had been laid in the loaded-line theory for the electric wave filter and circuit network philosophy. But lest the attainment of radiotelephony seem too easy, let us follow in a little more detail how the structure of the art was built. The scene is placed in America principally, for it was here that De

Forest was experimenting with his three-element audion tube, that telephony generally was developing apace, and that certain research laboratories were working upon problems which needed the tube.

The High-Vacuum Tube

Dr. Lee De Forest invented the three-element tube in 1906–1907, but it was not until about 1912 that he succeeded in adapting it under some circuit conditions to operate as a true amplifier. In the fall of that year he and an associate, John Stone Stone, demonstrated the audion to engineers of the Bell System in the role of an audio amplifier, a candidate for the solution of the telephone repeater problem. The device was still a weak and imperfect thing, had in the grid circuit the familiar blocking condenser of the audion detector, and was incapable of carrying any considerable voice load without blue hazing; yet, it *was* capable of amplifying speech.

Among those in the telephone laboratory who witnessed De Forest's demonstration was one H. D. Arnold, then fresh from the study of electron physics in Dr. Millikan's laboratory of the University of Chicago. Whereas there had always been confusion of thought concerning the effect of gas upon the operation of the audion, Arnold immediately recognized that what was wanted was a pure thermionic effect, free of gas complications. He set to work to produce a higher-vacuum tube, using evacuation methods then only recently available. He succeeded and, once and for all, took the three-element tube out of the realm of uncertainty and unreliability and made of it a definite, reliable, amplifying tool.

About the same time that Arnold was doing this in the laboratories of the telephone company, principally in 1913, Langmuir, in the laboratories of the General Electric Company, studying the problem of x-ray tubes and power rectifiers, arrived at substantially the same result. In a patent contest lasting many years the Supreme Court of the United States gave to Arnold the credit of having been the first to attain the truly high-vacuum tube and agreed with Arnold's original viewpoint, that this step, important though it was, did not constitute invention over the prior art.

By the time the high-vacuum tube was obtained several gaseous forms of tubes had appeared. One of these was of the mercury-vapor type, employing magnetic control, which was being worked upon by Arnold as a telephone repeater at the time the audion was first called to his attention. Another was the tube of von Lieben and Reisz, of Austria and Germany, which employed a grid element. All such gaseous devices were soon eclipsed by the high-vacuum tube.

The high-vacuum tube was further improved in 1913 by the application to it of Wehnelt's oxide-coated cathode. The filament electron emission was thereby increased, producing the dull-emitter type of long-life tube. The vacuum tube in this form, stable, with adequate filament emission and long life, set the pace in the amplifier art from that time forward and was the practical basis of the succession of further developments which resulted in practical radiotelephony. One of De Forest's audions and one of the early high-vacuum telephone repeater tubes are pictured in Figure 1.

Oscillator

One of the next developments was, of course, the conversion of the vacuum tube amplifier into a generator of high-frequency currents. This was accomplished first by De Forest in 1912, according to a decision of the United States Supreme Court. Others did it independently about the same time, notably Armstrong here and Meissner in Germany. Armstrong's 1915 Institute paper upon the subject was a notable one, as was evidenced by the demand for the issue of the Proceedings in which it appeared. Particular forms of oscillating vacuum-tube circuits were developed by other investigators, including

C. S. Franklin and H. J. Round, of the British Marconi Company, and Colpitts and Hartley, in the United States.

The earliest uses known to have been made of the oscillator in radiotelephony are the experiments of Meissner in Germany in 1913, between Berlin and Nauen, using the von Lieben-Reisz tube, and of H. J. Round, of England, early in 1914, in experimental transmission between two ships.

Modulator

Another major step, the invention of the vacuum-tube modulator, soon followed.   This solved the problem of enabling low-power voice energy to control the considerably higher-power waves required for radiotelephone transmitting, and enable this control to be exercised remotely over a telephone line, thereby giving through transmission between wire and radio circuits.   The earlier attempts at radiotelephony had depended for modulation upon the carbon microphone, usually worked directly in the antenna-ground circuit.   Here, again, we have a case of several investigators arriving at the invention at about the same time, 1913–1914, with Alexanderson, of the General Electric Company, and Colpitts, of the telephone laboratories, sharing the honors.   Other modulating circuits followed.   The telephone engineers had in mind doing the modulating at low power and then amplifying the modulated current by means of a high-frequency amplifier.

High-Frequency Vacuum-Tube Telephony

By the latter half of 1914 there was within grasp in the telephone laboratories sufficient of the high-frequency technique, based upon the high-vacuum tube, to cause the telephone engineers to set about the development of high-frequency telephone systems.   The first attempt was at the wire carrier-current problem.   A two-channel multiplex system was set up using vacuum-tube oscillators, modulators, amplifiers and detectors.   The result was decidedly encouraging.   Since the

249

same instrumentalities were applicable to radiotelephony, there was next undertaken the development of a vacuum-tube radio-telephone system.

These early wire carrier-current and experimental systems proved to be the precursors of our modern art. They mark a climax in what is perhaps the most rapid accretion of technique known in modern electric communications, from the condition, in the fore part of 1912, of there being no suitable generator nor modulator, to that of 1914–15 where these essentials had become available and were being synthesized into operative high-frequency telephone systems.

Long-Distance Tests of 1915

Vacuum-tube radiotelephony was now to be taken out of the laboratory for a field trial. A vacuum-tube transmitter of a few watts output was developed and installed at Montauk Point, Long Island, and an amplifying receiver was located at Wilmington Delaware, 200-odd miles distant. The distance was then stretched to some 600 miles by receiving the Montauk transmitter at St. Simons Island, off the coast of Georgia. These were one-way transmissions. For some of them the reception was brought back to New York by wire lines. The speech was itself clear, but was sometimes buried in noise due to the small transmitting power and the fact that it was the spring of the year. Wavelengths of 800 to 1800 meters were employed.

The success of these preliminary tests, together with the promise of laboratory developments for higher-power trans-mitting tubes, now led to a bold attempt on the part of the telephone engineers to overcome that great natural barrier of telephony, the oceans. Through the cooperation of the United States Navy Department, on the one hand, and the French Administration, on the other, appropriate field stations were made available for the tests. The large antenna of the naval station at Arlington, Virginia, was used for transmitting. A new vacuum-tube radiotelephone transmitter was developed, employing hundreds of tubes, each having a capacity of the order of 15 watts, and installed at Arlington. For reception the Navy Department made available their stations at the Canal Zone, on the Pacific Coast and in Hawaii. Through the kindness of Gen. Ferrié, of the French Administration, use of the Eiffel Tower station was permitted the American telephone engineers for receiving purposes. Thus did the French collaborate in the interest of technical advance and international good will by accepting foreign engineers in their most important military station during the life-and-death struggle of the Great War.

By June all the distant receiving points were covered by engineers who had been dispatched from New York provided with the then latest receiving apparatus; the new telephone transmitter had been installed at Arlington; a great effort was being made in the laboratories to produce the necessary quantity and quality of power tubes. The tests continued on and off during the entire summer on a reduced power basis, during which the difficult atmospheric conditions were studied by the receiving engineers. As the conditions improved with the coming of fall and as the transmitting power was built up, results began to be obtained, first, from Panama; next, from the Pacific Coast, representing transmission across the continent; then, from more distant Hawaii; and, finally, in November from Paris, where the receiving conditions had proven to be most difficult.

These were, of course, one-way transmissions. The reception was so uncertain and so subject to noise as to make it evident that the art would need to be advanced greatly before the requirements of a service could be met over such long distances.

Some of the technical features of the apparatus of these early tests were:

In the transmitting station, the use of the master-oscillator, power-amplifier type of circuit, operating in the 30 to 100-

kilocycle range, with circuits designed to accommodate the "carrier and sideband" aspect of the modulated wave.

The development of power tubes of the order of fifteen watts, requiring new designs and more thorough pumping and degassing.

The operation of large numbers of tubes in parallel (as many as 500), in order to build up the necessary transmitting power. The problem of operating these tubes in parallel and preventing singing can well be imagined. An average power of two or three kilowatts was obtained in the antenna. A photograph of two banks of 250 tubes each is reproduced in Figure 2, the tips of some of the tubes showing on the right.

Receivers employing a radio-frequency amplifying stage, plus two audio-frequency stages. Heterodyne detection was employed to find the carrier. Homodyne reception of the telephone signals was used at some of the receiving points.

The following year, 1916, tests of radiotelephony were made for the United States Navy, which included what is believed to have been the first attempt at tying together radio and wire lines for through two-way radiotelephony. The Secretary of the Navy, Josephus Daniels, talked from his desk in Washington, D. C., with the master of the *U. S. S. New Hampshire,* off the Chesapeake Capes. During this year Heising devised his now well-known "constant current" system of modulation, the simplicity of which led to its use in the radiotelephone sets which were produced during the war and in the early radio-broadcast transmitters. Incidentally, early in this same year there was undertaken anew the problem of carrier-current telephony and telegraphy, this time looking toward commercial designs, utilizing the newly acquired instrumentalities of the vacuum-tube and the electric wave filter. The application of the vacuum-tube amplifier to voice-frequency telephone circuits was also proceeding apace.

Radiotelephony was now progressing rapidly, building upon and, in turn, stimulating its antecedent and contemporary arts of wire telephony, wireless telegraphy and electronics. Something of the content of these related arts is indicated below:

ARTS UNDERLYING RADIOTELEPHONY

Wire Telephony	Wireless Telegraphy	Electronics
Electroacoustics Transmitters, receivers, characteristics of sound, high-quality reproduction	Generators and receivers of high-frequency currents; selective circuits.	Discovery and study of the electron (Crookes, J. J. Thomson and others).
Wire Transmission Propagation constant, characteristic impedance, transmission measurement, interference, carrier, wave filters and network theory.	Antennas Dipole (Hertz), grounded (Marconi). directive.	Thermionics (Richardson, Wehnelt and others).
	Wave Propagation Spreading and absorption, ground and sky waves, effects of solar and meteorological phenomena.	The Edison effect and the Fleming valve.
Amplification Microphone, repeaters.		De Forest 3-electrode tube. High-vacuum, high-power and multi-electrode tubes.

THE WAR PERIOD

The war came to Europe before the new vacuum tube art and radiotelephony had been fully born. Vacuum tubes were employed in the war by the European countries for radiotelegraphy, but radiotelephony is not known to have played a part on the continent. This may have been due in part to the lack of secrecy of this form of communication.

In the United States the normal development of radiotelephony continued, as we have seen, up to the time of this country's entry into the war. The new vacuum-tube radiotelephony had by then assumed real promise. The United States Government undertook to develop two-way radiotelephone sets on a large scale for dispatch purposes on submarine chasers and airplanes. In the short space of a year or so hundreds of thousands of tubes and thousands of sets were developed and manufactured. Several of the larger laboratories of the country were in effect taken over by the government for this purpose. The apparatus was featured technically by:

The general use of the high-vacuum, oxide-coated filament type
of tube.

Employment of the constant-current type of modulation.

The attempt to make the operation of the sets simple and fool-
proof, as by the elimination of filament rheostat and the
standardizing of tubes and circuits to permit of ready inter-
changeability.

Such apparatus was used in some quantity on submarine
chasers of the Navy, but the large production program for airplanes was not completed in time to enable radiotelephony to
come into play in the Army on the battle front. From the
technical standpoint the program stimulated apparatus design
and gave a useful experience in the standardization and quantity production of tubes.

Through the many military training schools in the United
States the new vacuum-tube radiotelephone art was "broadcast" to the most likely young men of the country, many of
whom developed a real interest and after the war helped to
swell the peacetime development.

POST-WAR DEVELOPMENTS

The peacetime development of the art was now immediately
renewed, especially in the United States where the technical
effort had been sustained through the war. It became evident
to the several large companies which were pursuing the vacuum-tube art, particularly the American Telephone and Telegraph Company and the General Electric Company, that their
inventions so interleaved as to require an exchange of patent
rights. This took the form of an inter-licensing agreement,
entered into between these two companies in 1920. It enabled
the telephone company to use tubes on its lines and to proceed
with the development of two-way radiotelephony. The General Electric Company and its affiliates, including the Radio
Corporation of America, were free to proceed in other fields,

principally radiotelegraphy, and, as it turned out, in broadcasting.

Early Ship-to-Shore Telephone Experiments

The telephone company had by this time undertaken development work in marine radiotelephony, partly as a means of advancing the art and partly with an eye toward the eventual establishment of a mobile public telephone service connecting with the land line system.   Experimental shore stations were provided (one of which, that at Deal Beach, New Jersey, is shown in Figure 3), and ship apparatus capable of duplex operation was devised and tested on coastal vessels and on one of the transatlantic liners.   This work was done in the frequency range then most available, that of the order of a million cycles.   Shortly thereafter broadcasting preempted this range and because of this and of the post-war depression in shipping, these experiments did not then materialize into a service. Trial connections with the land line network extending across the continent and to Catalina Island served to demonstrate the possibilities of combined wire and radio working.   Some of the technical attainments in this work were:

The development of duplex systems for ship use.

The development of superheterodyne receivers.

Progress in placing radio transmission upon a quantitative basis by the measurement of received field strengths and the overall circuit equivalent of radio links, and in the setting up of radio links as integral parts of long landline connections.

The beginning of the volume indicator, used to insure the voice loading of the radio transmitter and later employed extensively on wires, as well as in radio.

First Public Telephone Service by Radio

Another pioneering undertaking about this time, 1920, was the development of what proved to be the first use of radio-

255

telephony for public service, in the form of a point-to-point link on the Pacific Coast between Catalina Island and Long Beach on the mainland, connecting thence to Los Angeles. Service was given over this link for about a year, when the frequency band being used was wanted for the then newly developing service of broadcasting. The telephone service itself came near being a broadcast one, so extensively were the conversations listened to by amateur radio enthusiasts. The system was replaced by a submarine cable.

From the standpoint of technical progress, this installation included a number of interesting features:

Full-duplex operation in the sense of separate channels for the two directions of transmission, joined at the terminals to the two-wire telephone network by means of hybrid coils.

Through voice-frequency ringing, the first application to radio.

Superheterodyne receiving sets, incorporating wave filters in the intermediate frequency stages which separated out:

A telegraph channel which was superimposed upon, i.e., multiplexed with, the telephone channel and used independently for telegraph service with the Island.

The provision toward the end of the period of means for rendering the telephone transmission private, comprising voice inverters, plus carrier-frequency wobbling, the first installation of this combination to have been made.

The picture of the Long Beach receiver in Figure 4 shows at the top a portion of the loop receiving antenna; in center foreground, the circuit control desk; above, to the right, the speech inverter for privacy; and, in the left background, the apparatus of the superimposed telegraph channel.

Broadcasting

By 1920–1921 the stage was set in the United States for radiobroadcasting. A radiotelephone technique was becoming available in the relatively empty portion of the frequency range centering about one megacycle. Something of an audience

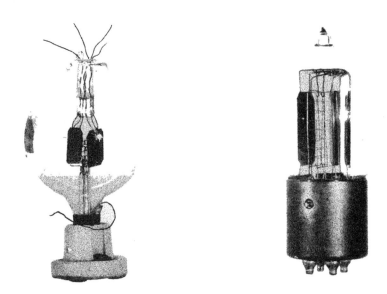

FIG. 1. ONE OF DeFOREST'S AUDIONS AND AN EARLY HIGH-VACUUM TELEPHONE REPEATER TUBE OF TWENTY-FIVE YEARS AGO.

FIG. 2. AT THE RIGHT OF THE PICTURE ARE SOME OF THE 500 TRANSMITTING AMPLIFIER TUBES USED TO PROJECT THE FIRST HUMAN VOICE ACROSS THE ATLANTIC IN 1915.

FIG 3   AN EXPERIMENTAL SHORE STATION FOR MARINE RADIOTELEPHONY WAS ESTABLISHED AT DEAL BEACH, N J SHORTLY AFTER THE CLOSE OF THE WORLD WAR

FIG. 4.   THE FIRST USE OF RADIOTELEPHONY FOR PUBLIC SERVICE—LONG BEACH, CALIF., RECEIVER FOR CONVERSATION WITH CATALINA ISLAND IN 1920

FIG. 5. HISTORIC SCENE AT THE ORIGINAL TRANSMITTER OF KDKA ON THE OCCASION OF ITS FIRST CAST, THE PRESIDENTIAL ELECTION ON NOVEMBER 2, 1920

FIG. 6 ONE OF THE FIRST 5000 WATT, WATER-COOLED TRANSMITTERS USED IN STATION WEAF

Fig. 7. Powerful Water-Cooled Radio Telephone Amplifier Installed in 1922 at Rocky Point, L. I., for Transatlantic Experiments which Culminated in Commercial Service in 1927.

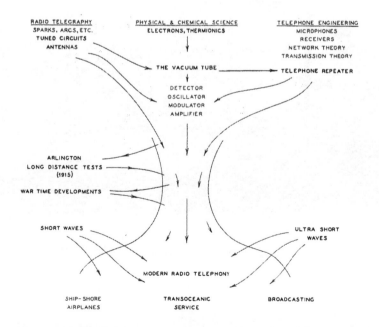

existed in the thousands of amateur radiotelegraphists spread throughout the country, a lively public interest in radiotelephony had been aroused during the war, and all that was needed to excite the public generally into providing itself with receiving apparatus was to have the experience of hearing speech and music on the air. These essential elements of an appropriate technique and of a widespread audience were lacking in the earlier years when De Forest and others broadcast speech and music upon a number of occasions with considerable success.

Public interest was first fanned by amateur listening to the experimental telephone transmissions being conducted by various people, amateur and professional. Engineers in making tests frequently availed themselves of reports written in by listeners, as a means of checking in a general way the effectiveness of their transmitters. For example, in the fall of 1919, tests made between New York and Cliffwood, New Jersey, of a pair of 500-watt transmitters intended for shipment to China, were reported by many amateur listeners. Tests of ship-to-shore radiotelephony, which were being made on more or less regular schedules from Deal Beach, New Jersey, were listened to and reported by hundreds of amateurs throughout the eastern part of the country. In the vicinity of Los Angeles listening to the radiotelephone link to Catalina Island was becoming enough of an indoor sport to be embarrassing to the public telephone service, as has been mentioned.

Of all the experimental activity at the time, it happened to fall to the personal efforts of Frank Conrad, an engineer of the Westinghouse Electric and Manufacturing Company, at Pittsburgh, to give rise to broadcasting of a continuing nature. Starting with transmissions from his home, the activity was taken up by his company, which had been engaged during the war in making radio apparatus for the government, and the experimental emissions were evolved into a continuing program, accompanied by the entering of the company into

257

the business of supplying receiving sets. The original transmitter of the now well-known station of KDKA is pictured in Figure 5 as it appeared on the occasion of its first broadcasting, when it sent out the returns of the presidential election on November 2, 1920. Note that the room which housed the transmitter served also as the studio. Public interest mounted rapidly and within a few years transmitting stations were growing up throughout the country and a boom was on in receiving sets. So great was the demand for transmitting station equipment that the telephone company was called upon to provide what proved to be most of the installations in these earlier days.

This great burst of activity brought with it real concern as to the character which broadcasting might assume and as to how it could be supported as a continuing service. As it was a form of telephony, the telephone company undertook to explore the field from the sending end by engaging in broadcast transmitting. There evolved the idea of putting the transmitter at the disposal of others for hire (toll broadcasting), the sponsored program, and arrangements for the syndication of programs over the wire telephone network. Thus was demonstrated the ability to support broadcasting from the sending end.

One of the first 5-kw, water-cooled transmitters, that was used in the telephone company's Station WEAF in 1924, is shown in Figure 6. Aside from representing an advanced design at the time, this transmitter is associated with an interesting bit of technical history. A 500-watt transmitter, which had been used just before it, had shown bad quality when received in certain outlying sections of the city on the far side of groups of skyscrapers. This gave rise to the making of one of the first studies of the broadcast transmission medium, including the element of fading and of coverage. The trouble proved to be due to the effect of the tall buildings in attenuating the direct transmission and making apparent interference between multiple paths. The effect of the interference upon quality proved to be exaggerated by a degree of frequency modulation occurring in the transmitter. The latter trouble was removed by the adoption in the 5-kw transmitter of the master-oscillator type of circuit, employing piezo-electric crystal control, one of the first transmitters so provided.

The intimate technical relationship which existed between broadcasting and telephony in general is shown also in the high-quality side of broadcasting, involving studio acoustics, high-quality microphone pickup and high-quality amplifiers. In the beginning of broadcasting the pickup and amplifying means were taken more or less bodily from the high-quality speech-study work which had been going on in the telephone laboratories, and from public address systems. In 1919 a great public address demonstration had been made in New York upon the occasion of a Liberty Loan; and in the summer of 1920 such systems had played a prominent part in the two national political conventions. Addresses delivered over such systems from a distance emphasized the need for high-quality lines. As a result of such experience and the considerable amplifier-network technique which had been built up in the long-distance telephone field, it was possible at an early stage of broadcasting to adapt telephone lines to handle as wide a sound-frequency band as the economics of the situation justified.

Broadcast Receivers

A realization of the progress which has been made in broadcast receivers is had by contrasting the modern, stable and selective loudspeaker set with the ticklish crystal or regenerative battery set with which listeners first heard whispers in head-phones. One of the first advances was to the high-frequency amplifying set, whereby sensitivity was achieved together with simplicity of adjustment. The stabilizing of these sets against singing stimulated the art of tube-balancing circuits and is remembered by Hazeltine's neutrodyne. The superheterodyne, the indirectly-heated cathode tube permitting operation from the a-c supply mains, the screen-grid tube, automatic gain control, featured the rapidly evolving receiving-set technique. Loudspeakers progressed from the old horn type to the armature-driven cone, to the electrodynamic, and multiple-unit system. While many of these advances had their origin elsewhere than in broadcasting, certainly the quantity production of broadcast receiving sets has been a powerful leaven in advancing the weak-current technique generally.

Transoceanic Telephony

As broadcasting was getting started, continuing research in the telephone laboratory gave promise of considerably greater transmitting powers, in the form of the copper-anode, water-cooled tube. This and the other advances which had occurred since the original transoceanic experiments of 1915 indicated that it might be timely again to undertake the problem of extending telephony overseas.

A powerful water-cooled amplifier, the first of its kind, was developed and in 1922, in cooperation with the Radio Corporation of America, was installed at the transatlantic transmitting station at Rocky Point, Long Island. It is pictured in Figure 7. Success attended the first objective of developing an antenna power of the order of 100 kilowatts and the transatlantic project was vigorously pushed. This work being in the then relatively low frequencies, it was possible to adopt single-side-band, carrier-suppressed transmission by borrowing that feature more or less bodily from the wire art, whereby the transmitting effectiveness was multiplied by a factor of about ten. The transmitting path to England was studied by making measurements there, in collaboration with the engineers of the British Post Office, of the diurnal and seasonal variations received and of the noise levels. A further improvement was obtained by borrowing from the wireless telegraph art the newly-developed directive antenna known as the Beverage wave antenna. There were, of course, other problems in getting started, and these and the manner in which service was established, beginning in 1927, and, in time, extended by the use of high frequencies, are told in a companion paper entitled "Transoceanic Telephone Developments," by Ralph Bown.

Higher Frequencies and Mobile Services

The extension of radio to the higher frequencies, or shorter waves, gave new opportunity for the development of radio telephone services because of the greater message-carrying capacity of the higher frequencies and the greater transmission range.

Following the introduction of short waves to transatlantic telephony, the ship-to-shore problem was undertaken anew on a short-wave basis and service was initiated on the North Atlantic in 1929. On the shore end the essential facilities comprised a duplicate of one of the transatlantic point-to-point installations, including directive antennas pointing out along the transatlantic shipping route, and means for effecting two-way operation and for connecting into the wire network. The ship installation included a transmitter of 500 watts capacity, employing a new screen-grid power tube. As a result of "stay noise," there was adopted the "cut carrier" method of transmission. Most of the larger vessels are permanently equipped for service and marine telephone service is being given from both sides of the Atlantic.

A related form of marine telephone service is that to small boats. In the United States this started somewhat as a continuance by the Coast Guard of the submarine chaser installations of the war. In Europe fishing trawlers have been provided with simple radio telephone sets in considerable numbers. In these installations the intention has been to enable the boats to talk with each other and with certain land stations; not with the land line telephone users. Small-boat telephony linked with the land line network is a more difficult matter. It is now under active development in the United States on both the East and West Coasts, and on the Great Lakes, and in some countries in Europe. The installations in the United States are of crystal-controlled sets, designed to be used directly by the officer of the ship without technical attendance. Many of the ships are equipped to be "rung" selectively as wanted by the shore station. The small-boat telephony works generally in the medium-frequency range of two to three megacycles.

Another type of mobile service is that being used throughout the airways of the United States in maintaining contact between the planes and the ground stations. Telephony has proven particularly useful here because of the facility it offers the pilots of communicating directly on a two-way basis with ground stations. The service is operated generally in the three to six megacycle portion of the spectrum. The apparatus is crystal-controlled, of special design for lightness, simplicity of operation and reliability. This type of service was well started about 1929.

A third type of mobile radiotelephone service, and one which has become quite important in the United States, is that of the various city and state police departments, used to direct patrol cars. Most of these services are limited to one-way talking to the cars, and operate on intermediate frequencies. Now that ultra-high frequencies are becoming available, some of these systems are being extended to two-way service. The apparatus is generally similar to that employed in the aviation service.

Ultra-High Frequencies

The recent extension of the radio technique to ultra-high frequencies brings new opportunities and also new problems for radiotelephony. One of the earliest practical trials of these frequencies for telephony, and one representing at the time a very large jump in frequency, was the 17-centimeter wave propagation across the English Channel in 1931, accomplished by the system developed by the laboratory of "Le Matériel

Téléphonique" of Paris, using the Barkhausen type of oscillator. Further experience has shown frequencies as high as this to be susceptible under some circumstances to rather serious transmission instability, resulting, it has been suggested, from changing moisture content of the air or from turbulent atmospheric conditions. A number of short radiotelephone links are now being operated in various parts of the world on somewhat lower frequencies, generally in the range of 40 to 100 megacycles.

It appears that as rapidly as the message-carrying capacity of radio is enlarged by extension to the ultra-high frequencies, the demand increases on the part of older services and of entirely new services, such as television. How much of the spectrum may be available for telephony will naturally be influenced by relative usefulness and economics. One problem is that of how to obtain radiotelephony sufficiently economically to "prove it in" for the shorter distances which characterize the useful range of these waves. Another is the one of preserving the privacy of communication by relatively simple means. It may be that the principle use of these waves for telephony will be for mobile services, thereby helping telephony keep pace with our increasingly mobile way of living.

Leaven of the Art

In describing the rise of radiotelephony we have spoken principally of physical things such as the vacuum tube, the filter circuit, etc. Another cross-section of the art would be the leaven of ideas which gave rise to it; the analyses and the reductions to measurement which enabled results to be obtained by design. That radiotelephony is particularly rich in this respect will be evident from the following citation of some of the more outstanding analytical contributions.

One of the first is that of van der Bijl's early study of the operation of the vacuum tube. In 1913–14 he derived approximate expressions for the plate current in terms of plate and grid

263

voltage, and presented the concept of the amplification factor μ. This work was published toward the end of the war and was the forerunner of his 1920 book on the vacuum tube, an authority for many years.

One of the earliest elucidations to be published of the operation of the audion as detector was the 1914 paper of Armstrong.

Next there is the more exact mathematical solution of the plate current in terms of the tube constants and grid voltage variation, given in an Institute paper in 1919; and the treatment of the vacuum tube as a part of a circuit network published the same year.

A potent factor has been the growing appreciation throughout the electric communication art generally of Fourier's theorem and the steady-state concept of transient phenomena. Related thereto is the band idea of wire telephone transmission which developed out of the frequency-band nature of speech itself, the characteristics of lines, and the necessity of suppressing reflections at circuit junctions. Campbell, using the loaded-line theory, combined the band idea of telephony with the sharp selectivity feature of radiotelegraphy to secure the wave-filter characteristic of a uniform transmission band, plus a sharp cutoff. This was a milestone in the development of circuit network theory.

Related to both vacuum tubes and the band conception were Carson's analysis of the modulated wave into the component carrier and sidebands and his invention of single-sideband transmission, made as far back as 1915, and the general extension of the side-band idea to high frequencies, which has meant so much to both wire carrier-current telephony and radiotelephony.

In the field of measurement and standardization there are the technique of making single-frequency measurements throughout a band, the decibel unit of attenuation, the volume indicator and the concept of volume range, and the measurements of the field strength of desired signals and of noise.

264

Figure 8 represents an attempt to diagram the flow of the art as a whole.

FUTURE

Radiotelephony may be said to have "arrived" and to be still young. Looking toward the future, the writer likes to think of radio and wire telephony as increasingly dovetailing together to form one general front of advance. The principles and technical tools being fundamentally the same for both, a technical advance in one is likely to help the other. Thus radio has led the way to the higher frequencies and this has benefited wire communication, as we see in the carrier-current and wide-band coaxial cable development. As regards services, we observe that radio and wire telephony are one and the same thing in respect to the overall result, that of the delivery of sound messages. Where one or the other is to be used will be a matter of natural adaptability of the medium of transmission and of the economics of the situation, with the meeting line shifting from time to time, but with the main emphasis upon integration rather than differentiation. Thus does radiotelephony become an integral part of telephony and of the whole field of electric communications.

LLOYD ESPENSCHIED

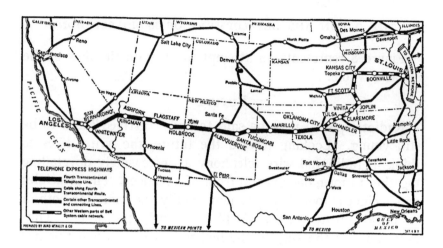

Southwest Passage

" KNOW that on the right hand of the Indies," wrote the quaint Spanish writer Rodriguez de Montalvo " there is an island called California, very close to the side of the Terrestrial Paradise."

This was early in the Sixteenth Century. Subsequent explorations of his countrymen and others showed that he was off on his geography, and there are differences of opinion as to the proximity of California to the Terrestrial Paradise. But at all events, it soon became a Promised Land to great numbers from the East. Its gold, its climate, its commerce drew them as a magnet draws iron filings. They came seeking the fountain of youth and the well of gold, by way of the Horn and the covered wagon. Their nieces and nephews followed on the Iron Horse and through the ditch across Panama.

Born nearly three decades after the Forty-Niners had trekked westward, the telephone set out in pursuit of these lusty enthusiasts who had passed out of earshot. Pushing steadily across prairie, mountain and desert, it thrust its way through the Sierra Nevadas, reached the Golden Gate in 1915, in time for the celebration that marked the opening of the Panama Canal. " Hello Frisco " was not only a popular lyric, but an historic event in the development of communications.

266

For a year or so it threatened to remain an historic event, with a trickling traffic of two or three calls a day. But the East and the West had a lot to talk about. Timber from the forests of the Northwest was piling into the eastern lumber yards. Oregon orchardists were shipping their products eastward a good deal faster than an apple a day. Down in California, citrus fruits, teeming with unsuspected vitamins, were being packed eastward. Motion pictures had already reached the "colossal" stage. It was soon evident that more telephone lines were needed.

The first line to the Coast, now known as the Central Transcontinental, terminated at San Francisco, whence calls were switched to Oregon, Washington and Southern California. In 1923 a line was thrown across the southwestern corner of the country, thus providing a second line terminating at Los Angeles for service to the Coast. In the Northwest, lumber, apples, salmon and a busy route to the Orient gave the businessmen of Washington and Oregon a good deal to talk over with their eastern friends, and in 1927 the Northern Transcontinental was opened across Minnesota, North Dakota and Montana to Seattle.

These three highways of speech—Northern, Southern, and Central—give access to all parts of that teeming western shoreline, and by means of a system of lateral north-and-south lines, traffic can be diverted from one route to another, giving a flexibility highly advantageous in emergencies—storms or unprecedented peaks in traffic.

Hundreds of people now talk across the continent every day. And with the accretion of busy years, these three routes now provide more than one hundred telephone channels which cross the western states;—but they are not enough to meet the estimates of the not-so-distant future. So a few months ago surveyors went out, blue prints were unrolled and a new telephone express highway was evolved that followed in the shadow of the transport planes across the great open spaces between Oklahoma City and Los Angeles.

The new "talkway," a straightening and widening of an older telephone route, is designed principally as a "through" way for long-haul traffic. In two notable respects it is well qualified for this important duty. In the first place, it will traverse a country rarely visited by the sleet storm, whose strangling coat of ice about the wires pulls the sturdiest poles to crazy angles. Second, it will employ a "carrier current" system of larger capacity, recently developed by the Bell Laboratories. By combining this new system with existing methods, it will be possible for *sixteen pairs of subscribers* to carry on, simultaneously over a single pair of wires, sixteen conversations as neatly and effectively separated from each other as the layers of a club sandwich.

The project is the largest construction job undertaken by the American Telephone and Telegraph Company since 1930. Briefly, it consists of a line of some 12,000 poles across a 290 mile stretch between Amarillo and Albuquerque, and the stringing of wires through these points from Oklahoma City to Whitewater, California;—thus providing a large capacity open wire line between the fine-mesh telephone network of the eastern half of the continent and the West Coast system. Several hundred men are employed in the work, the cost of which will exceed $2,000,000. The wire-stringing job will require some 3,500,000 pounds of copper, making up into 8,000 miles of wire. It is rough country, in spots. Between Amarillo and Albuquerque some five tons of dynamite have been used to blast out holes in which to set the telephone poles. At not infrequent intervals the line crosses rivers and creeks, and dry washes that at certain seasons are worse than several creeks and rivers put together. These must be crossed by a "catenary" or suspension construction for the crossarms, whose design often requires not a little ingenuity.

While Bell System engineers and linemen have run many lines across this kind of country, the preparations necessary in this case were on the scale of an expedition to the headwaters of the Amazon or into the less frequented regions of the Iranian plateau. The preliminary study, in the words of one of the field engineers, consisted in determining "the inaccessibility of the various routes." It meant breaking through a region that the hardy Spanish and American explorers had either avoided or penetrated with great difficulty and hardship.

In the making of the new route, A. T. and T. surveyors experienced two phenomena that are somewhat of a handicap to survey work. In the Panhandle they encountered rain. The special fact about this rain, in the words of one of the surveyors, was that "when it rains in the Panhandle it all falls at once."

Another thing that made survey work something less than a summer lark was the dust storm. According to one of the party, the Long Lines survey party, in the course of two and a half months, saw about eight days free from dust storms. They varied from a faintly perceptible haze to a murk that shut them in like fog. While these storms seldom lasted long. the party was generally too far out of town to quit work, and they worked on, in goggles and masks. And the dust was with them everywhere. Some of it was quite fine and had a choking biting odor. It filtered in through the windows at night, so that at first they slept with sheets over their heads and then in their masks. The dust even got into the tight joints of their transits and gave them a day's work cleaning them.

Another unpleasant manifestation of the dust storm was the static generated by the fast-moving particles. This was sufficient to give one a distinctly unpleasant shock, if one chanced to lean against a wire fence.

An unusual feature of the preparation for this undertaking was the survey of facilities that had to be made. Travelling from one end of the projected route to the other, the construc-

269

tion forces collected information about store-rooms, garages, machine shops, sidings, hospitals, boarding houses, restaurants, water and all the other facilities that are requisite in construction work. Operating in such rugged country, with long jumps between towns, information of this kind made it possible to work with a high degree of efficiency and economy.

The Fourth Transcontinental is being constructed so as to take advantage of the latest refinements in long distance telephony. Chief among these is the new type of high frequency "carrier current" system—the "J" type—that in the future will be used on it. This carrier, operating on frequencies ranging from 36,000 to 140,000 cycles, will provide twelve voice channels. It will operate on a pair of wires already carrying the regular voice telephone channel and a Type "C" carrier system, that gives three voiceways, using lower frequencies than the Type "J." Thus a total of sixteen circuits will ultimately be obtained from one pair of wires.

When the new carrier system is applied it will be necessary to increase the number of "repeater" stations along the route, and will greatly increase the problem of coordinating all the factors affecting the service on such long circuits. These repeaters are the vacuum tube amplifiers inserted at selected points along a telephone line to replenish the energy lost in transit. While these stations are generally spaced from 100 to 300 miles apart, depending upon the size of wire and other practical considerations, the distance will be cut materially on the Fourth Transcontinental when the "J" system is applied. Between Oklahoma City and Whitewater, a distance of about 1,200 miles, it is expected that a total of sixteen to eighteen repeater stations will be required on the new carrier channels. This is an average spacing of about 65 to 70 miles, compared with an average of some 240 on the existing type of open wire line along this route.

Another modification of equipment along this line is necessitated by the high frequencies to be used. Because of these, the cross-arms are placed three feet apart, instead of the usual two feet, as a means of minimizing the " cross-talk " between adjacent pairs of wires. It is also necessary to have frequent " transposition " of each pair of wires, the wires crossing each other, in the case of some pairs, at every other pole. It recalls one of the first technical problems tackled by the American Telephone and Telegraph Co. Back in 1885 this phenomenon of cross-talk made its appearance on the newly constructed New York-Philadelphia line, one of the first metallic-circuit lines. The idea of transposition was hit upon and has since been a universal practice on long distance lines —though it has never before been necessary to cross the wires at such short intervals as in the case of the new carrier lines.

The Type " J " has introduced other refinements into the construction of the line. Poles must be spaced evenly, or very nearly so, on both existing and new sections of line—not always an easy task over such terrain—and the " sag " of the two wires of each pair must be uniform. To produce the desired accuracy, two systems of adjustment are employed. In the first, a wooden target, marked with equally spaced horizontal lines, is mounted on one pole; on the other, is a telescope, through which a lineman sights on the wires and gives orders— over the wire, to a man on the ground some distance beyond the other pole—to pull up or slack away. Incidentally, to be sure the adjustment is correct, the lineman must refer to a temperature chart which shows the varying sag at different temperatures.

In the second method each wire of the pair is plucked in such a way as to cause it to vibrate. The period of oscillation of each wire is compared with that of the other wire of the pair. If these periods are found to be alike, the wires have the same sag.

The Fourth Transcontinental is expected to prove a useful route, not only for telephone traffic, but for the many other communication facilities which the Bell System is called upon

271

to provide—circuits for broadcasting networks, for telegraph and teletypewriter service, and picture-transmission. It is expected that the line will be in commercial operation by the end of the year, although the twelve-channel carrier systems will not be provided until a later date.

Writing on the twentieth anniversary of transcontinental service (QUARTERLY, October 1935), J. J. Pilliod cites some interesting contrasts that are even more striking in relation to the new line. Speaking of the first circuit across the continent, he says: " Cable was avoided as far as was physically possible, because of the greater transmission loss which it introduced, and the eastern open wire terminal was brought to within three blocks of the Hudson River." The circuits of the Fourth Transcontinental will enter a cable at Oklahoma City, stretching Eastward approximately 1,600 miles to the Hudson River. Again, Mr. Pilliod points out that " no direct circuit from Chicago or New York to San Francisco was set up because the number of calls did not justify it." The new facilities of the Fourth Transcontinental will bring the total number of direct circuits from New York to San Francisco and Los Angeles up to 20, while from Chicago there will be nearly 30 direct circuits to West Coast cities. These are only a part of the voice channels to the western slope of the Sierra Nevadas. In addition, there are the coast-to-coast broadcasting network channels and scores of circuits for telegraph and teletypewriter services.

There are other evidences of notable technical advances. Back in 1915 the man in New York who wanted to call up his partner or his girl in San Francisco had to wait quite a while for the connection—probably half an hour or more. Today the average time to put through a long distance call, whether it's across a state line or across the continent, is less than two minutes. Technical improvement has also been reflected in another feature of great interest to everyone using the service,

272

STAKING OUT THE AMARILLO-ALBUQUERQUE SECTION OF THE FOURTH TRANSCONTINENTAL LINE ON TH
ESTACADO, OR STAKED PLAINS, SO CALLED EVER SINCE CORONADO MARKED WITH STAKES THE PATH
LOWED OVER THESE VAST SPACES IN 1542

POLE HOLE DIGGER MAKING ITS OWN DUST STORM IN GOOD GOING BETWEEN MORIARTY AND SANT
NEW MEXICO.

WOUND ON "HIGH HATS," THE WIRES ARE PAYED OUT FROM A MOTORIZED HAT RACK AS THE LINEMEN ADVANCE ACROSS COUNTRY THROUGH CIBOLA NATIONAL FOREST.

SURVEY CREWS WERE EQUIPPED WITH GOGGLES AND MASKS AGAINST DUST STORMS WHICH WERE AN ALMOST DAILY OCCURRENCE.

DYNAMITE FOR THE NEXT POLE. IT MAY BE ROCK THAT MUST BE BLASTED OUT OR MUD OR SAND, BUT THE POLE MUST GO IN.

HAVING BORED A HOLE TO THE PROPER DEPTH, THE TELEPHONE TRUCK PICKS UP A POLE AND DROPS IT INTO PROPER POSITION.

HOISTING WIRES AT THE LEFT NEAR WINSLOW, ARIZ. SEPARATELY SPACED CIRCUITS AND MORE FRE
TRANSPOSITIONS ARE CHARACTERISTICS OF THIS LATEST CONSTRUCTION JOB. THE LINEMAN AT THE
IS PLUCKING THE TWO WIRES OF A PAIR TO START THEM DANCING IF THEY KEEP STEP WITH
OTHER FOR A FEW SECONDS THEY HAVE SUBSTANTIALLY THE SAME "SAG"—A NECESSARY REFINEME:
THE NEW CARRIER CURRENT SYSTEM

THE WIRES HAVING BEEN STRUNG OVER A NEW CROSS-ARM, THEY ARE PULLED TAUT BY TACKLES. ALOFT ON THE POLES, LINEMEN CHECK THE SAG OF EACH PAIR AND SIGNAL ORDERS TO THE MAN ON THE GROUND.

PUTTING THE FINISHING TOUCHES ON A SECTION OF THE FOURTH TRANSCONTINENTAL LINE NEAR ASHFORK, ARIZONA

namely the cost. It was almost the grand gesture of a prodigal to make a call in 1915, for a three-minute chat from New York to San Francisco cost $20.70. Today that same call, on a daytime station-to-station basis, costs $6.50. Or, if it be Sunday, or after the magic hour of 7 P.M. when the night rates go in, it would cost $4.25.

Another development of considerable importance has been the improvement in the quality of speech transmitted. In mathematical terms, the frequency band transmitted over the first transcontinental circuit was about 900 cycles. Today these circuits handle frequency bands ranging in width from 2,200 to 5,000 cycles. In perhaps more familiar terms, this means that the voice or music at the other end of the line, instead of sounding like those cylinders in the early phonographs, is not only recognizable, but pleasingly like the original.

Such an improvement has advantages too numerous to mention. It assists in the ready identification not only of voices, but of other sounds, and thus minimizes the risk of awkward moments. There is a story that shortly after the first transcontinental line was completed, General J. J. Carty determined upon a demonstration calculated to appeal to the imaginative mind. He was going to let the people listening at the San Francisco end hear the surf breaking on Rockaway Beach, near New York City. This new and magic wire would carry to the distant shores of the Pacific the sound which welcomed Henry Hudson as he entered New York Bay.

Since the effectiveness of such a demonstration depended in some measure on how smoothly it went off, General Carty arranged for a "dress rehearsal." The circuit was built up, all the way from New York to the Golden Gate. At each end of the line and at numerous intermediate points were skilled technical men, carefully testing each link in this chain.

At length all was in readiness. General Carty was at New York, an associate was in San Francisco. All the way across the continent, pairs of ears listened carefully, intent upon maintaining the circuit. General Carty spoke to San Francisco. A moment later he "turned on" the roar of the surf at Rockaway.

The man at the Pittsburgh testboard started. He listened intently for a moment, threw a key and listened again. Then he cut in on the line: "That noise in the line," said he, "must be east of Pittsburgh."

GEORGE G. BREED

The International Radio Meeting of 1937

LATE last spring there was held at Bucharest, Rumania, an international conference on the subject of the technical regulation of radio. This was the fourth of a series of meetings held by the International Radio Consultative Committee (CCIR), an advisory body which originated at the Washington International Radio Conference of 1927. The object of these meetings is, in general, by international agreement to promote an orderly world use of the radio medium and minimize interference, and to prepare technical advice for subsequent more formal international administrative conferences, the next one of which is to meet in February, 1938, at Cairo, Egypt.

One of the principal subjects considered at these conferences is that of the constancy to which the frequency of a radio transmitting station should be held. At Bucharest the permissible variations were tightened up somewhat from those previously agreed upon. For example, for high-frequency (short wave) stations in the fixed services the permissible variations (tolerances) were recommended to be reduced from 0.02 per cent, the value given in the Madrid Regulations, to 0.01 per cent for new transmitters installed after 1938.

Another question upon which progress was made is that of indicating the limits of the harmonics of transmitting stations to which suppliers of equipment should work. A previous meeting of the CCIR, held at Lisbon, had recommended that for frequencies lower than 3 mc. a harmonic should not exceed 300 mv./m. at a distance of 5 km. from the transmitting antenna, equivalent to a harmonic power of about 0.25 watt in the antenna. The recommendation which was adopted at Bucharest applies to stations operating on frequencies above 3 mc., except for mobile stations, and requires any harmonic to be at least 40 db down as compared with the fundamental and not to exceed in power 200 milliwatts. It was recognized that these limits will not insure against interference and that it remains an obligation on the part of the nations of the world to undertake special measures for suppressing harmonic interference where this becomes necessary.

A knowledge of the characteristics of wave propagation is, of course, fundamental to the planning of the use of radio channels. There were before the conference a number of treatises and curves on wave transmission. It became evident that the state of knowledge was as yet too incomplete to enable the subject to be presented in a comprehensive and yet simplified and practical form. It was left that the members of the subcommittee studying this question would continue their labors after the Bucharest meeting under the guidance of the administration which had centralized the subject, Great Britain, in an attempt to present it to the Cairo Conference in as useful form as possible.

On the subject of the field intensities which are necessary for the reception of various types of radio services, there was submitted to the conference a mass of data showing the field intensities actually being used, particularly in the United States. No conclusions were drawn and the subject was left upon the basis that further data of this kind, including noise levels, would be accumulated over the years and build up a picture of world-wide conditions as to received fields and noise levels.

One of the accomplishments of the Bucharest meeting was the classifying of the work of the CCIR along lines which will permit of the logical grouping of the recommendations of the committee and which can be followed to advantage in the setting up of subcommittees. The classification is as follows:

Organization and general matters.
Propagation of radio waves.
Transmitting station characteristics.
Receiving station characteristics.

Coordination, as between transmitter and receiver and as between different radio channels.

Standardization and measurements, involving terminology, definitions, measurements of fields, frequency, etc.

This classification is expected to help in better organizing the work of the CCIR. The more fundamental review of the field of competency of the CCIR and the further defining and planning of its work were left for the next administrative conference, that of Cairo.

A number of the twenty questions which were before the conference were found not to be subject to conclusions and were continued for further study. Some twenty new questions were proposed for the next meeting of this body. Several of these, which the United States was instrumental in getting adopted, are concerned with the important question of the band widths which are necessary for the various types of services and the minimum frequency separation which is practicable as between stations working on adjacent channels. These questions are, of course, fundamental to the more efficient use of the radio medium.

The United States Government was represented at this conference by a group of government department representatives, headed by Dr. J. H. Dellinger, of the Bureau of Standards. A number of the American operating companies were represented. For the Bell System there were present Messrs. C. O. Bickelhaupt, G. C. Barney, F. M. Ryan and L. Espenschied.

The Rumanian Administration was extremely kind in the arrangements made for the conference and for giving the delegates recreation and something of a picture of the remarkable country of Rumania. With the accretion of territory resulting from the War and the exploitation of oil, Rumania is developing rapidly. The activity and new buildings throughout the City of Bucharest were so striking as to present considerable of a " boom " appearance.

LLOYD ESPENSCHIED

Notes on Recent Occurrences

OPENING OF TELEPHONE SERVICE WITH HAITI
EXTENDS CARIBBEAN SERVICE

HAITI, upon whose shores Columbus' flagship the *Santa Maria* came to grief on Christmas Eve, 1492, was brought within reach of Bell System telephones on September 29, 1937. Ceremonies inaugurating the new radiotelephone link included an exchange of greetings between Secretary of State Cordell Hull, speaking from Washington, and August Turnier, Acting Secretary of Foreign Relations for Haiti, who talked from Port au Prince.

Mr. Hull referred to the Republic of Haiti and the United States as the oldest independent countries in this hemisphere. "At the time of their independence, it required weeks to communicate from one capital to another but in recent years first the airplane and now the radio telephone have made possible immediate communication and are strengthening the historic bonds between us."

"The growing perfection of the means of international communication can only bring the peoples closer together," Mr. Turnier said. "And the Haitian Government rejoices that the Pan-American governments henceforth can count on still another factor in the service of their ideas of solidarity and of the development of their moral and material interests."

The service with the Caribbean republic is handled by means of a short wave circuit between radio stations of the American Telephone and Telegraph Company at Miami, Fla., and stations of the West Indian Telephone Company near Port au Prince. Thirteen Caribbean islands and adjacent countries are now reached by radiotelephone connections from Miami.

S. C. WILLIAMS ELECTED DIRECTOR OF AMERICAN TELEPHONE AND TELEGRAPH COMPANY

AT a meeting of the Board of Directors of the American Telephone and Telegraph Company held on July 21, S. Clay Williams, of Winston Salem, N. C., was elected a director to fill the vacancy caused by the death of George F. Baker. Mr. Williams is Chairman of the Board of the R. J. Reynolds Tobacco Company.